Advanced Prais
'Viking' Farmer

MW01118919

A thriller, a family adventure, a Viking heritage story
that kept me turning pages and asking for more...
—Alice C. Schelling, Author of HIDING ALINKA

***

A riveting tale about Norwegian settlement
featuring strong women who carried their families
forward even when their men failed them.
—Carol Bradley Bursack, Author of
MINDING OUR ELDERS

***

Award-winning author Robert Dodge doesn't just
write history, he paints it in true story-telling style.
—Jodi Bowersox, President of the
Colorado Authors League

***

Peace Corps gives opportunities to take risks, value new
cultures, and build trust across communities through
shared vulnerabilities. What I appreciated about
Robert Dodge's book is his exploration of Norwegian
culture, hardships families faced adapting to a new
country, and how the drive to survive shows the depth
of immigrants' influence in the northern mid-west.
—Jody Olsen, Peace Corps Director, 2018-2021

***

FIELDS OF FORTUNE

VIKING FARMERS IN AMERICA

ROBERT DODGE

WILDBLUE
PRESS

WildBluePress.com

FIELDS OF FORTUNE published by:
WILDBLUE PRESS
P.O. Box 102440
Denver, Colorado 80250

ISBN 978-1-957288-66-6 Hardcover
ISBN 978-1-957288-67-3 Trade Paperback
ISBN 978-1-957288-68-0 eBook

Cover design © 2023 WildBlue Press. All rights reserved.

Cover Design by Tatiana Vila, www.viladesign.net

Interior Formatting by Elijah Toten, www.totencreative.com

FIELDS OF FORTUNE

ACKNOWLEDGEMENTS

My gratitude to WildBlue Press for bringing this project to the public. Special thanks to Stephanie Johnson Lawson for her oversight and guidance and to Donna Marie West for her insightful editing. I am grateful to Dag Arne Danielson for providing me information from Norway to which I would not otherwise have had access. Though they are no longer with us, I express my appreciation to my mother and grandmother for the preservation of records that tell the story of the family in Norway and its homesteading days and life in the America of an earlier time.

For Anne and Jim Carpenter

TABLE OF CONTENTS

INTRODUCTION

This story of homesteading and small-town life begins with a Norwegian family who for generations moved from place to place seeking a better life. When the 1800s came, they were swept up in "American fever" as they learned of opportunities for free land where they could have large farms of their own. Some made the voyage, but with the free land came the political complications for the Americans, since when they arrived in the early 1850s, the slavery controversy was dividing their new home. The Civil War soon followed. During that war and after, wherever they moved and settled, conflict continued. This time, the major focus was on the indigenous people whose land settlers were claiming to turn into farms. Pushing westward first in Wisconsin, then to Iowa, on to the Dakota Territory, which became South Dakota, then to North Dakota, the family relocated. The struggle of resettlement moved them west and the story reduces to fewer characters until it focuses on Caroline Olson in Dakota.

Caroline's daughter Nettie then moved on to a homestead near the new town of Garrison, North Dakota. There she met Oliver Fortune, whose ancestors had come to America from Norway in the 1860s. They married and homesteaded in Alberta, Canada, where their daughter Irene was born. Their homesteading was interrupted by attempts to start a small-town general store in Mohall, North Dakota.

Perhaps it was his name. Did it define some quest that was beyond his reach? Was it some cruel joke played by fate to continually mock him? Or was it a mere coincidence? In any case, Oliver Fortune was a fortune-seeker who never found the fortune he sought. Though he was born the son of a poor farmer, he was determined to work hard, take chances when they arose, and become "his own man," prosperous and beholden to no one. Instead, his attempts at homesteading and becoming a successful farmer failed. His attempts to become a merchant ended with going under due to bank failures, compounded by his mismanagement and ineptitude. His marriage to Nettie Williams deteriorated into a state of mutual contempt. Failure, rather than fortune, became his hallmark.

As the failures in Oliver's life continued to pile up, he began to lose heart. More and more, his former hopefulness gave way to despondency. He increasingly turned to alcohol to cope with the pessimism and depression that accompanied the dismal future he saw looming ahead.

Although Oliver Fortune did not acquire the kind of fortune he had envisioned throughout his life, he and his wife Nettie did leave behind a treasure—their daughter Irene.

With Oliver gone, Nettie at last was completely on her own. The neurotic tendencies that had been slightly below the surface since her years of isolated living soon emerged. She had many negative experiences with men that contributed to her bitterness and, perhaps, had suppressed prairie madness from her three homesteading experiences.

Oliver and Nettie were children of the American Dream. This story goes back to their ancestors in Norway, who moved from place to place seeking better lives. They ventured to America in search of opportunity in a land where they were not limited by their pasts. In the United States of the late nineteenth century, it was possible to believe that determination, hard work, and ingenuity might lead to a better life, perhaps even to great success and wealth. By the late 1800s, freed slaves were heading north from the South, the Eastern Seaboard was teaming with immigrants from Ireland and Southern and Eastern Europe, while gold and logging had long since brought large immigrant populations to the West. The great era of American industrialization and urbanization were well underway, and the United States was about to begin flexing its muscles as an imperialist power.

The last area of the continental United States to be settled by non-Native Americans was the Great Plains, the area between the Mississippi River and the Rocky Mountains. Although some miners and ranchers had moved into this area, until the post-Civil War era, nomadic Indian tribes still dominated the region. Permanent settlements of Whites existed in isolated farms near small villages and became largely concentrated in towns where cattle drives crossed railroad lines, with completion of the transcontinental railroad and the increased railroad network that followed. The Homestead Act of 1862 also drew White settlers to the Great Plains. It was this legislation that attracted Oliver and Nettie Fortune's ancestors to middle America.

The Homestead Act drew a population from the American coasts and from Europe into the central plains of America by offering free land to those willing to turn the prairie into farmland. It provided the opportunity for independence and a new chance in life for people who would take on the challenges of the frontier, living on the open prairies. It was so successful that following the Census of 1890, the leading historian of the time, Frederick Jackson Turner, proclaimed that the American frontier had come to an end. That was stated in the famous paper he read at the 1893 meeting of the American Historical Association entitled "The Significance of the Frontier in American

History,"[1] where he defined that frontier as "the meeting point between savagery and civilization."[2]

Turner's paper reflected the presumptions of the Europeans who settled the prairie that those who had long existed there had no rights and were inferior beings, non-Caucasian "savages," and it was the "manifest destiny" of the Whites to rule the continent of North America from coast to coast. The destruction of Native American culture and native animals were unavoidable consequences.

Nettie Fortune was born just as this great transition was documented and announced by Turner, while Irene Fortune was the product of those who had participated in the changes. The leading editor Ola Thommesen had written in 1908 of Norwegians like Irene's family, that America was "the great land of the future, where so many of my countrymen have found a home."[3]

While the stories of their lives are familiar, they are unusual. Like many others, they deal with the challenges and patterns of prairie life that came with homesteading and residing in small villages on the Great Plains, which was the story of the ancestors that preceded them. Stories such as this often paint a romantic portrait of a hearty man with a plow, a rugged individual turning the natural prairie into fields of amber waves of grain, with the difficult times and damage to the existing cultures and environment glossed over. But frontier life was harsh, marked by the courageous and often brutal struggle to "tame the land" and become self-reliant,

---

1. Frederick J. Turner, "The Significance of the Frontier in American History," Chicago, 1893, *American Historical Association*, https://www.historians.org/about-aha-and-membership/aha-history-and-archives/historical-archives/the-significance-of-the-frontier-in-american-history-(1893).

2. Ibid.

3. Quoted in Ingrid Simmingsen, *Norway to America* (Minneapolis: University of Minnesota Press, 1978), 131. Ibid.

whatever the cost. The Fortune stories are exceptional because they mirror what had taken place decades earlier in most similar stories. It is a nineteenth-century story that took place at the onset of the twentieth century. Isolated pockets of the Midwest remained relatively unchanged by the rapid modernization of America, and Nettie and Irene grew up in one of those pockets. While it eventually destroyed her parents, Irene emerged triumphant.

Although her fortune-seeking father Oliver never seemed to recognize it, Irene was the Fortunes' fortune, and this is the story of how she came to be.

CHAPTER 1: ARE THE TIMES A-CHANGIN'?

Nettie was nineteen and her pregnancy was just beginning to show. She had been shunted around since her father abandoned their family and her mother died, and now she was living on her own. The slick, mature Oliver seemed to offer some security, but then, that is how she ended up in her current situation. He did not run out on her like men tended to do. Both Nettie and Oliver were small in stature. During her 98-year life, she never exceeded 5'1" and 95 pounds. By the time she met Oliver, people found her unusually attractive, her even features and smooth skin framed by her most admired attribute, her dark, curly hair. Oliver was 5' 6" and 142 pounds, though due to hard work combined with stress and medical complications, this would decline to the mid 130 pounds when he reached his forties. He was a handsome man with deep-set eyes the blue-gray of many Norwegians. His hair and complexion were dark by Norwegian standards. That was something they had in common; both were descendants of immigrants from Norway who had arrived in America not long before they were born.

Nettie and Oliver were married in May of 1911 in Minot, North Dakota. At the time, prospects were dismal for both of them. Oliver was always searching for a new opportunity, something that would make him a big success and admired by those who met him or had looked down on him. Though getting Nettie pregnant had changed things, he had two new possibilities to consider, and he asked Nettie for her opinion since this time, she would be going along. He was known as the local pool shark and had been offered a job managing a pool hall in Sherwood, a town of several hundred people near the Canadian border. Also, his cousin Billy had recently sent him a letter with a proposition. Billy was one of several of Oliver's family members who had given up their earlier homesteads in southwest Minnesota to head north and homestead in southern Alberta, Canada. The Dominion Land Act of 1872 provided for Canadian homesteading, requiring a $10 fee and five years' occupation of 160 acres for title to the land. In the 1880s, the Canadian Pacific Railroad reached Calgary, giving Alberta a direct connection with Vancouver and the Pacific coast, so there was access to markets other than in the immediate area. Billy told Oliver he was going to give up his homestead so he could return to Minnesota. If Oliver wanted the homestead, he could head to Canada and take it over before anyone else had a chance to settle on it and file a claim.

Oliver asked Nettie what she thought. Nettie and Oliver knew that homesteading was a physically and emotionally challenging life since they had both lived on homesteads in North Dakota.

A book written about this time, Torger Anderson Hoverstad's *The Norwegian Farmers in the United States*,[4] said Norwegians like Nettie and Oliver constituted the largest proportion of second-generation farmers in North Dakota, with 63% on farms, and surprisingly, that number was increasing.[5] This was so because "In the development of any new country there are five stages the pioneers have to go through." In an idea that has not stood the test of

---

4. Torger Anderson Hoverstad, *The Norwegian Farmers in the United States* (Fargo, ND: H. Jervell Publishing Company, 1915).
5. Ibid., 11.

time, Hoverstad outlined that first came the "savage stage," which involved overcoming the Indians. This was followed by the "hunting and trapping phase," where some smaller animals were killed, but buffalo were eliminated as "the white hunter took the place of the savage hunter" until the great animals were almost extinct. This stage was followed by the "ranching phase" in sparsely populated areas, where domestic sheep, cattle, and horses were raised on the short buffalo grass. The fourth stage was the "bonanza farming phase," where population centers were nearer and involved very large fields on large farms growing very few crops and using machinery, with many immigrant laborers employed in the fields. From this came the fifth and final stage, the "small farm," which was the size a family could operate without hired labor, growing a variety of crops and keeping some domestic animals.[6]

Hoverstad's view is what the attitude of immigrants heading west in a new land thought and while looking back, many questions arise about whether homesteading on indigenous land could be part of a natural, five-step process. There can be little doubt that those in the late nineteenth and early twentieth centuries did not consider that question.

Nettie and Oliver were two of those people. To Nettie, the idea of being a property owner sounded like a big step up from her current situation, and she said it was a better opportunity than going to Sherwood, which was just what Oliver wanted to hear.[7] His cousin Billy had not succeeded in Alberta, but his older, blowhard brother Jack had been extremely successful and made sure everyone knew about it. Jack had also written to Oliver, telling him he could get a half section if he took Billy's land. That would be 320 acres. Once he got it cleared, the rich prairie soil could grow

---

6. Ibid., 13-17.
7. Nettie Fortune, "Personal Memories," transcription of interview of with Irene Dodge, Mohall, ND, Oct 22, 1979, 62.

plenty of wheat to harvest and the hard work it would take was nothing new.

The newlyweds packed what little they owned in a buggy and headed off on the 95-mile ride to Portal, a town with only a few wood-frame buildings, that had become one of the crossing points in North Dakota for traffic between the US and Canada. Oliver did a strange thing in Portal and he must have had some motive, or he was ignorant of Canadian homesteading requirements: he filled in an application for Canadian citizenship. Being a Canadian citizen was not required under Canada's homestead act and when he did file for Billy's homestead, he did so as an "alien." In what would be one of a number of things that would shape Nettie's very hostile view about men, when Oliver's Canadian citizenship was finalized in 1914, she lost her United States citizenship and also became a citizen of Canada. This happened without her ever being consulted, taking an oath, or signing a document. She was very unhappy about it and remained so for decades. It would much later trigger a long search for proof of where she was born and that her mother had lived in the United States.

They reached the remote, isolated village of Bow Island, Alberta, where they would settle. This village had only been officially established the previous year, though settlers had been congregating there since 1900. Nettie and Oliver increased the population from 307 to 309, and on February 1 of the year following their arrival, the village was declared the Town of Bow Island.[8] This was the community nearest Billy's homestead and those of other Fortune relatives. Located on a flat prairie that stretched in all directions as far as the eye could see, it consisted primarily of a wide main street that allowed space for turning around buggies and wagons, with six lackluster, wood-frame, single-story buildings of varying heights on each side facing each other.

---

8. "History," *Bow Island*, https://www.bowisland.com/history.

They were connected and had hitching posts near their entrances. There was a wood walkway in front of them elevated several inches above the broad dirt street, which would turn to mud during summer rains. Several had the business names painted above the entryways, interrupting the monotone blandness of the weather-beaten wood, while others, like the town's diner, had an extended narrow board jutting straight out, identifying it with hand-painted letters.

They rented a place to live, described by Nettie as "a one-room shack with a shanty roof down by the coulee."[9] Oliver got a job in the livery barn that paid $60 a month for sheltering, feeding, and watering the horses that farmers and others brought to town when they visited. On November 10, 1911, Irene was born in that rented, one-room shack. She would write of her father years later, "I understand that he was more than disappointed when I turned out to be a girl."[10]

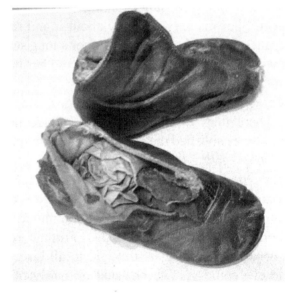

"Irene's first shoes" - 1891. (Property of the Author)

---

9. Nettie Fortune, "Personal Memories," 61.

10. Irene Fortune Dodge, unpublished memoir, 1984, 52.

Farm equipment and stock were going to be the initial problems for the Fortune family to begin life on the homestead, and they turned to Oliver's father in Minnesota for assistance. He agreed to sell Oliver some equipment and stock and to help him out, to pay for half of a boxcar and ship it on the new railroad line that ran from Minnesota through North Dakota to Alberta. Oliver went to Minnesota to buy horses, a cow, and some machinery from his father's farm. For the return, Oliver could not afford to do anything other than live in the boxcar with the animals. When they reached the Canadian border at Portal, there was a lengthy inspection of the animals to prevent diseases being brought in, so Oliver was confined to the boxcar for over a week. He had to milk the cow every day and did not know what to do with the milk, so he gave it back to the cow, who drank her own milk. Cows initially drink their mother's milk but when they mature, they become lactose intolerant and one problem with drinking milk, including their own, is diarrhea.[11] The remainder of the trip in the confined space might have been even less pleasant for Oliver than the beginning had been.

Oliver returned to Bow Island and in the spring, they left town and settled in the two-room tar paper shack with a pitched roof on the homestead that Billy had abandoned. Nettie recalled that antelope still grazed on the open range, and "the coyotes used to howl all night there."[12] Irene was too young to have memories of this stay, but both she and Nettie describe the majority of the homesteaders that had claimed land near them as "the Russians," or "the Roosians." The families they recall seem to make this doubtful, as their neighbors bore the surnames Hegel, Degenstein, Hoeffert, Singer, and Beckholtz. There is, however, reason to believe

---

11. "Do Cows Drink Their Own Milk," *AgricAite.com,* https://agricsite.com/do-cows-drink-their-own-milk/.
12. Nettie Fortune, "Personal Memories," 61.

they were correct in this assertion. Both Catherine the Great and Czar Alexander I had invited the efficient German peasants to resettle in Russia and by 1870, some 450,000 Germans had done so, more in Ukraine than anywhere else, and their economic success and desire for more land had brought one-third of South Russia's arable land under their control.[13] The 1870s reforms by Alexander II halted the influx and were accompanied by rising nationalism that included forbidding sale of lands to non-Russians. Canadian and United States railroad recruiters offered opportunities for land in North America, and 300,000 Germans left Russia. Half of the Germans who settled in Canada in the pre-1914 era were from the German areas of Russia.[14] That matches Nettie's recollection that the Russians came about the time Billy had originally filed for his homestead in Alberta.

These neighbors being Russian eventually left a gruesome memory with Irene from when she became old enough to be aware and retain what she saw. As an adult, she needed to confirm it with Nettie. The Russians, even if their heritage was German, brought with them to the New World a paranoia about military conscription. In the eighteenth century, each village was responsible for a certain number of soldiers, and their conscription was for life. Since these were nearly all illiterate peasants, once they were called to join the army, they never saw or heard from their families again. From 1793 through 1874 service was for twenty-five years, still a life conscription for many. Self-mutilation was common, and many recruits failed to meet minimum physical requirements.[15] An 1874 law reduced service time to five years, but many remained suspicious. Among those

13. "The Geographical Origins of the German Speaking Immigrants," *AlbertaHistory*, https://sites.ualberta.ca/~german/AlbertaHistory/Georigin.htm.

14. Ibid.

15. Walter M. Pintner, "The Burden of Defense in Imperial Russia," The Russian Review," Vol.49, No.3, Jul 1984, 251-252.

suspicious were the Russian homesteaders near Bow Island, Alberta.

What Irene recalled about her neighbors, she became aware of once they were her playmates and in class together at school. According to Nettie, "In Russia every boy, when he got to be sixteen or eighteen, had to serve in the army. So, when they were born, they would take a pin or needle and scratch out one eye to put the sight out of one eye. Then they wouldn't have to serve in the army. Can you imagine that?"[16] By doing so, the young man would be a good farm hand, but ineligible for military service.

What is likely the most amazing thing about Nettie and Oliver's story to this point is that their lives were in so many ways identical to those of their ancestors in Norway over a century earlier. As has been true for much of history, life for the poor involved working hard to provide some food for survival. Medical care was mainly home remedies. The couple reached a small village of wood structures in the middle of a very rural area where the population consisted of struggling small farmers dependent on the whims of nature where there were extremes that made life challenging. They traveled by a horse-drawn cart, and their daughter was born in a one-room shack. Their Norwegian ancestors of a century earlier knew about working hard on the land to survive. They traveled and resettled with their belongings on buggies and wagons, going to the village for necessary supplies and to see others socially. Both mainly ignored the problems beyond their small locale but were affected by them even so. Eventually, their ancestors moved on to a new country for greater opportunity, hoping to do what they had been doing in Norway but be rewarded for it much more. That was also Nettie and Oliver's hope in heading to Canada. Oliver's trip by train in the boxcar was

---

16. Nettie Fortune, "Personal Memories," 73.

one experience that would have been new to their earliest known relatives.

Oliver and Nettie's Norwegian ancestors possessed the skills one hundred years earlier that, had it somehow been possible for them to be transplanted to where Oliver and Nettie were in 1911, would have helped them live life successfully since all would have been familiar. By contrast, if the Oliver and Nettie of 1911 could have been transplanted to 2011 and the lives of their descendants, they would have almost no understanding of anything, from transportation, medicine, entertainment, and all that has followed the digital revolution. In the present, each new generation is given a label, from Baby Boomers following World War II, to Generations X, Y, Z, and currently, A[17] because it is different from the previous one. Constant, increasing acceleration in rapid change is now the norm, widening gaps between what generations know and the skills they have. Nettie and Oliver were a young couple who moved off to a new place they did not know in search of a better life. They saw many changes in the time following this resettlement in Bow Island. How their situations developed requires returning to their roots.

---

17. Kasasa, "Boomers, Gen X, Gen Y, Gen Z, and Gen A Explained," The Kasasa Exchange, https://www.kasasa.com/exchange/articles/generations/gen-x-gen-y-gen-z, Jul 6, 2021.

CHAPTER 2: NETTIE'S NORWEGIAN HERITAGE

Nettie's ancestry goes back to the time of the Vikings, meaning her descendants also have a Viking heritage. Perhaps the risk-taking, courage, and fatalistic attitude that characterized Nettie, Irene, and so many of the women in this saga owe something to the bit of Viking that was passed down to them over the many generations. A distant relative, Dag Arne Danielson of Flovåg, Norway, who has access to Norwegian records, traced Nettie and Irene's [and the author's] direct ancestry back for over 1000 years to the dim hazes of the Middle Ages. The book he created[18] begins with what he termed "the starting person," Irene F. Fortune, and includes 846 individuals who are direct line ancestors, providing date and place of birth and death. This leads directly to Nettie's very many times great grandfather as the earliest known forefather.

He was Viking på Torsnes, who was born in the 1100s.[19] Naming a person by his role, craft, or vocation had been introduced to Norway by this time from outsiders in territories throughout Europe the Vikings had conquered in previous centuries.[20] This was the same as Smith, Miller,

---

18. Dag Arne Danielsen, *Ancestors of Irene F. Fortune* (Florvåg, Norway: self-published, 2020).

19. Ibid. 388.

20. Solveig Wikstrøm, "Surnames and Identities," *Names and Identities, Oslo Studies in Language*, Vol. 4, No. 2, 2012, 258-259.

Carpenter, Thatcher, Taylor, Hunter, and many more names in Britain, where Vikings long occupied large areas of the isles. The Vikings were in decline by the time of Viking på Torsnes, as their era of great overseas conquest, known as the Viking Age, had begun at the start of the ninth century and is commonly said to have ended in 1066 with the defeat of King Harald Hardrada in England. Many Vikings had returned to Norway and carried on, still raiding England for a time, and raided Iona, Scotland in 1209-1210.[21]

Viking is actually a verb for raiding that describes pirates who traveled in sleek longboats and conquered many territories in Europe and Russia. While the Vikings were raiders and traders, they were most spectacularly great sailors. Unlike most other early sailors, they traveled great distances, daring to navigate out of sight of land. While Viking remnants have been found in Istanbul and Athens, by the year 874, they had reached Iceland,[22] which today includes many descendants in its population. These Scandinavians famously carried on and their stories have been derived from two Icelandic sagas, *Eric's Saga*, written in the thirteenth century, and *The Greenlanders' Saga*, written in the fourteenth, both from oral history, but parts verified by later research.[23] According to Icelandic histories and the study of records and ruins, a Viking living on Iceland, Eric the Red, had a son named in traditional Norwegian fashion Eriksson, first name Leif. Eric was

---

21. Ian Beuermann, "The Norwegian Attack on Iona in 2009-10: The Last Viking Raid?" *Medievalists.net*, https://www.medievalists. net/2016/02/the-norwegian-attack-on-iona-in-1209-10-the-last-viking-raid/, Apr 11, 2012.

22. Brian Handwerk, "New Dating Method Shows Vikings Occupied Newfoundland in 1021 C.E.," *Smithsonian Magazine*, Oct 20, 2021.

23. For an explanation of the sagas and their histories see Brigitta Wallace, "The Norse in Newfoundland: "L'Anse aux Meadows and Vinland," *Newfoundland and Labrador Studies*, https://journals.lib. unb.ca/index.php/nflds/article/view/140/236.

banished from Iceland for killing a neighbor and in 985, he sailed west with nineteen long boats, eventually founding a settlement on Greenland that grew to 500 Vikings and their descendants.[24]

It has long been said with little evidence that Erik's son Leif took discovery a step further and led Vikings to become the first Europeans to set foot on the Americas, arriving 500 years before Columbus.[25] Columbus Day became a public holiday in 1937, but there was pressure from states with significant Scandinavian heritage to recognize Leif Erikson. In 1964, President Johnson signed a proclamation that made October 9 Leif Erikson Day, and it has remained so since, but was little noticed, as it is not a public holiday and also falls on Beer and Pizza Day.

Evidence that dated Viking presence in Newfoundland in 1021, or that the Vikings "discovered" America, was scientifically proved and described in the journal *Nature*[26] and also reported by *The Smithsonian*.[27] This study by nine scientists presented exactly one thousand years following the time of the specific presence of these adventurers, examined what had been scraps from a reconstructed site. In 1960, a Norwegian explorer named Helga Ingstad discovered early Viking relics at L'Anse aux Meadows in Newfoundland, Canada, and the site had been remade into a tourist attraction by building it as it might have looked at the time of occupation. New technology allowed examination of the original trees removed for attraction of what was called

24. Tim Folger, "Why Did Greenland's Vikings Vanish," *Smithsonian Magazine*, Mar 2017.

25. Christopher Klein, "The Viking Explorer Who Beat Columbus to America," *History*, https://www.history.com/news/the-viking-explorer-who-beat-columbus-to-america. Sep 2, 2020.

26. Margot Kuitems *et al.* "Evidence for European Presence in the Americas in 1021," *Nature*. Vol. 601, Oct 20, 2021.

27. Brian Handwerk, "New Dating Method Shows Vikings Occupied Newfoundland in 1021 C.E."

the 993 cosmic radiation anomaly when a storm on the sun released an enormous pulse of radiation that affected plant life around the world. It left evidence in tree rings that could be detected by scientists, so they only needed to count the rings to know when the trees had been cut down. The chops were made by a sharp metal ax when no such tools existed in America and they had three trees surviving, all yielding the date 1021 for having been chopped down. The Vikings were the first Europeans to land in the New World.

So, the story of this family's Norwegian heritage begins with a Viking. Not all of life can be nurture. Some Viking nature is in the genetic code from long ago that seems to have resurfaced on occasion over the years, and that nature was of undaunted courage in the face of unknown challenges. It seems appropriate that from the earliest known instance, the lineage was carried on by a woman. Viking på Torsnes had only one child, his daughter Inga Vikingsdatter Torsnes. The story would have ended there if she had remained childless, but she married Kalv Torsnes. It is appropriate that there is a Vikingsdatter to begin this saga, as over the many years, and especially when there are recorded memories of the lives of the families, it would be the strong, determined datters that would keep the family from passing into the oblivion of families that have ceased to exist. The only son of Vikingsdatter Torsnes and Kalv Torsnes was Guttorm Kalvson Torsnes, born in 1220, so the heritage continued.

Among the early ancestors, there were nobles in the late Middle Ages who had coats of arms, and also many common people who were likely peasants. Danielsen includes maps, paintings, photos when they became possible, and extra information he located in his impressive work. This record includes the parents' birth and death dates, all their children in the known cases, and the number of children. As that period transitioned to the Renaissance, the longest-living family members overlapped. Gyrid Torbergsdatter Berge was born in 1390 and lived to age 107, dying in 1497. In the last years of her life, Jon Trondson Benkestok was a young man, living from 1480 until 1593, a span of 113 years.[28] They contrast greatly with the many immigrants who would come later, where so many did not survive childhood. Of course, the same was no doubt true and likely worse for many of those from longer ago.

Most of this story excludes the first sixteen generations of Fortune progenitors in Norway, other than some speculation, and is based on the following four who made the move to America. In this case, generations are not terms that relate to a social/cultural relationship between people of similar ages, like Generations X, Y, Z, but to the steps in the line of ancestry.

The ancestry line is complicated, as Norwegians frequently changed their surnames from generation to generation and within their own lifetimes as well. Traditional practice was for an individual to use a forename, such as Ole, a patronym such as Olson. Patronyms or surnames often ended in "-sen" or "-son," meaning "son of," so there were many Johnsons who were sons of John, Petersons who were sons of Peter, Olsons who were sons of Ole, and so on. There were also many "datters," or daughters, such as Nettie's very early relative Inga Vikingsdatter, a girl given the name Inga whose father still was called a Viking. But these names, like Petersdatter, vanished after marriage. There was also a toponym, or place name, which was often a farm such as Forde in Nettie's ancestry. While not common, a Norwegian who moved around a good deal could have used a dozen or more last names. Though Norway attempted to remedy this situation in 1870 by prohibiting the changing of surnames, the custom was well established and did not completely vanish.

---

28. Danielsen, *Ancestors of Irene F. Fortune*, 15.

On the Olson side of Nettie and Irene's mother's family, the earliest of her known close US relatives to their family of American immigrant transplants are Halver Finne of Voss, Norway, born in 1731, and his wife Inga.[29] Their only son, Joe, was born in 1779 when Halver was forty-eight. Being Halver's son, he was known as Joe Halverson. There were many Joe Halversons in Norway, and he was the one from the farm called Finne in the southwest region of Norway known as Vestland, so his name was Joe Halverson-Finne. When Joe was a man, he left Finne and resettled near the village of Vinje, and his name was increased to Joe Halverson Finne Vinje.

It was not only Joe Halverson Finne Vinje's last name that was subject to frequent change. His nationality was altered by events in the world around him, though he was only aware of the small area around the farming communities where he worked. Rural Norway was not integrated into Europe, and a peasant in or near a village might have no awareness of the world beyond the surrounding area and perhaps a nearby village. At the time of Joe's birth, Norway was part of the Kingdom of Denmark. One thing that distinguished Norwegians from Danes of this time is that small farmers in Norway like Joe and Halver owned the land they cultivated, while in Denmark they were mainly peasants on the property of a noble lord.[30] When he was a young man, unbeknownst to Joe, Napoleon launched his disastrous invasion of Russia (ninety-nine years before the marriage of Nettie and Oliver and Irene's birth). That was soon followed by the Battle of Leipzig and the defeat of France. In the Treaty of Kiel of 1814, Denmark gave its control of Norway to the king of

29. Violet Anserude, letter to Nettie Fortune, "The Family Tree of Halvor Finne from Voss, Norway" RR#2, Case Lake, Minnesota, May 5, 1978.

30. Gudleiv Bø, "The History of a Norwegian National Identity," University of Oslo, https://www.tsu.ge/data/file_db/scandinavian-studies/Nation-building-the-Norwegian-way.pdf, 7.

Sweden, so Joe became subject to Swedish rule, though Norway retained internal self-government. Throughout this time, Joe was never aware that he was anything other than a Norwegian.

When Joe lived in Finne and was single, his parents felt it was their responsibility to find him an appropriate bride, someone who would provide a suitable inheritance or dowry. Romantic love was not considered a main reason for marriage at that time especially in rural areas, where marriages of convenience were arranged by parents. Joe was on the young side, as marriage for men commonly took place over the age of twenty-eight.[31] His parents were in their late fifties and well beyond the life expectancy of the time of thirty-five,[32] and a good marriage could bring in the income to hire help for the farm as well as having someone else to do daily chores.

There was a woman, Ingeborg Andresdatter Lillethem, who caught Joe's eye. Ingeborg was a servant on a nearby farm. Hers was a common life as there were 95,000 young Norwegians who were servants in Norway.[33] Being sent into service dates back to the poor laws in the Middle Ages and was really increased with the labor shortage that followed the Black Death that hit in 1349. Christian V's Norwegian Law of 1687 made service compulsory, and this was still in force when Joe met Ingeborg. It had been clarified by a 1754 law that prohibited farmers from having more than one son

31. Jon Gjerde and Anne McCants, "Fertility, Marriage and Culture: Demographic Processes Among Norwegian Immigrants to the Middle West," *Journal of Economic History*, Vo. 55, No. 4, Dec 1995, 863.

32. Aaron O'Neill, "Life Expectancy in Norway, 1765-2020," *Statista*, https://www.statista.com/statistics/1041314/life-expectancy-norway-all-time/, Sep 19, 2019.

33. Monica Miscali, "What Happened in the North? Servants and Rural Workers in Norway," *Mundo Agrario* Vol 18, No 39, Dec 2017, 2.

and one daughter at home above age sixteen,[34] so since Joe was an only child, he was not forced to be involved.

Joe had seen enough of Ingeborge to realize that she would make a fine partner for survival and perhaps even success. They met for the Norwegian tradition of "night courting" as the weather warmed. In night courting, Joe would come to Ingeborge's sleeping quarters in her master's barn at night without informing his parents or her master. It was a way of testing their attraction and compatibility. It was only a Saturday event since she was allowed time off on the Sabbath to get to church.

On other days, she had to be up by 5 a.m. to start her sixteen-hour day. Ingeborge, being female, probably started her years in service earning one *riksdaler* per year, but she would have worked her way up to two or three. A *riksdaler* was the cost of a barrel of grain. Along with that she was given some clothes, food, and a place to stay.[35] Life was undoubtedly hard for her.

In 1807, Ingeborge and Joe were married and moved to the village of Vinje, where they purchased a small plot that came with a *hytte*, or hut. The unpainted country cabin had a hole in the roof to let out smoke from their fireplace. Though some more successful peasants had added chimneys, which had come to Norway earlier, most common people got by with the traditional and less efficient ceiling holes, so when the weather became cold, there was often a smell of smoke on everything. Furnishings were limited to a stove, benches, a bed and bedspread, a table, and the painted chests they had both brought with them from Finne containing what they owned.

---

34. Sølvi Songer, "The Legal Status of Servants in Norway from the Seventeenth to the Twentieth Century," in Antoinette Fauve-Chamoux, Ed., *Domestic Service and the Formation of European Identity* (Bern: Peter Lang AG, 2004), 182.

35. Ibid., 4.

Vinje was notable among the small peasant villages that dotted the country as it was where the first Norwegian *Svarte Bok*, or Black Book, had been found centuries earlier. The Black Book was a book of *sorteboksfonnler,* supernatural charms, and incantations, some dating back to ancient times, as well as associated formulas for potions.

Joe and Ingeborge, like most Norwegians, would have known of Black Books from tales of dread in their youth. The Norwegian weekly magazine *Skillin Magazin* reported in 1859 when their son was living in America, "Who in childhood did not hear about Black Books and who was not then frightened and shaken by the 'true' reports of this book's unmatched mystical properties?" That same article stated, "Faith in the Black Book still flourishes . . . among the honorable common folk whose livestock or children suffer from one or another illness caused by witchcraft or evil spirits."[36] Throughout history, the Norwegian Black Book has been associated with Satanism and witchcraft.[37] Black Books combined white and black magic with folk medicine and religion to heal both human and animal ailments, prevent misfortune, curse others, and attempt to affect the owner's future.

When Ingeborge and Joe resettled in Vinje, there would have been a heightened awareness of the Black Book by people of all ages, as a number of the books had recently been discovered[38] under the floorboards of the choir in the stave church. Stave churches were the great wooden cathedrals of Norway, where so many of the Black Books, or *grimoires*, had been stored. The small community had accumulated

---

36. Kathleen Stokker, "Narratives of Magic and Healing: *Oldtidens Sortebog* in Norway and New the New Land," *Scandinavian Studies,* Vol. 73, No. 3, Fall 2001, 400.

37. Mary S. Rustad, *The Black Books of Elverum* (Lakerville, MN: Galde Press, Inc., 2009), XI.

38. Ibid., 400.

Books since the time they first appeared there in 1480,[39] when witches were presumed to be prevalent throughout Europe. It had been common to think that witchcraft or evil spirits caused illness in children or livestock, a belief that carried on among the common folk in rural districts for centuries. By the 1800s, there were hundreds of Black Books in circulation in Norway, and others concealed and accumulated for centuries beneath the floorboards in choir lofts and under altar cloths of stave churches such as Vinje's, as that was thought to guarantee salvation for their owners.

While the Black Book and its magic powers were common knowledge to Norwegians, there were many stories about its origin. One belief that had been held for centuries was that Black Books were connected to the sixth and seventh books of Moses. Many people believed that Moses had written the first five books of the Bible: Genesis, Exodus, Leviticus, Numbers, and Deuteronomy, often called "the books of Moses," or the Torah. However, some believed Moses had written books six and seven about the powerful magic he had learned to combat the wizards of Egypt when he struggled to free the Israelites from their captivity.[40] It was said that the Church chose to hide these from the public since they were too dangerous, but the perception of Moses as being a wizard was common in early Christianity through medieval times.[41] The so-called "original Bible" with all the books of Moses was believed

---

39. "Vinjeboka: The Very Oldest Svartebok Manuscript, 1480 - 1520," *Grimoire Archives*. https://booksofmagick.com/vinjeboka/ /. Oct 24, 2020.

40. Roald E. Kristiansen, "Two Northern Grimoires: The Trondenes and the Vesteaålen Black Books," *Acta Borealia*, Vol. 30, No. 2, Dec 2013, 209.

41. For a detailed look at the relationship between Moses and magic in early writing see Yuval Harari, "Moses, the Sword, and The Sword of Moses: Between Rabbinical and Magical Traditions," *Jewish Studies Quarterly*, Vol. 12, No. 4, 2005.

to reside secretly in Wittenberg,[42] home of Martin Luther's Protestant Reformation.

Some continental European scholars claimed the Book was an adaptation or translation of Heinrich Cornelius Agrippa's influential book, *De Occulta Philosophia,* [43] which was published on continental Europe in the sixteenth century and England in the seventeenth. Since the Black Book appeared in Vinje in the fifteenth century, that explanation is doubtful. While the Scientific Revolution of the seventeenth century and the Enlightenment in the eighteenth had rendered belief in magic and fear of demons redundant among the educated on the continent, that was not the case in Norway. There, the vast majority of the population into the nineteenth century was largely unaware of the existence of continental Europe and changing European culture, and belief in magic and charms for healing remained a part of popular culture.

The name Cyprianus appeared on many of the Books' covers. One explanation was that long ago Cyprianus had been a Christian bishop who studied at the Black School and became a powerful magician. It was said that he was described as "too evil for Hell,"[44] and when Hell refused to accept him, he was disgusted by his expulsion and returned home. There, he wrote nine books of *Trolldomskunstner*, or magic arts, which became the basis of the Black Books.

An anachronistic story believed by some was that the Cyprianus who had authored the Book was not an ancient bishop, but a beautiful and gifted Mexican nun who had come to Denmark. A degenerate Danish bishop tried to seduce her, but she rejected him. He eventually stuck her in a dungeon and left her for her refusal. She thought she

---

42. Kristiansen, "Two Northern Grimoires," 210-211.

43. English edition, Agrippa, Henry Cornelius, *Three Books of Occult Philosophy* (London: Gregory Moule), 1651.

44. Stokker, "Narratives of Magic and Healing," 406.

would never escape, so she shredded her clothing to form pages and used her own blood to write down the secrets known only to her. Though she was devout, among the things she knew was *djevelmaning,* conjuring up the devil.

Cyprianus never escaped but died in the dungeon with her writings. In 1400, Black George, a medieval knight and renowned magician, was on the Jutland peninsula in northern Denmark at the time of the excavation of an old castle. He came upon the writings Cyprianus had left and realized what he had found. When he died, the chants, potions, and incantations were secured in a golden box that was placed next to his burial linen, the casket of the time, and he was laid to rest in the castle's foundation wall. The knight's death box remained there, and over time the castle wall eventually disintegrated. Ultimately, all that remained where the castle had once stood was reduced to farmland. A peasant plowing his field found the death box with the Book still intact and learned the Book's secrets. He became a powerful lord and shared the Black Book's secrets, which was how it became distributed.

Whatever happened, in Norway many pastors owned both a Bible and a Black Book.[45] Their congregations called on them in many difficult situations, and the Black Book offered advice for healing the sick, both animals and people, and recovering lost items, among other useful things.

There is no reason to believe that Black Book awareness was anything beyond a curiosity for Ingeborge and Joe, but the Books made their way to America with Norwegian emigration. In Minnesota, they continued to be used by some into the early twentieth century. Minnesota is where Oliver's ancestors settled. Whether they ever encountered Black Books is uncertain, but his mother was recalled as being a believer in similar mystical folklore that originated

---

45. MS.801059 "Vinjeboka". - *Nasjonalbbibliotetek*, https://www. nb.no/nbsok/nb/c596c7c4925c127cdef017847b5b17ad?index=1#0, from Dag Arne Danielsen. Bergen, Norway, March 18, 2022.

in Norway. A woman born in the Minnesota city of Duluth in 1901 remembered her mother using the Black Book in her youth to find a cure for her warts, taking her out under a full moon at midnight to apply the formula, then burying it.[46] A man born in Moorhead, Minnesota in 1926, inherited a Black Book he believed to be "an evil power and of the devil."[47]

Joe and Ingeberg were ready to move on from Vinje. They had selected a new town in the west of Norway and while there was farmland, it was surrounded by forests and snow-capped mountains, with lakes and fast-flowing rivers nearby for fishing, with the sea not so very far away. That was the parish of Førde. With packed wagon and plow horses, the couple headed off on the 250-mile trek to Førde. The two-week journey north took them into terrain that was unlike anything they had ever seen. There were rivers to cross and they had to change directions when they came upon a fjord. Lakes interfered with their route and waterfalls cascaded from high above, so water seemed to be everywhere as they came closer to the Atlantic coast and fishing country. There were towering peaks, the greatest of all being when they approached Førde and Hafstadfjellet Mountain, rising well over 2000 feet above the flat plain. Also, something they had not previously encountered was the mountains of ice, the glaciers. It was a surprisingly different world that was completely new to them.

After making it to Førde, the couple bought a small farm in the countryside. Joe again had a new name, becoming Joe Førde. Soon pregnancy became a near-constant condition for Ingeborge. First came Stor-Ola, followed by Andres. Peder, also known as Per, was third, and Erik was next. Joe, then Lars and Ole rounded out the family of all boys, born every other year. The first recorded memory Nettie later

---

46. Stokker, "Narratives of Magic and Healing," 412.
47. Ibid. 414.

collected beyond genealogy of her family was a specific event involving one of the sons from this time in Førde. From that, it is clear that they remained farmers. Farming was fine for subsistence and barter, with their butter and eggs, their corn, and especially their potatoes. Since the rise of distilling and the vast amount of vodka being produced, it was not possible to grow too many potatoes. Farmers and fishermen had traditionally lived in a barter economy, and it is estimated that only 17% of the population existed in a money economy by this time.[48] However, things in Norway were changing, and the country and business dealings were moving to money and banking.[49]

It is probable that Joe learned to fish, especially as the boys grew and could help with the farming before they left to start their own lives and families. Fishing would have been a way to provide the family with additional money. While they were surviving, one of the things that required money was the new fascination that enveloped them. "American fever" had come to Førde and the rest of western Norway. Like everyone else, Joe was swept up in it.

"American fever" was the term people used, as though the obsession was a contagious disease or, as some thought, demonic possession. In any case, there was little else people talked about. It conjured up visions of opportunity for improved lives that would never be possible in Norway. The word of America and opportunity spread through valleys and villages by letters and word of mouth along centuries-old paths. As people like Joe began to move from parish to parish, the talk spread with them of this land with endless

---

48. Reidar Østesjø, "The Spring Herring Fishing and the Industrial Revolution in Western Norway in the Nineteenth Century," *Scandinavian Economic History Review*, Vol. 11, No. 2, Dec 20, 2011, 136.

49. Oyvid Eitrheim, Jan T. Klovland and Jan F. Qvigstad, eds., *Historical Monetary Statistics for Norway 1819-2003* (Oslo: Norges Bank, 2004), 24.

expanses of cheap, fruitful soil waiting to be taken. A letter from America was news for a whole village, regardless of its recipient, and would be passed around, read out loud. In school, when children learned geography and the names of countries, few were told of France, England, Spain, but like their parents, they could rattle off with ease the "countries" they had heard of from emigrants: Wisconsin, Iowa, Illinois, Minnesota.

Early on in the century, the Haugeans, Quaker religious dissenters from traditional Lutheranism, had resettled in America. There were also notable leaders at the time pushing Norwegians to venture forth, such as one who exclaimed, "We have some schoolmasters at home who say we are a peasant land. This is a lie. Norway is a Viking land. We are not bears to sleep in winter; we make our nests in the mountains, but the flight of our wings and our longing goes over the whole world."[50]

Joe decided that the future for his family was in America. It was obvious. He and Ingeborge were too old to start over, but this wonderful place held the destiny of his children. He was one of many Norwegians who made this choice. Jan Myre noted in *Nordics Info* that Norwegians were not especially poverty-stricken by European standards, but they would rank second [to Ireland] on the percentage of their country that would emigrate in the great migration of 1830 to 1920. Myre argues that the lure of America was stronger in Norway than elsewhere, and those who left retained contact with their home country. Norwegian-Americans sent letters, money, and tickets for relatives' trips.[51]

50. Andreas R. Graven, "The Horrific Disease That Won't Die," *sciencenor.no*, https://sciencenorway.no/bacteria-diseases-forskningno/the-horrific-disease-that-wont-die/1464510, Apr 13, 2012.

51. Jan Eivind Myhre, "Emigration from Norway 1830-1920," *nordics info*, https://nordics.info/show/artikel/emigration-from-norway-1830-1920, Sept 8, 2021.

Joe was going to be the first in his family Førde to leave Norway, and no one was sending them tickets or money, so he was going to get some. But to earn *speciedalers*, or silver currency, it is likely he devoted time to fishing while his sons maintained the farm.

There were trout in the lakes and in the rivers, fast-swimming salmon. If he or any of his sons had familiarized himself with taking a boat out to sea, they could drop in a net and return with cod and herring in large quantities. The waters off the west coast of Norway had the largest concentration of cod in the world, and they were slit and dried until rock hard, which was called "stockfish" and could stay in stock for nearly a decade. The livers were boiled in an iron cauldron to extract liver oil, which had many uses and was very much in demand. Assuming Joe did or supervised this, after accumulating more stockfish and cod liver oil than was necessary for bartering for the necessities, he would have set off to sell it where he could earn real money. That would have been his first trip to a city, Bergen.

Joe's first visit to Bergen was no doubt a totally incomprehensible experience. The city had been Norway's capital centuries earlier and with a population of over 35,000 people, it was completely unlike the tiny villages he had known. Colorfully painted houses and shops lined its streets that had wooden plank walkways. A powerful fortress with cannons and ancient churches stood as reminders of when it had been a prominent center in the major medieval trade organization of northern Europe, the Hanseatic League. People dressed much differently and lived in a more complicated manner. The old guild area was occupied by merchants who bought and sold goods. Searching here, Joe could have found a buyer for both cod liver oil and stockfish, or his surplus potatoes. In the harbor were huge sailing vessels, with stacks of chests and boxes piled high next to them.

Then there were these frightening people the likes of which Joe had never seen before. They were begging, but what had happened to them? Had they been cursed in some evil way? Were they devils? It is likely Joe encountered a victim of leprosy, perhaps a desperate beggar, in Bergen, as Norway had the greatest concentration of people suffering from leprosy in Europe at that time,[52] many with its most disfiguring manifestation. It was assumed that they were either cursed by God or possessed by evil spirits and if Joe encountered them, and assuming his response was typical, he likely found them both frightening and repulsive. Leprosy had existed in Norway since the time of the Vikings, and the country's first leprosarium was built in Bergen in 1411, followed by its first hospital.[53] By the nineteenth century, conditions in the hospital were described by its chaplain as "a graveyard for the living."[54] Leprosy and its stigma would follow Norwegian emigrants to America, with a substantial number ending in Minnesota.[55] Later in the century, it was a Norwegian, Dr. Gerhard Hansen, who discovered the microorganism responsible for the disease, giving it its proper name: Hansen's disease.

Having enough money for the resettling of his family in America was no small project, and it was time for the boys and their families to head off on their own and find their futures and fortunes in America. Joe and Ingeborge had made it to sixty, well beyond their time. The trip and

52. Andreas R. Graven, "The Horrific Disease That Won't Die," *sciencenor.no*, https://sciencenorway.no/bacteria-diseases-forskningno/the-horrific-disease-that-wont-die/1464510, Apr 13, 2012.

53. Paul and Brenda Cohen, "The Leprosy Museum at St. George's Hospital in Bergen," *Journal of College Science Teaching*, Vol. 28, No. 1, Sept/Oct 1998, 70.

54. Ibid., 71.

55. See "Leprosy in Minnesota" 124-137, in Walter L. Washburn, "Leprosy Among the Scandinavian Settlers in the Upper Mississippi Valley, 1864-1932," *Bulletin of the History of Medicine*, Vol.24, No.2, Mar-Apr, 1950.

resettlement would have been too much for them to handle. The boys realized they all wanted to eventually go, and did, but only Peder was set to make the trip. He and his family prepared to leave in 1853. He would be the family's explorer and find a location, then write back for the others to follow and join him; or that was the plan.

Peder made his choice among the mysteriously named places based on what he heard from others, and he picked Wisconsin, a popular choice for Norwegians. Peder's wife Guri busied herself making ample quantities of flatbread, salting meat and herring, drying pork, packing containers of peas, potatoes, grain, flour, whey, cheese, and making or repairing sheepskin coverlets and blankets. She picked out what she was going to need, including her spinning wheel, iron griddle, and cooking utensils. Peder sold his share of the farm, stock, and tools, got a good ax, and made the arrangements. They boxed their things in chests and painted "WISCONSIN" on the side as an address along with his name.

CHAPTER 3: NEW WORLD

On May 10, 1853, Bergen was crowded with people from inland farms, dressed in brightly colored homespun clothes as they searched the city seeking last minute provisions. Peder and Guri took their wagon to the wharf and located the loading area for their ship, the *Virgo*. They unloaded what they had packed along with the stacks of other boxes and chests labeled, AMERICA, MINNESOTA, ILLINOIS, MICHIGAN, NEW YORK CITY, or CHICAGO. There were also other passengers from Førde who were on this voyage, so there was hope they would make for good companionship. After spending a little time walking around Bergen, they returned and boarded the ship. Others were doing the same and emotions were mixed. Some were happy and excited as they walked the plank onto the *Virgo*, while others looked solemn and sad, knowing they would never see this country, their Norway, again.

Peder's concern, which was shared by many, was not so much for his future in America as for how he and his family would survive for two or three months on the ocean. He had been fishing with his father and had been off the coast for brief periods only. Guri, who at forty-two was two years older than Peder, had seen plenty of water, but she had never been on it. The same was true of their six children, whose ages ranged from three to thirteen. Like the other passengers, they were giving up everything for a place they really knew of only in rumors and secondhand tales from people they did not know. Even more frightening was leaving dry land and the prospect of living in cramped conditions that were alien and a complete mystery.

It was up to Peder to lead the way and reassure his family. They walked the plank onto the deck of the ship, then went below and staked claim to their sleeping quarters where their family could remain together, and piled bed clothes on them. The ship had two rows of bunks fastened to walls on starboard and port sides, with space for five in each bunk. Peder and Guri would keep three-year-old Ole in their bunk while another was taken by their daughter named for Peder's mother, Ingeborge, along with John, Anders, and Brithe. Peder had brought several tools with him and hammered in nails that served as pegs for hanging bags, coverlets, and dried food. They were among the seventy-seven passengers in steerage, the cheapest way to travel, while twelve were in what was called "houses on deck" and nine had cabins.[56]

Soon the ship was full and crowded with hopeful, nervous Norwegians. Many went up on deck as they left the quay and watched anxiously, hoping they had made the right decision as their homeland disappeared in the distance.

Not long after departing, seasickness was rampant and Master Meidel, the ship's captain, had the passengers help the crew with scrubbing decks, cleaning, and sweeping as they slowly adjusted. The once optimistic voyagers spent much time early on lying in their bunks and moaning. When the sea was gentle, though, the wind moved them along well. Following good sleep, Peder and his family felt much better and their spirits rose. Before long, they joined the others on deck when the weather was good, where some were using chests as tables and chairs. Soon fiddles were brought out, and before long dancing began. The adults and

---

56. "Passenger List 1853 -brig Virgo," *Norway Heritage*, NARA Roll # 128, arr. no. 600, http://www.norwayheritage.com/p_list.asp?jo=2045.

some of the younger people did country dances, waltzes, polkas, schottisches, the "spring dance," and the "halling." Children ran races and young men, including John and Anders, wrestled to get exercise in the confined space. On May 17, Norway's national holiday, "Syttende Mai," or Constitution Day, they were well out in the ocean and there was considerable celebration. The flag was hoisted and courtesy of the captain, there were rounds of brandy.

When the weather turned bad, they all had to stay below, the deck and the hatches were battened down, the quarters were dark, and the air became stale. On the occasions when persistent stormy weather kept them confined, the passengers not only were uncomfortable, but they began to worry about their health. Their captain also was concerned about typhus and dysentery, given how crowded they were, and so poorly equipped with toilets. Some of the older people got sick and several who were the age of Peder's parents Joe and Ingeborge did not make it, their dreams of America cut short. Respectful ceremonies were held before they were buried at sea.[57]

On June 23, 1853, Peder Forde and his family entered the mouth of the Hudson River as their long journey came to an end. The *Virgo* docked and the family gathered its belongings, then set foot in America for the first time on Ellis Island.[58] While some came to take advantage of them, they had been told of a group called the Scandinavian Society that had been founded in 1844 by Norwegians in

---

57. The description of the crossing is based on Ingrid Semminsen, "The Long Journey," in *Norway to America: A History of the Migration* (Minneapolis: University of Minnesota Press, 1975).
58. "Arriving Passenger and Crew List," *Virgo*, June 24, 1853, Castle Garden and Ellis Island, New York, *National Archives and Records Administration*.

Manhattan and could be trusted.[59] If Bergen had been a shock when they were leaving, New York City was totally unreal. Peder found a room in a Norwegian area where his family could stay, and he went off to make plans. Ingeborge and the other children tentatively saw some of the city of 600,000 that was preparing to host the first World's Fair in the United States in three weeks. Guri worried about whether they could belong in this very strange new world. Peder was successful in making arrangements for getting to the interior of America via the Erie Canal and before long they were off again, making their way to Wisconsin.

Other Norwegians took this route, while some took a longer water voyage all the way to New Orleans, then up the Mississippi River. They reached Wisconsin and settled, as it was a common destination for Lutherans, but found it had many settlers and soon moved on. The Fordes next settled in Big Canoe, Iowa in an area that had numerous Norwegian settlers, which was comfortable. Soon they moved to Chickasaw County in the northeast of the state, the most unsettled section in the area. Peder and his family built a log cabin on the prairie, acquired a team of oxen and a plow for them to pull, and turned the land into a farm. There, they raised a family that expanded rapidly, as was common with many Norwegian families of the time. They eventually had six sons, though Nils died at age three, and four daughters. Since they had settled in this remote area, the family could remain close together. The area had land for the boys to claim and start out on their own when the time came. The farming was good and there were also other Norwegian immigrants in the area.

The 1850s were a very difficult time in the United States and things were only getting worse. Norwegian settlers could not avoid the politics of their new home. The country

59. Lars Nilsen, "Norway's Presence in New York City - The Norwegian Immigration Association, Inc.," *Scandinavia Review* in *NIA*, https://niahistory.org.

was equally divided between states where slavery was relied on in the South and those where it was not allowed in the North. This kept the US Senate balanced and the government functioning. It had originally been established by the Missouri Compromise of 1820 that slavery was prohibited above the sacred line of 36° 30'. Eight years before Peder and Guri arrived, the territory of Iowa had been admitted to the union as a free state to maintain the balance in the Senate after Florida had been admitted as a slave state. The size of the country had been greatly increased by victory in the Mexican War of 1846-48, and new states coming in would threaten the balance, which led to the Compromise of 1850. This allowed California, which had rapidly gained a large population with the discovery of gold and the Rush of 1849, to enter the union as a free state, and "popular sovereignty," wherein the territories of New Mexico and Utah residents would vote to decide whether to allow slavery in those future states. There was a Fugitive Slave Act included in the compromise, stating that when slaves escaped to freedom in places like Iowa, fugitive slave hunters could demand help from US marshals. Additionally, the act stated that "all good citizens are hereby commanded to aid and assist in the prompt and efficient execution of this law."[60] Peder and Guri certainly wanted to be good citizens, but was this right? Still, for most of their Norwegian neighbors, the Compromise of 1850 seemed to have solved the slavery problem by keeping it confined to the South, and perhaps the Democratic Party was best prepared to see that this condition remained.

The whole Norwegian community had two sides pulling on it. Of course, they remained good Lutherans, and the leading members of the Norwegian Synod, influenced by the German Missouri Synod's position in favor of slavery,

---

60. "Fugitive Slave Act 1850," *The Avalon Project: Documents in Law, History and Diplomacy*, https://avalon.law.yale.edu/19th_century/fugitive.asp.

officially adopted that position in the 1850s.[61] Even so, most Norwegian immigrants did not seem to follow their church's lead, hoping for status quo and no problems to interfere with their pursuit of the American Dream. A number were like Peder and Guri, who had come to Iowa after settling elsewhere. Some who had previously been in Wisconsin or Minnesota helped spark the popularity of the Free Soil Party and its call for "free soil, free speech, free labor, and free men." In Wisconsin, which had the largest concentration of Norwegian settlers at the time, this group launched America's first Norwegian newspaper, *Norlyset*, or *The Northern Light*, promoting the Free Soil agenda since the late 1840s.[62] Norwegian papers of this time were written in Danish.[63] A much more widespread and influential Norwegian paper began publication in 1852 with the purpose "to hurry the process of Americanization,"[64] impacting Iowa and all the upper Midwest. This paper was *Emigrantin*, meaning "The Emigrant." It originally took a pro-Democratic, pro-slavery editorial stance.[65]

Then came 1854 and everything changed. Another political party, the American Party, emerged as a national force at this time. Members were commonly referred to as the "Know Nothings," since they were required to say "I know nothing" when asked about the party. Their anti-

61. Arlow William Andersen, "Venturing into Politics: The Norwegian-American Press of the 1850s," *Wisconsin Magazine of History*, Vol.32, No. 1, Sept 1948, 64.

62. Theodore C. Blegen, "The Early Norwegian Press in America," *Minnesota History Bulletin*, Vol. 3, No. 8, Nov 1920, 509.

63. Anrnstein Hjelde and Benthe Kolberg Jansson, "Language Reforms in Norway and Their Acceptance and Use in the Norwegian American Community," https://library.oapen. org/bitstream/handle/20.500.12657/54132/external_content. pdf?sequence=1#page=297, 2016, 298.

64. Andersen, "Venturing into Politics," 63.

65. Theodore C. Blegen, "The Early Norwegian Press in America," *Minnesota History Bulletin*, Vol. 3, No. 8, Nov 1920, 509.

immigration policy was not attractive to most Norwegians. The Kansas-Nebraska Act was signed into law, authorizing popular sovereignty, meaning the public would vote to determine whether slavery would exist in the massive territory bordering Iowa and nullifying the Missouri Compromise of 1820. In Kansas territory, a running guerilla battle between pro-slavery and anti-slavery forces labeled "Bleeding Kansas," broke out. The Free Soil Party gave up and joined others to form a new political party, the Republicans. *Emigrantin* switched allegiance to align itself with most Norwegians who supported the new Republican Party's position of antislavery, not merely anti-extension.[66] Lutherans in general favored the new party and supported it as well. The country was clearly divided and without sign of compromise.

Six years later, in November 1860, a Republican, Abraham Lincoln, was elected president. Peder could write to his homeland where they still had a Swedish king, that a rail splitter now ruled this new country with its open spaces for farms that would welcome Norwegian settlers. Soon after Lincoln's election, seven southern states seceded from the Union and on April 2, 1861, the American Civil War erupted. Though they had not been in America long, the Forde family was soon involved.

Throughout this time period, Peder and Guri's children had been growing up. Their firstborn was Ingeborge Forde, commonly called Inga, who had been born before they emigrated. Among the settlers in the area by this time was a man Inga had met years before in Norway, though it was an occasion that her parents were more likely to remember than was Inga. In Norway, his name was Ole Selland, but he

---

66. Ibid., 514.

changed it to Ole Olson upon moving to America.[67] When Inga was a five-year-old child and living near Oslo, Ole was fifteen.[68] Her parents had left her sleeping in the house while they were working in a hay field, and Ole passed by and heard her crying. So, he carried her out to her folks. Inga and Ole had both since emigrated and resettled in Iowa, and that acquaintance was eventually revived and soon became a romance. Irene's aunt, who knew Ole from when she was a child, described him as a big man for his time, standing well over six feet tall and with a "dark complexion and medium build."[69] Not all Ole's family survived resettling in America. Two of his three brothers had died tragically, as one drowned at a very early age and the other broke his neck and died instantly after falling off a platform on a barn. He also had three sisters.

After the Civil War broke out, eighteen-year-old Ole enlisted in the Union Army to fight for the cause of the North. He joined an infantry unit from the Dakota Territory in 1862 and eventually served as a private on the Crow Creek Indian Reservation on the Missouri River, and in Buffalo County until June of 1864. While on duty in the spring of 1864, he slept on the frozen ground, which he felt contributed to his contraction of pneumonia. Although he was given a medical discharge from the army, he continued to aid the war effort by bringing baked goods to Union soldiers.

After Ole was discharged, he and Inga became a couple. Soon, his third brother Eric, his remaining sibling who had emigrated from Norway and survived to adulthood,

---

67. Mildred (Millie) Reister Wilson, Nellie Fortune's first cousin, letter including family history, to Millie Purdy, March 21, 1954. Writer was granddaughter of Ole Olson and remembered him from her youth. This is disputed in other records that list him as from Førde farm, but they are not personal memories, 1.

68. Ibid., This is disputed in other records that list him as from Førde farm, but they are not personal memories.

69. Ibid., 3.

entered the picture. Eric joined Ole and Inga as they set off to begin a new life and left Chickasaw County, headed west, and homesteaded near Lake City, closer to Minnesota and Dakota. With little available timber, they built sod houses. These were made by cutting strips of sod and piling them in layers to make walls that were often over two feet wide. Floors were commonly dirt, though some homesteaders invested in wood and some also wrapped the house in tar paper. With such thick walls, windows were very small. Some thought they were warmer than log cabins when winter came, but the dark interior only furthered the inhabitants' sense of isolation.

During their time as neighbors in the distant terms of prairie settlers, they did some farming together. Relatives say Eric spent much of his life jealous of his brother Ole, and that was exposed when there was a dispute over a hayrack. While Ole still had pneumonia, he was entitled to a pension for his Civil War service and continuing disability that was to be sent to him monthly. Eric prevented him from receiving the payment. Eric picked up the mail in town for Ole and Inga as well as himself and, out of spite, when the money arrived, he held onto Ole's payments for six months.

Three years after the war, and a year after the birth of Ole and Inga's firstborn child, Caroline, the couple was married in 1868. Ole was twenty-eight and Inga eighteen. On their northwest Iowa homestead, they had fourteen children. In this very patriarchal world, their roles were well defined. Ole was the boss and Inga the helpmate. But as would be the case of early settlers and homesteaders, women's work was essential to success in agriculture. Abundant evidence indicates that from colonial times through the nineteenth century, White women on the moving frontier were engaged in from a third to more than half of all the food production on family farms and homesteads. They commonly helped men with the field work, especially at planting times. Women were solely responsible for all food preparation, childcare, household chores, production and repair of clothing, textiles, and more.[70]

As a father, Ole was in his granddaughter's words, "good to his smaller children but quick-tempered and sterner with his older children."[71] His health remained a challenge in a world where health, hard work, and surviving physical challenges without available medical health care beyond home remedies was what one accepted by moving to homesteads. Inga's resettlement in America carried on, and her eldest daughter, Caroline, was among those who followed her farther westward into Dakota, but the story was complicated by those who had arrived there first.

"Ingeborge in her later years" - (Property of the Author)

---

70. John Mack Faragher, "History from the Inside-Out: Writing the History of Women in Rural America," *American Quarterly*, Vol. 33, No. 5, Winter 1981, 540.

71. Mildred Wilson letter to Millie Purdie, 4.

CHAPTER 4: WHOSE LAND WAS IT?

Ole's granddaughter's description of his role as a soldier was, "He protected the White people from the Indians."[72] While the expansion or abolition of slavery and the Civil War were America's major preoccupation when Nettie's Norwegian descendants arrived, the Manifest Destiny of Whites on prairie land that followed brought a conflict closer to home for her ancestors and their Norwegian neighbors. It would affect them more directly and also have enduring consequences. The land they were claiming and dividing into small sections had been occupied by America's indigenous people since late in the last Ice Age 17,000 years earlier.[73]

The conflict with Indians over land has traditionally been discussed in US history as the "Winning of the West" achieved by a "Nation of Immigrants." While those are topics of celebration and strength, Houston's Holocaust Museum labels the interaction between Whites and Indians since 1492 as a genocide.[74] America's indigenous people's contact

72. Ibid., 2

73. Michael R. Waters, "Late Pleistocene Exploration and Settlement of the Americas by Modern Humans," *Science*, Vol. 365, No. 6449, Jul 12, 2019, 138.

74. "Genocide of Indigenous People," *Holocaust Museum Houston*, https://hmh.org/library/research/genocide-of-indigenous-peoples-guide/.

with Europeans that began with Columbus was a tragedy that made Europe's worst population disaster, the Black Death of the fourteenth century, "pale by comparison."[75] Before Europeans arrived, Americans suffered no measles, no influenza, no smallpox, no chickenpox, no cholera, no malaria, no typhoid, no diphtheria, no scarlet fever, no whooping cough, no plague.[76] Jared Diamond's Pulitzer Prize winning book *Guns, Germs and Steel* states, "Diseases introduced with the Europeans spread from tribe to tribe far in advance of the Europeans themselves, killing an estimated 95% of the pre-Columbian Native American population."[77] Europeans asserting the right to ownership of lands they "discovered" was first justified by papal bulls to spread Christianity, in this case, Pope Alexander VI's Papal Bull *Inter Caetera* to Ferdinand and Isabella of Spain in

75. David S. Reher, "Reflections on the Fate of the Indigenous Populations of America," *Population and Development Review*, Vol.37, No.1, Mar 20, 2011, 172.

76. Nathan Nunn and Nancy Qian, "The Columbian Exchange: A History of Disease, Food, and Ideas," *Journal of Economic Perspectives*, Vol. 24, No. 2, Spring 2010, 165.

77. Jared Diamond, *Guns, Germs, and Steel: The Fates of Human Societies* (New York: W. W. Norton & Company, 1999), 78.

1493.[78] By the time of United States independence, taking land was justified by racism.[79]

Though many Indians died, using the term genocide for their treatment by White settlers such as the Norwegians moving to the Midwest is not accurate. There were incidents such as Horseshoe Bend, Sand Creek, Bear River, and Wounded Knee where many Indians were intentionally killed, and claims were made of intentional murder through

---

78. Pope Alexander VI, Papal Bull *Inter Caetera* to Ferdinand and Isabella of Spain in 1493. The pope said he had, "learned . . . [they] intended to seek out and discover certain islands and mainlands remote and unknown . . . to the end that you might bring to the worship of our Redeemer and the profession of the Catholic faith their residents and inhabitants."

79. Race as an aggregate of continental physical features as the term is currently used first emerged in the 18th century, formalized in Carolus Linneaus, *Systema Naturae* (Leiden: Johann Wilhelm de Groot for Theodor Haak, 1735). His 10th edition of 1758 classified all humans in four categories: Americans red-reddish, obstinate, and regulated by custom; Europeans white - white, gentle, and governed by law; Asians yellow - sallow, severe, and ruled by opinion; Africans - black, crafty, and governed by caprice. Printed in Sandra Soo-Jin Lee, Joanna Mountain & Barbara A. Koenig, "The Meanings of 'Race' in the New Genomics: Implications for Health Disparities Research," *Yale Journal of Health Policy, Law, Ethics*, Vol. 1, Art. 3, 2001, 6. As there are no red Indians or yellow Asians, permanent stereotypes that justified prejudice were given a "scientific" appearance. Added to this polygenism gained more acceptance at this time, adding religious justification. This belief stated Indians and blacks were descendants from someone different from Adam, the father of the white race. Terence D. Keel, "Religion, Polygenism and the Early Science of Human Origins," *History of the Human Sciences*, Vol. 26, No. 2, Apr 1, 2013.

giving Indians blankets infected with smallpox.[80] What was much more widespread in the United States was the mass deportation of Indians from the East to the West and within the West to confined areas. This geographic movement is now called *ethnic cleansing*. The settlers' opinion of Indians was not typically bloodlust, but more often that they were racially inferior, in the way, and the newcomers wanted their land. European settlement and Indian displacement were closely interrelated.[81]

Indians had been "others" in their homeland since European arrival and were enslaved in all the original thirteen British colonies up to independence.[82] When Thomas Jefferson wrote the Declaration of Independence from England and declared "All Men are Created Equal," the grievances he listed against King George III of England

---

80. A frequent claim is that during Pontiac's Rebellion smallpox infested blankets taken from corpses at Fort Pitt were collected on Jeffrey Amherst's orders and distributed to Indians, ending their resistance. This story finds some support in Amherst's notes. See Peter d'Ericco, "Jeffrey Amherst and Smallpox Blankets: Lord Jeffrey Amherst's Letters Discussing Germ Warfare Against American Indians," https://people.umass.edu/derrico/amherst/lord_jeff.html. There is reason to believe it never happened or would have been effective, given the recent smallpox epidemic in the area. Philip Ranlet, "The British, the Indians, and Smallpox: What Really Happened at Fort Pitt in 1763," *Pennsylvania History*, Vol. 67, No. 3, Summer 2000, 435-436.

81. See Gulög Fur, "Indians and Immigrants - Entangled Histories," *Journal of American Ethnic History*, Vol.33, No.3, Spring 2014.

82. Gregory Ablavsky, "Making Indians 'White': The Judicial Abolition of Native American Slavery in Revolutionary Virginia and Its Racial Legacy," *University of Pennsylvania Law Review*, Vol. 159, No. 5, Apr 2011, 1459-1460.

included lack of protection from "the merciless Indian Savages."[83]

The Constitution was written when the United States occupied a small territory on the Atlantic coast and Indians held lands all around. Tribes were considered foreign powers as stated in Article 1, Section 8, which includes the phrase on relations between Indians and the US government: "Congress shall have the Power . . . To regulate Commerce with foreign Nations, and among the several States, and with the Indian Tribes."[84] The United States soon expanded vastly with the Louisiana Purchase of 1803 and White settlers spread to the center of the continent. The relationship with Indians was spelled out in the Supreme Court decision *Cherokee Nation v. Georgia* when Chief Justice John Marshall wrote: "They occupy a territory to which we assert a title independent of their will . . . Meanwhile they are in a state of pupilage. Their relation to the United States resembles that of a ward to his guardian."[85]

French diplomat and scholar Alexis de Tocqueville visited the United States and released a book in 1835 that was very influential in America and Europe, *Democracy in America*.[86] In it, he described how Indians were exploited as land agents who went to tribes and gathered them, first providing them food and drink. Then the tribe members

83. In the list of grievances against George III, Jefferson included, "He has excited domestic insurrections amongst us, and has endeavoured to bring on the inhabitants of our frontiers, the merciless Indian Savages, whose known rule of warfare, is an undistinguished destruction of all ages, sexes and conditions."

84. "The Constitution of the United States: A Transcription," Article I§ 8, *National Archives*, https://www.archives.gov/founding-docs/constitution-transcript.

85. John Marshall, Cherokee M, *United States v. Rogers*, 30 US 1, 1831, 2.

86. Alexis de Tocqueville, *Democracy in America, Vol. I*, (originally London: *De la démocratie en Amérique:* Saunders and Otley, 1835). Trans to English by Henry Reeve (Cambridge: Sever & Francis, 1862).

were told their land was useless, but land far to the west was teaming with game. Agents then spread before the Indians "firearms, woolen garments, kegs of brandy, glass necklaces, bracelets of tinsel, earrings, and looking-glasses."[87]

This book was published the year the government signed the Treaty of New Echota with some members of the Cherokee Nation in agreement with the Indian Removal Act, though it was rejected by the tribe's chief John Ross and other leaders. The treaty called for Cherokees to resettle from the Southeast to an area in eastern Indian Territory, now Oklahoma, in exchange for a grant of fifteen million dollars. In 1838, the Cherokees were disarmed and General Winfield Scott was sent to oversee the forced removal of the tribe.[88] The removal of the Cherokee during the late 1830s included sometimes brutal, inhumane treatment, with tens of thousands dying along the way. The Cherokees later named it *Nunna daul Tsuny*, which means "Trail Where We Cried." This has become known in English as the "Trail of Tears."[89] Arriving in Indian Territory across the Mississippi, the survivors murdered the signers of the treaty who had agreed to their transfer of land.[90] This event was a case in America's past where the "Winning of the West" involved ethnic cleansing.

Beginning in 1836, about 12,000 settlers made their way by wagons or pulling and pushing two-wheel carts on a 2000-mile trip from Independence, Missouri to Oregon on the Oregon Trail to make their living, often trapping beaver,

87. Ibid., 437.

88. Russell Thornton, "Cherokee Population Losses During the Trail of Tears: a New Perspective and Estimate," *Ethnology*, Vol. 31, No. 4, 1984, 290.

89. "The Age of Jackson," *U.S. History*, https://www.ushistory.org/us/24f.asp.

90. Russell Cobb, *The Great Oklahoma Swindle* (Lincoln, NE, Bison Books, 2020), 113.

an especially popular fur of the time,[91] and compete with British-owned Hudson Bay Company outposts. This travel took them across the land of the Plains Indians. Beginning in 1846, members of the Church of Jesus Christ of Latter-day Saints, known as Mormons, were also crossing the plains of mid-America. The Mormons had been founded in New York in 1830 by their prophet Joseph Smith and, after being run out of towns and persecuted, Smith moved the church headquarters to Nauvoo, Illinois, where he was murdered. In February 1846, the Mormons departed, following Brigham Young as he pointed "Israel's needle" toward the West and believing God would guide their plans.[92] After over a year, the first group had exited what was then the United States and arrived at the Great Salt Lake in what was soon to become the Utah Territory. The Mormons settled, but the migration continued for two decades to an area where Utes, Shoshones, and Paiutes were already present.

James Polk, elected president in 1844, added more territory to the US government than any other president, and he did it quickly. In 1846, he provoked a war with Mexico over the Texas boundary. It was officially ended by the Treaty of Guadalupe Hidalgo on February 2, 1848, when Mexico ceded 55% of its territory to the United States. That included all or parts of present-day Arizona, California, New Mexico, Texas, Colorado, Nevada, and Utah becoming part of the United States. Mexico also gave up all claims to Texas and recognized the Rio Grande as the border between the countries. This immense addition of territory inflamed the question of where slavery would be extended as it was formally carved into states, and new settlements increased conflict with indigenous people.

---

91. History.com Editors, "Oregon," *History*, https://www.history.com/topics/us-states/oregon, Nov 4, 2019.

92. Lewis Clark Christian, "Mormon Foreknowledge of the West," *BYU Studies Quarterly*, Vol. 21, Iss. 4, 1981, 414-415.

Also, just days before the treaty was signed, gold was discovered at Sutter's Mill in northern California. By August, 4000 hopeful miners had shown up and a year later, 80,000 "forty-niners" were in California. Eventually, over 300,000 people headed to the west coast in the Gold Rush, mainly from the United States but also from Europe, South America, and China.[93]

Chief Justice Marshall's successor, Roger Taney, went further in reducing Indians' legal status in his 1846 opinion for *United States v. Rogers*. He wrote that Indian tribes had never been "regarded as the owners of the territories they respectively occupied."[94] Europeans had carved the continent up and occupied it as if it were vacant, "and the Indians continually held to be, and treated as, subject to their dominion and control."[95] It has been argued that from the Land Act of 1796 through the 1841 Preemptive Act, the Homestead Act of 1862, and following the Timber Culture and Desert Land Acts of the 1870s, it was the government's goal to get as many White settlers as possible in "enemy territory," where they would concentrate to confront "hostile Indians" and reduce the demands placed on the army, which was unable to protect individual settlers in isolated locations.[96]

As Taney announced this decision, the expression "Manifest Destiny" was entering usage. Manifest Destiny was a belief that became widespread in the 1840s and 1850s and especially popular after the Civil War until the end of the century. The belief was that White Americans were on a mission from God to spread their ennobling, democratic

---

93. Editors of Britannica, "California Gold Rush," *Britannica*, https://www.britannica.com/topic/California-Gold-Rush.

94. Roger Taney, *United States v. Rogers*, 45 US 567, 1846, 567.

95. Ibid., 572.

96. See Douglas W. Allen, "Homesteading and Property Rights; Or, 'How the West Was Really Won,'" *Journal of Law & Economics*, Vol. 34, No.1, Apr 1991.

civilization across the continent from the Atlantic to the Pacific and perhaps farther, combining greed for land with morality. For those who stood in the way, the Spanish and the Indians, it meant the United States granted itself the authority to take and exploit their territory and believe that not only was it justified, but ordained by Providence. Belief in the exceptionalism of Americans, or at least the inferiority of all others, was elevated to extreme heights as the century progressed.

The phrase "Manifest Destiny" was introduced in the presidential election of 1844, when expansion of America's territory was a major issue. Editor of the *Democratic Review,* John L. O'Sullivan, was the first to use the expression when he wrote, "The fulfillment of our manifest destiny [is] to overspread the continent allotted by Providence for the free development of our yearly multiplying millions."[97] Expansionist James Polk was elected, and the phrase entered common usage. Some would take the idea further as James Gordon Bennett's editorial in the *New York Herald* on April 3, 1865, proclaimed, "It is our manifest destiny to lead and rule all nations."[98]

Norwegians and other European peasants and small farmers who came to America to claim cheap land before and after the Homestead Act had no awareness of being involved in Manifest Destiny or what would later be described as ethnic cleansing or even genocide. They simply hoped to create better lives for themselves. It would not be fair to judge their actions by today's knowledge or standards. Still, it would be equally inaccurate to ignore the history of Europe's interaction with outside areas, especially

---

97. Robert J. Scholnick, "Extermination and Democracy: O'Sullivan, the Democratic Review, and Empire, 1837-1840," *American Periodicals,* Vol. 15, No.2, 2005, 124.

98. Lewis Eigen and Jonathan Siegel, *The Macmillan Dictionary of Political Quotations* (New York: Macmillan Publishing Company, 1993),145.

America, and not see that westward movement onto the Great Plains would be met with resistance, not because of heathen savage redskins, but because the people who lived there felt their homes were being attacked. This is worth examination in Nettie's case, as her ancestors were directly involved.

It is probable that when Peder and Guri boarded the *Virgo* with their family in 1853, they believed the central United States was open territory with free land for their taking and no Indian resistance. The most popular and influential guidebook for potential American settlers had been published in 1838 in Norway by an early visitor who spent eight months in the United States, primarily Illinois, in 1837. This was Ole Rynning's *True Account of America*.[99] Rynning spoke of Indians, writing, "These people are very good-natured, and never begin hostilities when they are not confronted."[100] More importantly, he stated, "The Indians have now been transported away from this part of the country [central plains] far to the west."[101]

Once Peder and Guri's family settled in Iowa in the 1850s, they were in the Great Plains and encountered the indigenous population, the Native Americans called the Plains Indians. When Inga and Ole moved to northwest Iowa, they were in Sioux territory.[102] Unlike many of the peaceful coastal Indian tribes who occupied specific, limited areas, the Plains Indians were migratory, following the movements of their basic source of food, clothing, and

---

99. Ole Rynning, *True Account of America* (Christiana, Norway: 1838).

100. Ole Rynning, *True Account of America,* Theodore Christian Biegen English translation (Minneapolis: Norwegian-American Historical Association, 1926), 91.

101. Ibid.

102. Bill Sherman, "Tracing the Treaties: How They Affected American Indians and Iowa," *Iowa History Journal*, http://iowahistoryjournal.com/tracing-treaties-affected-american-indians-iowa/, Jan 7, 2022.

shelter, the buffalo. Massive buffalo herds of 10,000 or more individuals pounded their way north and south across the prairies, feeding on the open ranges. A claim of a herd 100 miles wide was once reported, and a traveler in 1859 Nebraska claimed he passed over 200 miles through a continuous herd. Another report described a herd seventy miles long and thirty miles wide.[103] Estimates vary, but all agree there were tens of millions of buffalo on the Great Plains at the beginning of White settlement[104] and the Indian nations of middle America depended on them for survival.

These Indians—the Cheyenne, the Arapaho, the Pawnee, and the Sioux—were expert horsemen and courageous warriors. Once the United States gained ownership of this territory that had previously been claimed by France, the clash between the Plains Indians and new settlers who wanted the land they occupied was inevitable. White settlement grew enough that Iowa became a state in 1846, Minnesota in 1858, and the discovery of gold in Montana in 1862 increased traffic through Indian country.

Several of Ole's and Inga's relatives who had settled near them were killed by Indians during this time. Among these were a twelve-year-old boy and Inga's uncle, Ole Forde, who was killed in 1862. These incidents solidified family attitudes about Native Americans as savages preventing civilized settlement by hard-working, well-intentioned farmers who intended to make good use of the abundant land.

The year 1862 was pivotal. Congress passed the Homestead Act that gave 160 acres of government land to any citizen or intended citizen who had not taken up arms against the United States for a small filing fee and living five years on the land, making improvements.

---

103. James H. Shaw, "How Many Bison Originally Populated Western Rangelands?" *Rangelands*, Vol.17, No.5, Oct 1995, 148.
104. Ibid., 150.

Also in 1862, the Sioux War, or Dakota War, began in Minnesota, bringing the conflict between claiming free land and the indigenous people to Nettie's ancestors. Sioux negotiators had been convinced to sign the Treaty of Traverse des Sioux and the Treaty of Mankato with the Minnesota government in 1851, giving up thirty-five million acres of land and only retaining a twenty-mile-wide strip on the Minnesota River. The remainder was to be open for Euro-American settlement. In exchange, they were to be paid $3,750,000, which they never received. At the signing, there were two copies, but traders handed the Indians a third document that the Indians thought was another treaty copy. It said that all the Indians' payments would go to them.[105]

In the summer of 1858, the Sioux territory had been reduced to a ten-mile strip on one side of the Minnesota River, leaving very little land for the nomadic people. They were entirely dependent on treaty guaranteed allotments. Due to graft and government bureaucracy, the allotments did not arrive or were not being distributed, and the Minnesota Sioux were desperate. Chief Little Crow went to the Lower Sioux Agency in August to tell the Indian agent, Andrew Myrick, that his people had no food and were starving. A missionary translated the message and Myrick's reply, which was, "So far as I am concerned if they are hungry, let them eat grass or their own dung."[106] Raids and reprisals followed, and shortage grew worse when the Civil War began. On August 17, 1862, four young Sioux of the M'dewakanon tribe killed three White men and two White women at a farm over an incident involving the theft of some eggs.

---

105. Priscilla Ann Russo, "The Time to Speak Is Over: The Onset of the Sioux Uprising," *Minnesota History*, Fall 1976, 101.

106. Francis Davis Millett, "The Treaty of Traverse des Sioux," *Minnesota State Capitol,* https://www.mnhs.org/capitol/learn/art/8961, 2005.

That night, the young Sioux reached Little Crow's camp, and he knew this meant war. Little Crow gathered 750 warriors while Governor Ramsey of what was by then the state of Minnesota sent 1,400 soldiers in pursuit of them under Colonel Sibley by the end of the month. The soldiers had help, as the *Minneapolis Star* recalls: "Parties of adventurers went out hunting Indians to collect the $25 bounty for each redskin's scalp offered by the governor of Minnesota."[107] On September 24, the editor of *The Daily Republican* of Winona, Minnesota wrote, "The State reward for dead Indians has been increased to $200 for every redskin sent to Purgatory."[108]

Six weeks after it began, the war ended. Sibley's soldiers surrounded Little Crow's camp while a number of Indians abandoned the cause. Though 400 surrendered, Little Crow and his loyal followers escaped. He was picking raspberries in northern Minnesota when a father and son, Nathan and Chauncey Lamson, shot Little Crow and scalped him, for which the Minnesota legislature awarded Nathan $500 for his "great service to the State," and Chauncey was given $75 as payment for Little Crow's scalp.[109] The scalp was put on display for public viewing at the state historical rooms in the capital, St. Paul.[110]

The army took many Indians, mainly women and children, the elderly, and noncombatants to Fort Snelling for the winter of 1862-63, where as many as 300 died in an internment camp, victims of illness and attacks by soldiers and civilians. In addition to this, 303 more were charged with

---

107. Star Journal Research Staff, "Indian Meeting Won't Match Old Days," *The Minneapolis Star*, Sep 12, 1941, 16.

108. "Indian Deserves the Same Rights," *Winona Daily News* (Winona, MN), Nov 22, 1972, 7.

109. Walter N. Trenerry, "The Shooting of Little Crow: Heroism of Murder?" *Minnesota History*, Vol. 38, No. 3, 151-152.

110. Frank Fiske, *The Taming of the Sioux* (Bismarck, ND: Bismarck Tribune, 1917), 52.

war crimes and sentenced to death in rushed trials without representation. That was rejected by President Lincoln, who eventually recommended forty be hanged.[111] One of the condemned died and another had his sentence commuted to life imprisonment. Mankato, Minnesota erected rectangular gallows in the town's public meeting area, and on December 26, 1862, thirty-eight Sioux Indians were simultaneously dropped and hanged in the largest execution in American history.[112] The army pursued the Sioux into the Dakota Territory and Indian resistance continued against White settlers, which made their situation unsafe throughout the region.

After Ole had been given a medical discharge during the Civil War, he found himself in the role of protector of White settlers on several occasions. After he and Inga resettled in a sod house, he went out on a number of expeditions that were part of what was called the Indian Wars that took him into Minnesota and the Dakota Territory. On one occasion, he picked up a widow and her child after the father was killed by Indians. At another time, Ole was returning alone and rescued a father and a child after tragedy struck. The family lived in an isolated, vulnerable area and was organizing a move to live where there were other settlers as protection against Indian attacks. As part of the final preparations, the father had been out on the range rounding up his cattle. While he was away, the Indians attacked his home. His wife was killed, and the Indians had swung his three young children by their feet and bashed their heads into a wall. The four were left for dead, and the mother and one of the

---

111. Daniel W. Homstad, "Abraham Lincoln: Deciding the Fate of 300 Indians Convicted of War Crimes in Minnesota's Great Sioux Uprising," *Historynet*, https://www.historynet.com/abraham-lincoln-deciding-the-fate-of-300-indians-convicted-of-war-crimes-in-minnesotas-great-sioux-uprising.htm, Dec 2001.

112. David A. Nichols, "The Other Civil War: Lincoln and the Indians," *Minnesota History*, Spring 1974, 11.

children were. However, when the father returned home he discovered two of the children still living. The distraught man could not ride carrying both children and in desperation was walking with one under each arm when Ole discovered them. Ole escorted them to safety, but one of the children died along the way.

Personal tragedy also struck Ole's home, as the tensions mounted between settlers and the Native people. His granddaughter said, "There was no Indian trouble when they came there."[113] That changed, as Nettie, who was also Ole's granddaughter, recalled, "When they [Ole and Inga] lived in Iowa, the Indians were on the warpath. They wanted to kill off all the White people."[114]

When Caroline was a little girl, the clash between settlers and Indians dangerously involved their settlement. Soon after the Indian Wars had spread across the border of Minnesota into Iowa, the men were away from home. Life on early farm settlements required cooperation, and even though there was the danger of Indian attack, the men, Ole, Eric, and other neighbors had to get out to work breaking the prairie, leaving the women to care for the children and clean, cook, and garden. On this particular day, the women and children, including Inga and Caroline, heard the Indians coming and immediately knew what that meant. They headed into the storage cellar under the small cabin before the Indians arrived.

This could well have been a successful strategy, as these Indians were apparently unaware of cellars. They were hidden quietly when the Indians entered and searched what appeared to be an empty cabin. However, among the hidden women and children in the cellar, there was a baby, and the baby began to cry. Their secrecy was no doubt lost. The

---

113. Mildred Reister Wilson to Millie Purdy, 3.
114. Nettie Fortune "Transcript of Conversation with Irene Dodge," 60.

baby's mother acted with self-sacrificing courage to save the others. To prevent the cellar from being searched and the others discovered, she went upstairs, entered the cabin, and presented herself and her baby to the Indians. With the others in the cellar below listening in horrified silence, the Indians slammed the baby's head against the wall and killed it. After that, they killed its mother. They then left, apparently thinking they had eliminated all the people in the cabin.

The surviving homesteaders and the lineage of Ole and Inga that was Caroline and her younger siblings emerged from the cellar following this gruesome event,[115] and Indian resistance became primarily concentrated west into Dakota.

---

115. Reported by Carolines' daughters, Mildred Reister Wilson to Millie Purdy, 5, Nettie Fortune, "Transcript of Conversation with Irene Fortune Dodge," Mohall, ND, Oct 22, 1979. 58.

CHAPTER 5: TO DAKOTA

Fighting increased in the next decade as the army pushed west through Dakota, and more tribes joined in the resistance. Ole had made trips to Dakota to participate in this conflict. The pneumonia that had long tormented him led to his death when he was fifty, the year before the Dakota Territory separated into two new states. After he died, because of his Civil War service, the family inherited a pension of $2 per month for their children until they were sixteen and $12 per month for Inga.[116] They'd had fourteen children, but "seven died when small."[117] Ingeborge, with a family to raise, decided to move west. With her children, including Nettie's future mother Caroline Olson, and other relatives, she headed out by covered wagon. They were destined for the Dakota Territory, where the Indian Wars were still taking place. Among the children on the voyage was Nettie's Uncle Oscar. While fording a river Oscar fell out of a wagon, but his mother managed to catch him and save him. Nettie's older cousin Pearl was less fortunate, dying from diphtheria at the age of eighteen months.

South of Madison, in the east of the Dakota Territory, the family settled in a sod house. A number of Inga and Ole's relatives established homes nearby, including one of Ole's brothers, who homesteaded in Minnesota on the

116. Mildred (Millie) Reister Wilson to Millie Purdy, March 21, 1954, 4.

117. Ibid., 5.

Dakota border. Another of Ole's sisters, Karen, married a man named Mart Magneson, who was financially successful and lived in Sioux Falls, the largest city in what was soon to become South Dakota. Karen and Mart had no children and apparently desired to have a family but were unable to do so. Ole's brother Eric resolved this by giving them Lena, his eldest daughter, to raise as their own.[118] The arrangements of this transaction are unknown. They also let another of Ole's sisters live with them. Also in Sioux Falls were two more relatives, including one described by Nettie's cousin as "a very fat woman," while both "were very refined women."[119]

Inga's oldest son eventually moved north to homestead in McHenry County near the Canadian border, where "there was no Indian trouble."[120] Others in the family soon followed, claiming homesteads in what would become North Dakota. Cousins intermarried and Inga considered moving north, where there was a second gathering of relatives. With four of her children in two covered wagons, carrying a large tent, she headed to McHenry County to look around and consider relocating near her son's homestead. After one winter, she'd had enough; it was worse than South Dakota, and she returned to Madison. Her remaining years were not golden. She remarried, again to a Norwegian immigrant, Ed Maltare. He proved to be a heavy drinker with a dangerous temper that threatened her safety. While enduring life on a homestead with him, she developed breast cancer. It would eventually kill her, but not until the twentieth century began.

Inga's life with Ed ended long before this as once in a drunken stupor, he shot at her and also at her young granddaughter Nettie. That event brought Ingeborge's second marriage to an end as she left her husband and returned to the Minnesota farm. Inga on her own was, in

---

118. Ibid., 2, 5.
119. Ibid., 3.
120. Ibid. 4.

her granddaughter Nettie's memory, "a good lady," with clear priorities. When Nettie and two of her aunts, Inga's daughters Bertha and Millie, went to stay on the farm for over a month one summer, they were only allowed free access to bread, butter, sugar, and coffee, and never milk. Also, "She never said anything to us."[121]

During all this time, other things had been taking place. Inga's daughter Caroline had grown up and was a woman. She had set off to start a life of her own. Nettie's life was about to begin in a perplexing manner.

In a larger context, this move from Iowa to Dakota appears to have been inspired by fear of Indian attacks. Inga and Caroline had been fortunate to survive an attack on their Iowa homestead during the Minnesota Indian Wars. While Ole had fought Indians in the Civil War and afterward, their moving to Dakota after his death had not moved them farther from conflict with Indians. Though Inga had only moved to the east edge of Dakota, the Armageddon of the conflict between Whites and Indians over control of the Great Plains was centered on the territory that had become their home.

Both the army and the Indians were suffering and had a real interest in bringing an end to the long ongoing warfare. Government agents met with twenty-four chiefs in eastern Wyoming on the buffalo grass plains that were interrupted by the 10,000-foot Laramie Peak, with the Rockies in the distance to the west. On April 29, they signed the Laramie Treaty of 1868.[122] This outlined the entire portion of what would become South Dakota from the Missouri River to the Black Hills as a reservation for the Sioux Nation. The Sioux were specifically granted possession of the Black Hills of

---

121. Nettie Fortune, "Transcript of Conversation with Irene Fortune Dodge," 70.
122. "Transcript of Fort Laramie Treaty (1868)," U.S. National Archives, < http://www.ourdocuments.gov/doc.php?flash=true&doc=42&page=transcript >.

Dakota that were sacred to them "for all time." It also said the land was for the Indians alone and no one "shall ever be permitted to pass over, settle upon, or reside in" the territory except for authorized government agents. Whites would be required to obtain special permission from the Indian agent to pass over it.[123]

This treaty lasted until Lieutenant Colonel George Custer (often referred to as "General," his previous Civil War rank) arrived from Fort Abraham Lincoln in 1874. General Philip Sheridan sent Custer to do a feasibility report on building a fort and reporting on the natural resources in the Black Hills. The *New York Times* published a report written by a *Bismarck Tribune* correspondent who accompanied Custer and the ten companies of the 7th Cavalry. It explained why Custer was confident the Indians would not interfere with his violation of the treaty by encroaching on Indian territory, emphasizing the danger to them of doing so. The force Custer led was armed with "the new Springfield arm just adopted for the army... the most perfect breech-loading gun yet manufactured." Along with this: "The Gatling guns will fire 250 shots a minute, and are good for 900 yards... The guns are ten-barreled, consequently, at each revolution, ten shots are fired. Should [Lieutenant Josiah] Chance open on the red devils with one of these guns they would think the infernal regions had broken loose on them."[124] Following his arrival and initial inspection, Custer reported on the area's great promise for farming and ranching.[125] He added, "Gold has been found at several places and it is the belief

123. Paul L. Hedren, *Fort Laramie and the Great Sioux War* (Norman, OK: University of Oklahoma Press, 1998), 1-4.

124. "Custer's Expedition: Its Objects, Equipment, and Personnel," *New York Times*, July 5, 1874, 3.

125. Doane Robinson, *A History of the Dakota or Sioux Indians* (Aberdeen [SD]: State of South Dakota, 1904), 413.

of those who are giving their attention to this subject that it will be found in paying quantities."[126]

That comment led to an unrestricted gold rush to the Black Hills. While US troops initially ejected the first arrivals, they soon gave up and thousands of prospectors poured in. Lawless towns, including Deadwood, were founded, and most treaty provisions were rendered void. Some larger mines went so far as to establish a reward for the heads of Indians who came too near them on reservation land that was restricted by treaty for Indians.[127] Farmers and ranchers followed.

Many of the different Sioux tribes were distressed by this influx of White people on the land they had been promised, and they understandably resisted. Some refused to go to reservations designated for them and headed to the Montana Territory to join and hunt with the Mandans and Arickarees along the Bighorn River. Near the end of 1875, the Commissioner of Indian Affairs issued an ultimatum to these Indians, ordering them to return to their reservations, which they ignored. The commissioner then asked General Sheridan to have the army round them up and bring them in. Sheridan devised a three-prong attack, each led by a general. General John Gibbon would attack from Fort Ellis in the Montana Territory, while General George Crook attacked from Fort Fetterman, Wyoming Territory. Finally, General Alfred Terry of Fort Abraham Lincoln, Dakota Territory, joined by the 7th Cavalry under George Custer, would attack from the east, trapping the Indians in a massive military operation. The Indian leadership the army faced included experienced warrior chiefs Gall, Crazy Horse, Inkpaduta, and Sitting Bull.

---

126. Ibid.

127. Harry H. Anderson, "Deadwood Effort at Stability," *Montana: The Magazine of Western History,* Winter, *1970,* 44.

In the spring of 1876, the armies entered Montana and the generals met on the Yellowstone River steamer, the *Far West*. They had information that there was a large Sioux camp on the Bighorn or nearby on the Little Bighorn. Assignments were agreed on for each army to advance through the wooded territory from different directions and to converge at the Bighorn on June 26. Custer had recently been humiliated for implicating President Grant's brother in a scandal during congressional testimony and was seeking to regain his reputation.[128] As a personal guest to record his exploits he brought Mark Kellogg, correspondent for the *Bismarck Tribune* and the *New York Herald*. When Custer saw the trail that had previously been reported, he split his cavalry off from General Terry and headed in the direction of the Little Bighorn. He was ordered by General Terry to send information on what he discovered.[129]

Custer's scouts spotted the Indian camp from a distance very early in the morning of June 25 at the Little Bighorn, known to the Indians as the Greasy Grass. During a candlelight meeting, Custer ordered Major Marcus Reno to take soldiers to the south of the camp to prevent them from fleeing and Captain Frederick Benteen to accompany him part of the way, stopping across from the camp, while he advanced on the village from the north and conquered it. The generals' armies were to arrive the following day, so he was in a rush to attack and win a victory that would have made him a national hero. Reno's advance was met with a skirmish that drove him and his men to high ground for safety. Custer led his troops down the foothills, where the Indian camp became visible from a distance. He likely saw only a small portion of it as it extended four miles, including

---

128. Mari Sandoz, *The Battle of the Little Bighorn* (Lincoln, Neb: Bison Books, 1978), 26.

129. Jim Donovan, *Custer and the Little Bighorn: The Man, the Myth the Mystery* (Minneapolis: Voyageur Press, 2001), 144.

approximately 10,000 people[130] from seven different tribes. He then led his troops down to the river on the opposite side of the Indian camp and ordered a charge, as there were a large number of Indians approaching. Rain-in-the-Face and Gall sent warriors around to get behind the soldiers, while Crazy Horse led his warriors against Custer's soldiers with the Lakota battle cry, *"Hoka hey!"* ("It's a good day to die.")[131]

All of Custer's men died with him. In all, including Reno's and Benteen's troops, 268 Whites were killed and forty-four wounded.[132] Indian scouts had spotted the generals' approaching armies and abandoned the camp that night, heading in different directions. The generals converged on an empty camp and found the wounded survivors. They also discovered among the many bodies a pouch of notes written by newspaper correspondent Mark Kellogg. Custer's soldiers were buried and Reno's and Benteen's surviving troops, along with Captain Myles Keogh's horse Comanche, who was the only survivor from Custer's attack, were brought on the *Far West* and returned to Bismarck the following day.

Kellogg's notes were rapidly constructed into a 50,000-word story by Colonel Lounsberry, editor of the *Bismarck Tribune*, which was published in his paper in a special edition[133] and sent by the one existing telegraph line to the *New York Herald*. It was published there on July 7, 1776,

130. History.com Editors, "Battle of the Little Bighorn," *History*, https://www.history.com/this-day-in-history/battle-of-little-bighorn, Jul 1, 2022.

131. Frank Fiske, *The Taming of the Sioux* (Bismarck, ND: Bismarck *Tribune*, 1917), 108-110.

132. Ralph K. Andrist, T*he Long Death: The Last Days of the Plains Indians* (New York: Collier Books, 1969), 265.

133. Merry Helm, "Colonel Lounsberry Scoops Bighorn," *Prairie Public Newsroom*, https://news.prairiepublic.org/show/dakota-datebook-archive/2022-04-25/colonel-lounsberry-scoops-bighorn, Apr 25, 2022.

under the headline "CUSTER'S TERRIBLE DEFEAT."[134] Much of the country learned of "Custer's last stand" and a legend of glory of sacrifice in the defense of civilization immediately followed. One day after this story, Walt Whitman had a poem in the *Herald*, "A Death Sonnet for Custer." It began, "Land of the wild ravine, the dusky Sioux, the lonesome stretch, the silence/Haply to-day a mournful wail, haply a trumpet note for heroes," and included, "The fall of Custer and all of his officers and men/ Continues yet the old legend of our race/ The loftiest of life upheld in death."[135]

"Rain-in-the Face" - Frank Fiske photograph, North Dakota Historical Society.

---

134. "First Account of the Custer Massacre," *Bismarck Tribune Extra*, July 6, 1876.

135. "A Death-Sonnet for Custer," *The Walt Whitman Archive*, <http://www.whitmanarchive.org/published/periodical/poems/per.00142>.

American poet Henry Wadsworth Longfellow quickly followed with "The Revenge of Rain-in-the-Face,"[136] with a completely invented story that Rain-in-the-Face killed Custer, cut out his heart, and thrust it victoriously in the air. His story served to further demonize Indians.

In Dakota, the paper nearest where Inga and Caroline had settled was the *Press and Daily Dakotaian* in Yankton, over sixty miles from their homestead. Yankton was a real wild west town that had been developed when Dakota first opened to White settlement in 1859 and had a three-story hotel, saloons, gangs and gunfights, and a railroad by the 1870s. Major land and political deals for Dakota were carried out there.[137] Their paper's report was likely where settlers in southeast Dakota, including Inga's family, first heard of what had happened. The paper had a story on what remained of the 7th Cavalry when its remnants returned from the Little Bighorn and docked in Bismarck, writing, "Tears came unbidden to many an eye, for Custer, the brave Custer his noble brothers and fellows, were not there."[138] Descriptions of Indians following the Little Bighorn further convinced Whites expanding into their territory that they were obstacles and extermination might be required to remove them. Custer's widow, Elizabeth Bacon Custer, eventually conducted a campaign to turn her husband into an American hero, including the writing of a book entitled *Boots and Saddles*.[139]

---

136. "The Revenge of Rain-in-the- Face," Henry Wadsworth Longfellow, <http://www.hwlongfellow.org/poems_poem.php?pid=208>.

137. Brian Gevikm, "Think Deadwood was wild in the 1870s? Try Yankton," *South Dakota Public Broadcasting*, https://www.sdpb.org/blogs/images-of-the-past/think-deadwood-was-wild-in-the-1870s-try-yankton/ May 5, 2022.

138. "Return of the Seventh," *Press and Daily Dakotaian* (Yankton, Dakota Terr), Oct 26, 1876, 2.

139. "Elizabeth B. Custer, *Boots and Saddles* (New York: Harper & Brothers, 1885).

In a time of growing Indian desperation, Wovoka, an Indian shaman of the Paiute tribe of Nevada who claimed to be a reincarnation of Jesus, spoke of having a vision. He declared that in 1891, White people would be eliminated from earth and the dead Indians would be revived, as would conditions from before the arrival of Whites. Hopeful believers adopted ghost dancing, as Wovoka encouraged, to assure that this happened.[140] Government allotments had been cut to Standing Rock Reservation, which crossed the boundary of what became the states of North and South Dakota in 1889, and it was among the places where ghost dancing was prominent. There, it was led by Sitting Bull, who had been confined to the reservation. Another was Pine Ridge in South Dakota. Indians claimed they were "dancing to Christ," but Whites saw it as a war dance and a threat. While over thirty tribes were involved in ghost dancing to some degree, Congress only expressed concern about the Lakota version in the Dakotas.[141] In November 1890, President Benjamin Harrison ordered General Nelson A. Miles to take "such steps as shall be necessary" to suppress the Lakota Ghost Dancers.[142] When the dancers converged in a camp of teepees near Wounded Knee, they were surrounded by the 7th Cavalry that mounted Hotchkiss guns capable of firing fifty two-pound shells per minute. The Indians were ordered to disarm and at the first sign of dispute, the soldiers opened fire. Between 250 and 300 Indians were killed, about half of

140. George Bird Grinnell, "Account of the Northern Cheyennes concerning the Messiah Superstition," *The Journal of American Folklore*, Jan. – Mar., 1891, 62; Raymond J. DeMallie, "The Lakota Ghost Dance: An Ethnohistorical Account," *Pacific Historical Review*, Nov., 1982.

141. Jeffrey Ostler, "Conquest and the State: Why the United States Employed Massive Military Force to Suppress the Lakota Ghost Dance," *Pacific Historical Review*, Vol. 65, No.2, May 1996, 217.

142. Myles Hudson and Michael Ray, "Wounded Knee Massacre," *Encyclopædia Britannica*, https://www.britannica.com/event/Wounded-Knee-Massacre, Dec 22, 2021.

whom were women and children. Some 146 were buried in a mass grave by the soldiers. The military's highest honor, the Congressional Medal of Honor, was awarded to twenty members of the cavalry who had massacred the defenseless Indians.[143]

Wounded Knee marked the end of Indian resistance and the Great Plains were open for White settlement, with Indians confined to reservations and no longer a threat to Norwegians or other Whites.

---

143. Ibid.

CHAPTER 6: NETTIE GROWING UP

In the midst of the time when this was occurring to the east of them, Inga's daughter Caroline had grown into a young woman in Madison. She eventually met and married Austin Williams. Austin, a butcher commonly referred to as "Bill," was born in Auburn, Iowa. He had an older sister and a younger sister Dotty, who died when she was a few days old.[144] Austin had deep-set eyes and a slightly protruding nose that cast a shadow over his upper lip. His thick, black hair was wavy and it is likely some described him as handsome in his younger days. This marriage would continue a tradition established by Caroline's mother when she married Ed Maltare of being attracted to men who became abusive alcoholics. First Inga's second husband Ed, then Caroline's husband Austin, and eventually Caroline's daughter Nettie all followed this pattern.

Caroline and Austin had three children. The first was Minnie, born in 1887. Minnie drank lye as a young child and soon went partially deaf. Whether the lye and the deafness were related in any way other than in Caroline's and Austin's imagination remains unknown. After Minnie came their son Oscar, born the year Dakota split into North and South Dakota, in 1889.

---

144. Nettie Fortune, Mohall, letter to Irene Fortune Dodge, Fargo, Dec 26, 1965.

Nettie Williams, the baby of the family and eventual mother of Irene, was born in Madison on September 2, 1891. At that time, Austin Williams worked as a part-time bartender and carpenter, which provided drinking money for him but left the family struggling. He spent little time helping Caroline with raising the children when they were young. Nettie described him as "just no good."[145] By the time she was five, he had abandoned the family without ever getting divorced from his wife and headed out to Utah to seek a new life on his own. Being abandoned was likely the first memorable event in the series of incidents in Nettie's life that would leave her embittered and distrustful of men.

Left alone following Austin Williams's desertion, Caroline gradually hardened into a stern, cross woman. Life for a single woman raising a family on the fringes of western society was challenging. Having attended school for only a few years and being female, her options for employment beyond their farm were limited. Women were typically regarded as "helpmates" and though a number from many places became homesteaders in the Dakotas, other work opportunities were mainly as teachers, domestic servants, seamstresses, or nurses. Caroline was unqualified to be a teacher or a nurse and had three small children, one of them deaf. Her only income came from selling rag rugs and she was desperate.

In the striving to make ends meet, Caroline had little time for her children, who came to believe that their mother resented and disliked them. Nettie viewed Caroline's sisters with more affection. Her favorite was the jovial and good-natured Aunt Tillie. She also liked Aunt Bertha, a generous woman with a frightening, explosive temper. While Caroline was struggling to get enough food on the table for the four of

---

145. Nettie Fortune, "Transcript of Conversation with Irene Fortune Dodge," 59.

them, let alone education or security, her wayward husband Austin's mother intervened.

Austin's mother Lucinda had once come to visit her son and his wife and children before he deserted the family. She came again after he had left to see how her grandchildren were getting along.[146] Lucinda was a very unusual woman to be living in a frontier town on the Great Plains. Her full name was Lucinda Caroline Smith Williams and later, Vile. Her heritage can be traced to Madam Campan and her husband Nathaniel. Madam Campan was a lady-in-waiting to Marie Antoinette, queen of France and wife of King Louis XVI. Marie had become a very unpopular and unsympathetic queen by the time of the outbreak of the French Revolution in 1789. When the Revolution entered its violent stage, the Reign of Terror of 1792-94, Marie and King Louis were sent to the guillotine and beheaded. Madam Campan was also beheaded by the guillotine, but her husband and their young son Nehemiah escaped to England, where they adopted the surname "Smith." Nehemiah eventually married Penima Cummins of England, and Nathaniel joined them in emigrating to America. Nathaniel became a teacher in Elmira, New York but drowned in a boating accident in the Delaware River.[147] Lucinda Caroline Smith, Nehemiah and Penima's daughter, was born in Pennsylvania.

Lucinda took great pride in her French heritage. Every day of her adult life she wore a white lace collar to distinguish herself from others. She moved to Iowa, where in 1846 she married a Welshman who worked as a carpenter, Almon Williams. Almon and Lucinda had eight children, five of whom died as babies, which was not uncommon at the time. [148]Among the surviving children was Austin. What

146. Ibid., 62.

147. O.K. Smith (Nettie's cousin), Nevsho, Missouri, letter to Nettie, May 25, 1952.

148. Lydia [no last name given, cousin of Nettie], Hawkeye, Iowa, letter to Nettie, Mohall, May 4, 1976.

eventually drove a wedge into this marriage was when this complicated woman became a devout and uncompromising follower of a Christian sect that had first appeared in 1863, the Seventh-day Adventists. Members of this faith believed in the imminent second coming of Christ, their Sabbath was on Saturday rather than Sunday, and they followed dietary practices based on the Old Testament.

Lucinda's husband Almon did not share her devout Seventh-day Adventist views or lifestyle. According to one of his relatives, "Almon never was an Adventist."[149] He soon deserted her and headed west, where prospectors were still making new discoveries and towns were springing up in the territory taken from Mexico. Opportunities seemed to be plentiful. Perhaps they were, but when Almon reached the Utah Territory he contracted pneumonia and became delirious with fever. This would lead to a strange confluence of two new religions.

In Utah, members of the Church of Jesus Christ of Latter-day Saints, or Mormons, nursed Almon back to health. His gratitude led him to become a convert to their religion. As a Mormon, Almon soon took a Mormon bride. In time, he decided to return to Iowa to retrieve his original bride, in keeping with the Mormon practice of polygamy that infuriated many Americans of the mid-nineteenth century. Lucinda had presumed Almon was dead, having heard nothing from him in years. She had remarried, her second husband being a wealthy widower, James Vile, and Lucinda and James had a son.

Almon Williams returned to a bizarre situation. He and his still un-divorced wife both had new spouses. To Almon, this may have been disappointing, but not sinful. The same cannot be said for Lucinda, whose religious views did not tolerate divorce, let alone polyandry. Almon had absolutely

---

149. Mrs. Ed (Ella) Miller [cousin of Nettie], Hawkeye, Iowa, letter to Nettie Fortune. Mohall, Aug 29, 1956.

no possibility of convincing Lucinda to leave James Vile and return with him to Utah. However, he did manage to convince Lucinda and James's son Frank to do so. As Almon had done before, Frank deserted his wife and family and headed west. This second deserted family included Nettie's future father, Austin.

The religious implications of being married to two men at the same time were extremely distressing for Lucinda. Her problem was eventually resolved in a fashion, when the unreliable Almon headed off on his own again, deserting his second wife as well. After doing so, once again he grew seriously ill, but this time, he had nobody to care for him. He died in what would become Arizona. Lucinda, a woman of conscience who took her Christian marriage vow as sacred despite the intervening circumstances, went to the site of his death to oversee the funeral arrangements.[150]

The irresponsibility of the husband who ran off on her grandmother Lucinda, and her step-uncle Frank, who deserted his family, was not lost on the young Nettie. It merely reinforced the view that had begun with her mother's abandonment and was to color her attitudes and relationships throughout her life: men had power and responsibility that they did not deserve; women were their victims.

Lucinda's second marriage to the wealthy James Vile gave her the liberty to live her life as she wished. She remembered her years of living in poverty and the values she thought she had gained from it. After remarriage, she had ample resources and could afford to attempt to make up for her son's failure as a husband and father. She had done this with Nettie's cousin Dotty, the second child of Austin's sister Emma. Emma died several days after giving birth, and Lucinda took Dotty to raise until her sister Ella was grown, married, and willing to care for Dotty. Lucinda

---

150. Bernese Johnson [Nettie's cousin], Aberdeen, South Dakota letter to Nettie Fortune, February 23, 1973.

was willing to do this again for the family abandoned by her wayward, irresponsible son. She invited her son's deserted family to leave Madison and come to live with her in Iowa. Caroline managed to get train tickets and packed a large dishpan, covered with a red-and-white checked tablecloth, that contained sandwiches made of nothing but bread and butter. With that, the Williams family headed for Iowa.

When they arrived in Union Prairie on the western border of Iowa, Nettie's grandmother and her husband took them into their home in the country and assumed considerable control over Caroline's family. The food situation that had been a challenge in Madison did not take a sudden turn for the better. In keeping with her religious views, Lucinda believed that eating could be a form of indulgence and, in spite of her wealth, she restricted the amount of food that Nettie and her sister and brother were allowed to eat. As a five-year-old child under the care of a wealthy family, Nettie cried herself to sleep from hunger every night. Lucinda and her husband decided that Minnie and Oscar belonged in school, so they rented the family a basement apartment in town with two beds for $2 per month.

"Nettie, Oscar, and Minnie in Iowa" -
1896. (Property of the Author)

The benefits that came with the move were nearly outweighed by the shortcomings. Caroline received some assistance from women in the community, who took up a collection to buy her a new flying shuttle carpet loom. Others provided her with rags from which she could make rag rugs to sell. Caroline first made use of her loom to make carpets for their damp rooms. The nearly unfurnished, clammy apartment contributed to her development of an acute skin infection called erysipelas that made her skin red, shiny, and swollen, and gave her fever and chills.

While her youngest child would never forget this, it was second in trauma to the presence of the large rats that roamed around the apartment. Caroline always kept rat poison on the floor in the pantry where they kept their food, but that did not prevent the rodents from getting into the living areas. Nettie recalled her encounters with them. First was, "Mother and I were alone there and the rat ran across the floor and it got scared when it saw us, and I stood in the middle of the floor and it ran up my leg. And there I stood, screaming. Well, the rat got scared and ran down my leg. Mother grabbed a stick of wood. She threw it at that rat and killed it dead!"[151] Next came, "One night one of those rats got in bed and started chewing on my cheek, right under my eye. I yelled and that scared the rat out of bed."[152]

Because of Caroline's illness, a doctor told her to move to the main floor, which she did. Nettie was still five but helped by carrying some dishes. They only had two beds, a stove, and a carpenter's chest of tools left from Austin. Their new room was located in the back of a house and, like the previous one, cost $2 per month. Although it came with water, the water had to be carried by hand from a hydrant behind the house, and there was no sewage system attached

---

151. Nettie Fortune, "Transcript of Conversation with Irene Fortune Dodge," 59.

152. Ibid., 62.

to the room. They kept two cats in the apartment to keep the rats under control.

Being on the main floor, Caroline recovered immediately from her skin ailment, but they sat on the floor since they had no chairs and ate bread and milk from the chest of drawers. The owner soon brought them furniture and Caroline's mother-in-law began providing them with milk from her cow. Life improved some for Caroline's children following this, and they had several years of somewhat stable life where they began school and were adequately fed.

Unfortunately, those years were few. Caroline became ill with a condition involving inflammation of the bowels that led to near-continuous diarrhea. Living in a place at a time when a local doctor was in the area, but home remedies were commonly relied on, her health deteriorated, and her sisters Julia and Bertha came to Iowa to care for her. By this time, Austin, Caroline's husband who had abandoned her years earlier, had returned to Madison, South Dakota. He had been informed of his wife's condition and came to her home. Caroline's sisters would not allow him to stay and they told him to go stay at his mother's home. Nettie's recollection of the time raises questions. She said that when Fourth of July celebrations came there was concern for how the fireworks noise would affect her mother. Since they were anxious to attend, their father was allowed to come pick up her brother and her and take them to the carnival. Nettie recalled her experience as an eight-year-old: "So there I stood, up on a wooden fence. He stood there with his arms around me, while my brother chased around, looking everything over. There I sat, didn't look at anything. Oh, he seemed to think a lot of me all right."[153] Was there anything improper taking place with this irresponsible man avoiding one of his children he had not seen for years while pinning

---

153. Nettie Fortune, "Transcript of Conversation with Irene Fortune Dodge," 59.

one to a fence with his arms around her and seeming to "think a lot" of her? Speculation is possible, but all evidence has long vanished.

As Caroline's health continually declined with no signs of things changing, the issue had to be confronted as to what would become of Nettie and her siblings if their mother did not survive. Although Caroline had initially been reluctant to consider this morbid possibility, the time had come to make choices.

America began a new century as Caroline's family ended its time together with the three children heading in different directions. When Caroline died at age thirty-five in July 1902, her son Oscar remained in Iowa, where he was taken in by a family farm. Minnie, who was fourteen and considered "grown up" and old enough to do housework and earn an income, returned to Madison, where she had the intention of becoming a dressmaker. Nettie was taken by her aunt Bertha, who was anxious to become her guardian and resettled with her in Madison.

"Caroline Olson when healthy" - (Property of the Author)

"Caroline near her death" - 1935. (Property of the Author)

"Bertha, Nettie, and Millie visiting Iowa" - Four years after death of Caroline. (Property of the Author)

Bertha and Nettie returned to Madison, where Bertha rented a one-room apartment. Bertha took in her sister Millie as well, while Millie was learning to become a dressmaker. The three relatives shared one bed. Nettie attended school, eventually finishing grade seven. Her father was living there at the time, initially in a free room with her aunt Julia. When he started coming home drunk she would no longer allow him in her house, but he continued to sleep in her barn.

Territory for homesteading opened up around the new town of Garrison, North Dakota, that had been formed in 1905, and Bertha's brothers headed north. The Homestead Act of 1862 had been specifically written to include both men and women who were willing to settle the expanded territory of the United States, stating, "And be it further enacted, That the person applying for the benefit of this act shall, upon application to the register of the land office in which he or she is about to make such entry, make affidavit before the said register or receiver that he or she is the head of a family."[154]

Before long, Bertha decided she also wanted to homestead, and she set out to file her claim. Bertha was the first woman in the new town of Garrison. She did not think it would be wise to take the maturing and attractive thirteen-year-old Nettie along with her, so she left her with exuberant Aunt Tillie, Nettie's favorite. Tillie had a daughter, Pearl, who had died at age two, and Tillie had kept all her clothing. Nettie used to spend time looking at Pearl's clothes. Bertha's first job once she arrived was to serve as a cook and housekeeper for the Taylor brothers' store, which traded with the Indian reservation. When the railroad added a stop at Garrison, the Taylor brothers moved

---

154. Act of May 20, 1862 (Homestead Act), Ch. LVIIIV, Sec. 2 General Records of the United States Government, Record Group 11; National Archives Building, Washington, DC. https://www.archives. gov/milestone-documents/homestead-act#transcript.

their operation into town, and Bertha moved to town with them.

Things went fine for Bertha as long as she was in Garrison, filing her claim and making preparations for farming. However, when it came time for her to actually take up residence on her homestead, which was a requirement of the Homestead Act, she was faced with a problem: she was afraid to stay alone at night. She could manage it in areas surrounded by people, but out on the prairie, with no human existence in sight, she had somniphobia, which is fear of sleeping alone. The simple solution was for her to return to Madison and pick up Nettie. So, Nettie began her first experience of life on a homestead.

Leading North Dakota historian Elwyn Robinson described homesteading on the state's prairie at this time. He wrote that new settlers "were awed by the vast, open, almost barren prairie. It increased their sense of isolation and loneliness. And long winters added to their hardships. . . The pioneers furnished their first homes simply. They substituted dry goods boxes for tables and dressers and used a small, four-lid stove, homemade beds, chairs, and benches. . . Settlers found fuel a problem on the treeless prairies. . . Many burned cow chips."[155]

What Robinson called "cow chips" were actually "buffalo chips," the dried buffalo excrement that dotted the prairie and served as the fuel for Bertha's stove, since they were without a cow when they started out. Nettie enjoyed the work she did in joining Bertha as they took grain sacks out on the prairie and filled them with chips. "They made a real hot fire, but boy did they make a lot of ashes," she said.[156]

---

155. Elwyn B. Robinson, *History of North Dakota* (Lincoln, NE, University of Nebraska Press, 1966), 156-160.

156. Nettie Fortune, "Transcript of Conversation with Irene Fortune Dodge," 61.

Living with Bertha and providing her with company was a life young Nettie enjoyed, but things became complicated when Bertha found a boyfriend, the strikingly handsome Jim Cheek. He had a homestead about six miles north of Garrison, which was not far from Bertha's house. At first he came to visit, then he provided them with a horse and buggy so Bertha could go to town. Bertha and Jim's relationship became more serious, but they could not be married while Bertha was completing the requirements of the Homestead Act, which included a five-year time requirement of her as "head of household," establishment of a permanent residence, and improving or "proving up their land by cultivating it so that crops could be planted." This was very difficult work.

"Bertha's homestead near Garrison"
- (Property of the Author)

It is said that in these early years of homesteading by Norwegians in North Dakota, remnants of the Black Book beliefs persisted. Barbara Anne Woods wrote in "The

Norwegian Devil in North Dakota,"[157] that in many rural communities, the use of Norwegian was promoted, legends and folklore were preserved, including things that could bring forth the devil, who at times appeared as a large, black bird. A person who had sold his or her soul to the devil would experience a horrible death. A particularly interesting feature of the North Dakota legend is the inclusion of a common Scandinavian motif: "to get rid of a haunting spirit or devil, burn or move the house," stated Woods.[158] On completion of her Homestead Act requirements, Bertha and Jim were married. Bertha abandoned her homestead and moved to Jim's, and they added a second room to his shack. By this time, all Bertha's brothers were living in the area. At Bertha's insistence, Nettie stayed on and lived in Jim's shack as well, where the attention Bertha gave to Nettie bordered on spoiling her. It is likely that these years on Jim Creek's homestead were the happiest in her ninety-eight years.

"Bertha's husband Jim Creek" - Nettie lived with them after they wed. (Property of the Author)

157. Barbara Allen Woods, "The Norwegian Devil in North Dakota," *Western Folklore*, Vol. 17, No. 3, Jul 1958.
158. Ibid., 196.

"Getting a living under difficulties" - 1908.
Labeled photograph from Jim Creek's
homestead. (Property of the Author)

Nettie's older sister Millie again became part of her life during this time. Millie's original hopes of becoming a seamstress when Caroline's children left Iowa had not gone well. After Bertha and Nettie had moved, she left Madison and went to Minneapolis, where she found work as a dishwasher in a hotel. At the hotel she met Arthur Wilson, who Nettie recalled "was nuts over her. He would not leave her alone. She had to marry him. He just insisted she marry him. She did, and she didn't like him even."[159] Millie and Arthur came to Jim Creek's homestead and Arthur was considering homesteading in Canada. Millie wanted to be around family again and convinced him to move to Garrison, where they got an apartment and he became a cook in a restaurant.

Bertha and Jim eventually had to leave North Dakota. Bertha had become very ill, hemorrhaging continually, and could not be on her feet. She made the sixty-five-mile trip

---

159. Nettie Fortune, "Transcript of Conversation with Irene Fortune Dodge," 63.

to the state capital of Bismarck, where she could be cared for in a hospital, but she did not improve. Bertha wanted to return to die in Madison. Her husband agreed, but Nettie was not invited to return with them.

"Madison, South Dakota, early 1900s"
- (Property of the Author)

Nellie was sixteen and considered old enough to take care of herself. Throughout all her experiences, her young adult personality and character had formed in certain ways, some of which would never change. She had become a reserved young woman who valued neatness, tidiness, and honesty. She was imaginative and creative, which she expressed in painting and drawing.[160] She enjoyed reading and listening to music. Another aspect of her that had become clear was that she resented the position of inferiority that came with being female at the dawn of the twentieth century.

Nettie stayed on in Garrison. It was a typical small North Dakota town, like many that were being formed

---

160. This is evident from the sketches and paintings in her "Lorna Doone" National Style Book from the time.

rapidly at this time with the boom in settlement inspired by homesteading and by railroads selling land cheap to earn profits from their investments in laying track across the prairie. The *Ward County Independent* described in October of 1905 the anticipated terminus of the Soo Railroad being established in Garrison and connecting with stage service there. This would provide a direct connection to the much larger city of Minot and the paper optimistically stated, "The threshing machine whistles are being heard in all directions and soon we will see our crops transferred from the stacks to the well filled granaries and consequently well filled purses."[161]

Robinson's seminal *History of North Dakota* describes what was common to these new homesteading, frontier towns as immigrants populated the new state. He wrote, "At the beginning a collection of small, boxlike frame buildings, cheaply built and without architectural pretention, would spring up on the bare, flat prairie." It often moved when a railroad entered the region, and some towns were served by stage lines. New towns quickly had general stores, hardware stores, harness shops, blacksmith shops, lumber yards, and livery stables. The dominant features in many towns were the grain elevators. There would be a doctor and a lawyer, sometimes a dentist, a veterinarian, and a photographer. Banks and saloons often vied for being the first building in a town, and newspapers were in almost all. In 1890, there were fifty incorporated towns and villages in North Dakota and 125 newspapers. "Many of the raw little towns, especially at the end of the railroad, were rough places with drifters, prostitutes, sporting houses, and gambling houses . . . fights, beatings, and shootings were common." For the

---

161. Edgar Weatherbee, "Rapid Development," *Ward County Independent* (ND), Oct 4, 1905, 5.

isolated settlers, the new towns disseminated mail and news and when mail came, it boosted the residents' morale.[162]

Mail would become a problem for Norwegian settlers who hoped to remain in contact with relatives from their homeland. They tended to communicate with each other in Norwegian and encouraged their children to retain the language and their heritage. Throughout the upper Midwest, Sons of Norway were common organizations in communities. The many Norwegian synods of the Lutheran church also promoted immigrant identity as Norwegian-American.

Notable to their claims were that the Viking Leif Ericson had discovered America centuries before Columbus, and the "discovery" of the Kensington Runestone that demonstrated to many the presence of Norwegians on the Great Plains in the Middle Ages. The Runestone story was born when a Swedish-born resident of Kensington, Minnesota wrote to a Swedish newspaper about a strange stone slab found in the roots of a tree that his neighbor Olof Öhman had dug up in 1898. His letter included pencil copies of 219 characters and a date of 1362 engraved on the stone, which was 130 years before Columbus reached America. The editor of the paper showed it to a Norwegian-born professor of Scandinavian languages at the University of Minnesota, who knew runes and translated the inscription while expressing indecision on its authenticity. In February 1899, the story was published in the Swedish paper and soon after it was picked up by Scandinavian papers and large English dailies, including the *Chicago Tribune*. The story of Vikings in Minnesota was born.

That year, a copy of the inscription was sent to Cristiana [Oslo] University where professors cabled their verdict that it was a clumsy forgery. This did little to conclude discussion on the stone's authenticity. Over time, scholarship and

---

162. Robinson, *History of North Dakota*, 163-165.

evidence continued to mount that the stone was a hoax, such as including runes that had ceased usage by 1362 and the writing of the year in Arabic numerals that had yet to come to Scandinavia by that time.[163] Still, argument continued on both sides and a Runestone Museum would be built in Alexandria,[164] Minnesota, which called itself "the birthplace of America." When professional football came to Minnesota, the team called itself the Vikings. Though American Heritage described the Kensington Runestone as "one of the greatest hoaxes in American history and one of its most persistent myths,"[165] questioning its authenticity would still offend some hardcore Norwegian Americans.[166]

Since Nettie's ancestors had left Norway, this spirit of nationalism had been a dominant theme, and that included Norwegianization of the language. Two competing proposals for a new written language meant that communications with the Old Country were more difficult. In 1907, two years after Norway gained its independence as a country by separating from Sweden, a reform act adopted Dano-Norwegian, Danish with minor changes plus Norwegian speech. Ten years later, the competing systems were combined and a written system was finalized.[167] On a related theme, Great Plains immigration historian and Charles J. Mach Distinguished Professor of History at the University of Nebraska, Frederick Luebke, has written that Scandinavians generally adapted rapidly to assimilation on the Great Plains

---

163. Erik Wahlgren, "The Case of the Kensington Rune Stone," *American Heritage*, Vol.10, Iss.3, https://www.americanheritage.com/case-kensington-rune-stone, Apr 1959.

164. For a discussion of the complexity of both points of view on authenticity see Henrik Williams, "The Kensington Runestone: Fact and Fiction, "The Swedish-American Historical Quarterly, Vol 63, No. 1, Jan 2012.

165. Wahlgren, "The Case of the Kensington Rune Stone."

166. Hjelde and Jansson, "Language Reforms in Norway," 301.

167. Ibid., 301-304.

and remained where their ancestors arrived in the nineteenth century. He notes, "Norwegians, in contrast to their Swedish and Danish cousins, were somewhat more retentive of their ethnic culture and often resisted language transition, even as they retained adherence to their Lutheran churches."[168] Robinson adds that Norwegian-Americans continued to use their own language, read Norwegian newspapers, attend Norwegian-American churches, join Norwegian-American societies, and even send sons to a Norwegian-American college.[169] As for newspapers, North Dakota at that time still had an active Norwegian press, including *Tidende* and *Normanden* published in Grand Forks and the *Posten* and *Fram* out of Fargo. The *Nord-Dakota Herold* had moved around but had ended in Dickinson.[170]

Nettie first found work in Garrison as a housekeeper in a rooming house, which provided her with room and board only. She then got a job in a hotel as a dining room girl. Dining hall girls in frontier towns mainly populated by men often served more than food. This was a hall where people who could not afford to eat at a restaurant would come and gather in an informal setting, though they had tables set aside in the back for regular customers. They were then all fed the same cooked meal by Nettie and other girls. She was eighteen when, to her surprise, her brother Oscar arrived unannounced. She had not seen him since they were separated ten years earlier and was initially delighted. They spent an hour talking and catching up before she needed to start work. Once she began serving the regulars at the dining hall, Oscar, who clearly had no idea about dining hall procedures, sat with the regulars and quickly finished his

---

168. Frederick C. Luebke, "Ethnic Group Settlement on the Great Plains," *Western Historical Quarterly*, Oct 1977, 426.

169. Robinson, *History of North Dakota*, 290.

170. Ibid., 317-318.

bacon and eggs plus dessert, then started helping himself to the food of everyone around him before walking out.

Nettie attempted to make up for her brother's boorish behavior by bringing out more from the kitchen for the diners to eat, but she was too late. They had also all walked out. Nettie recalled, "I was so embarrassed that I bawled most of the evening,"[171] and assigned the blame for her brother's lack of any social awareness to the farm family that had taken him in. She concluded that they had only wanted a free laborer on their farm and were "old fashioned," rarely went to town, and if they did, brought their meals with them, so if Oscar had accompanied them he had never entered a restaurant or dining hall. This event renewed the separation between the siblings so that it became a permanent condition.

Nettie's sister Millie also came to Garrison as a married woman with a daughter. Her bond to her sister was stronger than her ties to the man she had married, and she had stayed and filed for a homestead on her own, though her husband hung around long enough to get her pregnant again, this time with twins.

At that point, her husband abandoned her, and Millie took a job in Garrison as the "proving up" time began. Soon she developed chronic catarrh. In 1910, the year Nettie saw Halley's Comet, she convinced Minnie to head "to the city," Minot, one of North Dakota's few cities, with more than 6000 people, to get treatment. Millie quit her job and headed to Minot to seek better medical care. She landed a new job there doing laundry in Ward County Hospital. She did not want to be in Minot alone with her children, so Nettie quit her job in Garrison and moved to join her. Nettie got a job as an apprentice to a dressmaker, which paid no money but

---

171. Nettie Fortune, Mohall, Letter to Irene Fortune Dodge, Fargo, Nov 19, 1970.

provided room and board and taught her a valuable skill. Still, having no money was not viable, so she soon quit.

"Garrison, ND, Main Street, early 1900s" - (Property of the Author)

"Nettie (bottom) with dining hall workers" - (Property of the Author)

Nettie next found work as a chambermaid at the imposing landmark four-story Waverly Hotel on the corner of First Avenue and Main Street. The city was much more cosmopolitan than any she had experienced before and activities took place in the open. Minot was founded by railroad workers, then farmers and ranchers moved in along with businesses and traders stopping by frequently, many who found it a good stop because of the availability of prostitutes. This included a substantial number of African-American women at a time when they could not mix with the public. The community's High Third Street was a "red light district" known far beyond the region.

Several years before Nettie and Millie arrived, Minot had found it necessary to pass an ordinance to prevent people from keeping "a place of ill-fame or place resorted to for the purpose of prostitution, assignation, fornication, or for the resort of persons of ill-name, or ill-fame or dishonest conversation or common prostitutes."[172] The fines and jail sentences applied to both the prostitutes and their clients. This did little to change Minot's activities, as its reputation carried on well into the twentieth century.[173]

Soon Nettie had an active social life in the more modern and vibrant city. She had well-to-do friends who dressed in Edwardian era fashion with S-bend or S-curve corsets, blouses with puffed shoulders, skirts just above the ankle that exposed the high-heeled ankle boots, and most noticeably, the oversized hats. There was also the wealthy Clarence Foss, owner of one of those new motorcars. Though he was older, he was certainly interested in young Nettie. Years later as her frustrations grew, she would question herself.

172. "Disorderly Houses: An Ordinance Related to Disorderly Houses, and Houses of Ill-Fame and Common Prostitutes," *Ward County Independent* (ND), Sept 20, 1906, 4.

173. Kristine Kuntz, "High Third Street," Oral history special collection HQ146.M65 K86 2002, Minot State University, Mar 5, 2002.

Had she made a mistake by not marrying the affluent man, despite his age? At the time, she had considerable cynicism about men and marriage, considering that both her sister and her mother had been abandoned by their husbands. Then there was her grandmother, whose husband had shot at her.

"Nettie's stylish Minot friends" - (Property of the Author)

*"The man Nettie latter sometimes regretted
not marrying showing off his automobile"
- 1910. (Property of the Author)*

Nearby the hotel where Nettie worked on the corner of
Central Avenue and First Street was the 100-room Grand
Hotel. A dapper, worldly night desk clerk worked there and
at times filled in at the Waverley. He was Oliver Fortune and
on a night when he was working at the Waverley he met the
naive, petite nineteen-year-old Nettie. Oliver contributed to
another of Minot's activities that gave the city its reputation.
His bootlegging days in the dry state of North Dakota were
in full swing. While not wealthy like Clarence Foss, he was
young and charming. Whatever suspicions of men Nettie
had, things moved very quickly following her acquaintance
with Oliver.

CHAPTER 7: OLIVER'S HERITAGE

Irene's eventual father, and Nettie's eventual husband Oliver Fortune, was a compact, second-generation Norwegian. His strength came not from a healthy diet and good exercise, but from a lifetime of hard work. His earliest known relative in Norway was Nils Ingvardson Oye Hauge, who was born in the Vestland village of Laerdal in 1769 and remained there until 1810. Laerdal was surrounded by good farmland and towering mountains in a spectacular setting. The wooden buildings of the village bordered the south side of the Sognefjord, the longest and deepest of Norway's 200 fjords on its west coast, extending 127 miles inland.[174] Nearby was Borgund Stave Church, which had long existed for residents of the area.

Nils Ingvardson Oye's son Johannes Nilsson Hauge Fortun was also born in Laerdal just as the nineteenth century began. In 1834, he married a woman from his village, Gjertrud Knutsd Færestand, and apparently resettled in the village of Fortun, about sixty miles northwest by a channel of the fjord. Among their children was Oliver Nels, sometimes called Oliver N and at other times Oliver Nelson, born in October of 1852. In his later years, he would list this

---

174. Annika S. Hipple, "Exploring Norway's Fjords: The Sognefjord," *Real Scandinavia*, http://realscandinavia.com/exploring-the-norwegian-fjords-the-sognefjord/.

as "about 1853," then "about 1854," perhaps trying to take the edge off aging.

"Borgund Stave Church at end of the nineteenth century" - Public Domain/Wikimedia Commons

When Oliver Nels and many of his relatives emigrated to America in 1866,[175] like many Norwegians, he took the name of his European village home, Fortun, as his personal name, though he anglicized it to Fortune. He settled in southwest Minnesota, where he was a secretive, suspicious man who stuck to the motto, "Only believe half of what you see, and none of what you hear." Oliver Nels apparently had a great fear of how the Norwegian government, especially the military, might interfere with his future. It is likely

---

175. *Thirteenth Census of the United States, 1900*; National Archives and Records Administration, Census Place: Clifton, Traverse, Minnesota, Page 2, Enumeration District: 0285; FHL microfilm:1240794.

that he had left Norway to avoid military service. Once in Minnesota, he discouraged any sort of record keeping or discussions of heritage concerning his family. It is known that he had a one-legged brother named Ed who became a judge in Wheaton, Minnesota. Ed lost his leg when he fell from a buggy and caught it in the spokes of the moving wheel.

Another Norwegian family, the Mellems, emigrated to Wisconsin in 1855.[176] In Norway, they had been Rasmus Augundson Melheim of Sogn in Oppland and his wife Magdelene Pederdatter Hillstad of Halfslo. Their children included a young girl of five by the time they emigrated from Norway. After crossing the Atlantic, the Mellems had to change boats on the St. Lawrence River. The daughter was playing with other children who had been on the boat with her. When the announcement came that it was time to board the second boat and leave, the girl could not be found, so her father gathered the remainder of the family and said, "Come on, we've got to go. We can't wait for her." His wife replied, "No. I won't leave until I have all my children with me."[177] Eventually, the daughter was found. That daughter never forgave her father for the rest of her life for his willingness to abandon her as a helpless child. Her name was Hannah Mellem.

Hannah's family eventually moved on to Minnesota and Hannah grew into a woman who always parted her long, straight hair directly in the center. When she was nearly twenty-five, she married the heavily bearded Oliver Nels Fortune in the town of Owatana. They soon started a family that grew to twelve boys and one girl. The girl and one of the boys died very young in a diphtheria epidemic. That

---

176. Ibid.
177. Nettie Fortune, "Transcript of Conversation with Irene Fortune Dodge," 69.

boy's name was Jack, and Hannah and Oliver Nels named their next son Jack as well.

At a time when Minnesota farmland had to be carved out of the natural woods surrounding Wheaton, the town nearest them, sons were seen as great attributes and were expected to work from the earliest moment they were capable. Once he had a family of boys, Oliver Nels still had the paranoid notion that the Norwegians would somehow come after his sons in America and force them to return to Norway for military duty. As for farm labor, no one worked harder than Hannah, who did not rest even in the late stages of her many pregnancies. She gave birth to one of her children in the furrow of a field where she was helping with the farming.

The seventh of these thirteen children was Oliver, born on August 2, 1884. It is, perhaps, unusual that the son named after his father was not the firstborn son, but one born in the middle. Oliver was never called Oliver, Jr. or Oliver II. He was distinguished from his father by his complete lack of a middle name. The elder Oliver was referred to as "Oliver Nels." Young Oliver had never known his sister or the first of his two brothers named Jack. However, from the time he first saw her tiny baby-girl clothing, through his life he remained sentimental about his sister and despite his ambiguous religious views, he spoke of finally getting to see his little sister when he died.

Clearing wooded land was back-breaking labor for the Fortune family. Occasionally, it involved dangers as well, as the young Oliver was to discover. He used to tell of coming face to face with a bear one evening in the moonlight. The two of them were headed in opposite directions on a single path in the forest, and a possibly fatal collision was imminent. In his version of the story, he managed to overcome his initial panic long enough to recall his father's advice: do not show any fear. Clinging to that straw of hope, he walked straight down the path at the bear, and the bear retreated to allow him to pass.

The senior Oliver was an autocratic character who treated his sons as free hired help and clearly believed that there was "men's work" and "women's work." With eleven surviving sons and no daughters, this left Hannah in a position where her work was never done, and she could never rest. The younger Oliver, in his later years, could not recall seeing his mother ever walk. She always ran. This view of roles for men and women was one thing Oliver learned without instruction from his youth that he would retain when he eventually headed off on his own.

Hannah was a devout Lutheran who brought her Norwegian folk beliefs with her and "knew that the sun danced every Easter morning." She managed to have her sons "read" for the minister and become confirmed in the Norwegian Lutheran Church, though this had little influence on their adult characters. Her life as little more than a servant drove her further and further into finding her only solace in her Lutheran views. She had been reduced to seeking escape. Later in her life, when the younger Oliver returned to the Minnesota farm to visit her, he found that prairie life as a woman serving her husband and family had broken her. Hannah spent the last ten years of her life with her Bible every evening, praying to die.

Oliver grew up admiring his father, who did the very difficult work of clearing the land, then tending the fields and animals, supported by his boys as soon as they were old enough to help. His mother also worked from dawn to dusk, cleaning, cooking, scrubbing and washing clothes, and mending. Like many women, she did not make any decisions on what was happening or being planned. One of Oliver's siblings noted that while his father spoke frequently of his mother with love and affection, it never seemed to occur to him that her family need not make her whole life no better than that of a slave's.[178]

---

178. Ibid., 71.

The second oldest and most offensive of the sons was Jack. Other than determination and business sense, he was a man lacking in admirable qualities. Ruthless, brash, and cruel, Jack was willing to drive himself and all those around him to the limits in order to get what he wanted. He had a near religious belief that wealth somehow brought one immortality, and he saw his opportunity when homesteading was opened in southern Alberta, Canada. He headed north and managed to stake his claim on the most desirable of the available land. Jack met and married a widow, Mary Meyers. Mary had two sons from her original marriage, but Jack never adopted them. These boys were always seen as outsiders as Jack began building his empire, and other Fortune brothers headed to Canada to follow in his footsteps.

Jack's wife Mary was a devoted Catholic. In some ways, she resembled his mother. She silently suffered the degradation of her husband's arrogance, she worked continually from dawn to dusk, she was treated like a servant rather than a partner, and she retreated further and further into her religion as the years went by.

Jack's brother Howard and his cousin Billy were the first to attempt to follow in his footsteps. Billy's decision to go had been forced on him by his father, and he soon abandoned his claim to head back to Minnesota. It was at this point that Jack contacted Oliver to tell him of the available homestead Billy was leaving behind, and the recently married Oliver and Nettie headed north to claim it. Austin, Frank, and Ben also moved to Alberta but ended up as farm hands rather than homesteaders. Their stays were brief, and they all returned to "God's country": Minnesota. Allie, his wife Mabel, and his identical twin brother Dan eventually moved to Alberta as well, where they rented a farm. Like Billy, Frank, Ben, and Austin, they stayed only a couple years, then headed for southern Minnesota, vowing to never see Alberta again.

Jack's image was further tarnished with the younger Oliver when the twin Fortune brothers, Dan and Allie, and Allie's wife Mable were in Canada. They were in desperate need of money and had to swallow their pride and ask Jack for a loan. As often happened in the Fortune family, they turned to Oliver to intercede on their behalf. Jack asked, "How bad do they need it? Are they *really* hungry?"[179] Oliver and Nettie resented the cavalier attitude Jack displayed toward his own family.

Dan, Allie, and Mable were a curious threesome throughout their adult lives. They always stayed together and even when Allie died, Dan lived with Mable. Allie was relatively mild mannered, while his twin Dan was sober and touchy. Mabel was a good natured, cheerful woman who stuttered and seemed to carry a burden of self-imposed and in-law imposed guilt. She had always wanted a family, though Allie did not. When she gave birth to a stillborn baby for whom the name Walter had been selected, it was a very hush-hush event in the Fortune clan. Walter would have been the only grandson of Oliver Nels and Hannah. Although there were twelve sons in the family, the Fortune name had died out in a single generation.

As the United States moved from isolationism to support of the Western allies in the Great War, later called World War I, the three single repatriated brothers, Frank, Ben, and Austin, joined the US Army. Only Ben eventually ended up fighting in the trenches in France, suffering the miseries of struggling to survive while surrounded by the stench of death and the inescapable mud and gloom of northern Europe. The rheumatism that crippled his hands for the remainder of his life seems to have been brought on by the conditions he endured during trench warfare.

Frank, who wrote to his brothers that he "would be glad to go in the front lines for Old Glory any time," never

---

179. Ibid., 72.

got his chance. He was stricken with influenza and put in quarantine the month he was due to be shipped abroad. Austin's decision to enlist proved fatal. During training he contracted blood poisoning, and he subsequently died. The army presented his mother Hannah with $10,000 to atone for its mistake.[180] It was the only time in her life when she had any money of any significance that she could call her own.

"World War I Fortune doughboys Frank Fortune (left), Austin Fortune (right)" - (Property of the Author)

"Military funeral for Frank Fortune" - 1918. (Property of the Author)

---

180. Nettie Fortune, Mohall, Letter to Irene Fortune Dodge, Fargo, Nov 19, 1970.

In general, the Fortune boys were physically small, wiry people who were often cynical, ill-tempered, and philistine. Oliver's older brothers, especially Ed, the overbearing Chris, and Jack, often mistreated him. Ed was nearest Oliver's age, and he frequently bullied and taunted Oliver. On top of this, throughout their lives it seemed that their parents usually preferred Ed to Oliver. Ed was two years older, and when favors were handed out or one of the boys had to stay home from school to help put in the crop, things came out better for Ed. In spite of their occasional cruelness to Oliver, family members often looked to him to be the peacemaker in their frequent family squabbles, and he attempted to intercede and smooth over the frequent hostilities.

The most notable exception to the Fortune brothers' abrasive character was that of Ben, the thirteenth child. Oliver Nels's wife stood up to her husband very few times in her life, but when Ben was born, she insisted he was not going to work. She had seen what hard labor from an early age had done to her other twelve boys, and she was not going to allow it to happen to another. In spite of her husband's protests, she prevailed, and throughout his life Ben was much different from his brothers. He had a pleasant, congenial nature and a continuous smile on his face. He made friends easily, was well liked by all who met him, and had a happy-go-lucky attitude toward life. In an era and a place where it was "a man's world," the real head of the household in Ben's family was his wife Betty. This anomaly was the couple's mutual choice. Ben was a gentle person who showed genuine interest in others, unlike many of his self-absorbed brothers.

Young Oliver adopted the profane, quick-tempered character of his older brothers, but could not escape the taunts of his brother Ed. Ed had left the farm to get a job in St. Paul, and Oliver decided to follow. He dropped out during his freshman year of high school at Wheaton, Minnesota and eventually got a job with Swift and Company, the meat packers. During this time, he also took a night course at a business college in Minneapolis and worked as a night desk clerk at Minneapolis's finest hotel, the Nicollet. He was told by an instructor at the business college that he had a bright future if he worked his way up through the ranks at Swift. But Oliver had little interest in committing himself to a life as an employee. He wanted to be his own man.

Throughout all of this, Ed thought Oliver was naive and could easily be deceived and cheated once he was off the farm and continually taunted him. He loudly referred to Oliver as a "greenhorn" to anyone who would listen. The embarrassed and frustrated Oliver decided to eliminate that label permanently. He was seventeen when he decided to travel and see the world beyond the upper Midwest and experience places he had only begun to realize existed. If he did, he could never again be mistaken for a "greenhorn."

Seeing the world necessitated travel, and Oliver had no money. His solution was to become a hobo and head off in search of a life with exciting places and experiences. It was a desperate choice, but the option of remaining insignificant and barely getting by while being a low-level employee in Minneapolis with little respect from others and little respect for himself made his decision obvious. His four years as a hobo provided a kind of education that had many benefits.

Hoboes are sometimes thought of as bums or tramps, but they emerged in the late nineteenth century when the mechanization of industry forced many into unemployment, while the new railroad network made it possible for them to catch a ride and seek temporary employment in far-off places, then move on to the next spot where a job might be available. Hoboes' labor had contributed to the building of many of the railroads on which they hitched rides. There were so many in the late 1800s that they formed a union and adopted a code of ethics. Rule number one suited Oliver well: "Decide your own life. Don't let another person run or rule you."[181]

Hoboes had two common methods of hitching rides. One was to find empty boxcars on freight trains and hop in. The railroads hired guards to patrol their terminals and search the cars, then roughly throw out anyone they found, so avoiding being caught was a challenge. Oliver adopted the risky method of "riding the rods" to escape the Midwest and head for the West. Riding the rods involved hitching rides underneath the boxcars of freight trains. Boxcars had long iron rods under them and, as a train left a station, men and boys like Oliver would slip under a car, grab a rod to pull themselves into an obscure position, and hang onto the rods to prevent slipping to an abrupt and hideous death. This sort of danger was compounded by the fact that the railroads' crews looked for the freeloaders when they were about to leave a station, so Oliver and the others like him had to wait until the train was moving before they headed for the boxcar bottoms.

"Hobo riding the rails the way Oliver traveled country" - Public Domain/Wikimedia Commons

181. Roger Bruns, *Knights of the Road: A Hobo History* (London: Methuen Publishing, 1980), 54.

The ride was free, but the risks were considerable, as is illustrated by an experience Oliver had while still seventeen, heading through mountainous western Montana in the winter. This was a time of great engineering accomplishment in America, and nothing symbolized this better than the technical achievements involved in completion of the various transcontinental railroads. In Montana, this involved digging long tunnels through the Rocky Mountains.

Oliver had left Minneapolis on a freight train in an effort to reach California. As he traveled through Montana, he had to pass through a tunnel over a mile long. The rough terrain of the tunnel caused the train's steel wheels to continually throw off sparks, which would set Oliver's clothes on fire. He had to use one hand to beat off the fire, while holding onto a rod with his other hand. The weather was so cold that his hand grasping the rod could barely function, but he survived.

Things soon went badly for Oliver on his western adventure. Always a hard worker, he took what employment he could find, and he managed to get a construction job in Wyoming. This was short-lived, as he developed pneumonia and had to be hospitalized. When he was discharged from the hospital, he did not have a cent. He owned a good pair of overshoes that would have brought him a descent price in a saloon, but he was still only seventeen and unable to gain admittance. He ended up selling them to a pawn shop for fifty cents. With that money in hand, he first went to a restaurant and had a meal for twenty-five cents, then immediately walked down the street and had a second meal for the remaining twenty-five cents.

This left him with hospital bills unpaid, and he sought a second construction job. He was offered the job on the condition he had his own roll of bedding. Since he had no bedding, he went to a store and was given free gunnysacks that had been used for sacking potatoes, tied a rope around them, and went to work. His hospital bill had been only a dollar a day, and he paid it off, once again leaving himself with no money.

Over the next four years, Oliver drifted around the west, taking odd jobs for a time in one spot after another, then heading out again. He traveled through and made stops in Montana, Wyoming, Yellowstone National Park, Seattle, Tacoma, Spokane, San Diego, and San Francisco, which he left the day before the great earthquake of 1906. Seattle and San Francisco were his favorite spots.

Throughout this time, he usually lived in "hobo jungles," areas of unclaimed or vacant land sometimes sheltered by a bridge or in wooded settings and usually located near the railroad tracks or a river and near a town. Hoboes tried to remain inconspicuous as many towns and cities had laws against vagrants and they could be arrested. They slept on their blanket rolls if they had them, cooked their coffee in a tin can, and many camps had a communal soup, called "mulligan stew," for dinner. In these, each day, a hobo was expected to find fuel for the fire and also contribute something edible to put in the stew. When they camped near a river, they used the opportunity to wash their clothes. These camps commonly had a clothesline for drying their clothes, pots and other cooking utensils, and a mirror for shaving. Those passing through used the "jungle" as their base from which to hunt for some sort of work. These were often rough areas peopled by desperate and lonely men, so learning how to take care of oneself and one's few possessions was important.[182]

The hoboes had their own simple written language, a special set of symbols called the "hobo code" known only to them. These ciphers were used to leave messages for others who would pass after them and give them advice, warnings,

182. Lisa Hix, "Don't Call Them Bums: The Unsung History of America's Hard-Working Hoboes," *Collectors Weekly*, Apr 16, 2015, https://www.collectorsweekly.com/articles/dont-call-them-bums-the-unsung-history-of-americas-hard-working-hoboes/.

and suggestions. These could be left on trees, buildings, fence posts, or painted on walls. They were simple, since a fairly large number of vagrants could not read. Parallel lines with a wavy line running between them said, "Bad water," as a warning that drinking it could make a person sick. A circle with a diagonal line running through it from upper left to lower right said, "Good road to follow." A triangle with stick arms, each with three stick fingers, meant, "Man with a gun lives here," and it was dangerous to approach the property. A straight line rising from left to right with four perpendicular lines running through it signified, "Get cursed out here," warning that hoboes were likely to encounter verbal abuse and if they retaliated, the law would not be on their side. Two lines drawn parallel depicting spades meant, "Money for work here," indicating that previous hoboes had found what were likely low paying manual labor jobs or migratory farm work jobs. A tall, lower case "r" conveyed, "Good place if you are hurt/sick," which could be helpful since hoboes' survival depended upon them being able to get occasional work.[183] There were many more and it is likely that only the veteran hoboes were familiar with most of them, but there were some in the hobo jungle who could help while they were leaving new symbols for those who came next.

By the time Oliver returned to the Midwest, he was a changed man. He was a survivor and certainly no longer "green." Willing to do what was necessary to promote his own welfare, he had become a pool shark. Eager for opportunity, he briefly made an attempt at homesteading near Ryder, North Dakota[184] but soon abandoned it to move to the major North Dakota city of Minot and become a

---

183. Joel Diffendarfer, "Hobo Code: The Signs and Symbols Used by Travelers of Old," *Owlcation*, Jul 13, 2022, https://owlcation.com/humanities/All-things-HOBO-signs-and-symbols.

184. Nettie Fortune, Berthold, ND, letter to Irene Fortune Dodge, Fargo, ND, North Dakota, Apr 1, 1975.

hotel desk clerk. His income was soon augmented when he took on the role of supplying bootleg liquor to residents of, and visitors to Minot. North Dakota was a "dry" state, and bootleg liquor commanded high prices. As he prospered through his bootlegging, he began to be a sharp dresser, wearing only tailor-made suits. Oliver's concern about his personal appearance extended to the point where he would carry nothing in his pockets, to assure that the fit of his clothes remained perfect.

He also returned from his travels with well-defined prejudices that he retained from that time on. Although he was a great believer in the "melting pot" view of America, his melting pot excluded all but white Northern European immigrants. His daughter recalled that when she grew up, she heard "his intense dislike for a lot of different people—anyone who spoke with an accent ('can't even speak decent English'), Jews, niggers, Catholics, Dagos, Bolsheviks, only names he ever used."[185] She added, "As a child, I wondered a great deal about those tirades on all those subjects. I was puzzled as to how he could be so against all those people, most of whom he never saw or had anything to do with."[186] One of Oliver's favorite stories from his hobo days that he repeated often to his daughter and others concerned an incident he had observed somewhere out west at a restaurant. Irene described the event: "He went into a restaurant to eat. A black man ('nigger, of course') came in and was served. However, when he was through eating, the man in charge picked up the diner's plate and smashed it—so that no one else would have to eat off of a plate that a 'nigger' had used."[187]

Oliver's Minot bootlegging days were in full swing, and he was an impressive figure in the eyes of a country

---

185. Irene Fortune Dodge, unpublished memoir, 48.
186. Ibid., 47.
187. Ibid., 49.

girl working at the same hotel, Nettie Williams. Though she was soon pregnant and he felt obligated to marry her, his comment to her foreshadowed the future discord of that arrangement. Oliver told Nettie he would be ashamed to have his folks meet her.

The couple headed for Canada to homestead, and their daughter Irene was born.

CHAPTER 8: FIRST HOMESTEAD FAILURE AND RETURN TO NORTH DAKOTA

Life on the homestead came with many challenges. There was little rain, and the dry sod had to be broken with great effort. Isolation added to the problems. When Irene got the measles at eighteen months, her parents had to call on relatives from miles away for help doing the homestead duties. Irene was very ill and for three nights, she would only calm down when she was held by one of her parents and rocked. Although she improved, her ears grew seriously infected and began to discharge large quantities of pus.[188] There was nothing for her mother to do but keep her warm and make her wear a night cap, a practice she continued to enforce regularly in the winters that followed. The threat of illness was ever present, as trained medical care in Bow Island was twenty miles away.

Homemade remedies had to be designed or remembered to cope with most illnesses. Hot water with sugar and whiskey, even for the youngest of children, was standard treatment for colds. If the cold was in the chest, poultices of flannel and goose grease were added. A woolen sock around the neck was the right thing for a sore throat, and a hot water bottle was standard treatment for nearly all aches and pains. Queasy stomachs and intestinal distress were treated with

---

188. Nettie Fortune, letter to Irene Dodge, Feb 21, 1968.

Epsom salts, which were guaranteed to "clean you out," and a dose of sulfur and molasses in the spring was good for one's general health.

"Nettie and Irene at age two on original Alberta homestead" - 1913. (Property of the Author)

Yet illness was not the only hardship of isolation. Another was loneliness. When Irene wrote her memoir of her and her mother's life on homesteads, she introduced it with a quote from anthropologist and educator Loren Eiseley, who had spent his early years in the rural prairies of Nebraska. He described how this isolation could destroy women's lives: "I have seen beaten, toil-worn women staring into immensity, listening to the wind. We were mad to settle the west in that fashion, hopelessly vulnerable. You cannot fight the sky. In the end you will hear voices, you will weep, or you will kill, or abandon what you struggled to for and flee, but by then the sound of the wind will always follow you."[189] Perhaps she saw in hindsight that the isolation and demands that this and the following homesteading experience her mother endured as an adult contributed to her mental illness in her later years of life.

Irene had one dress in her early years made from a flour gunnysack dyed blue. On one trip to town her mother, who was a fine seamstress, had a little extra money and bought cloth. She made some dresses for her daughter and when she had finished, she hung them on a line. She then invited Irene to choose which one she would like to wear, but she was not about to wear any of them. The blue flour sack dress was her attire. Nettie had a challenge convincing her daughter to try any of the new ones but eventually prevailed.

For Irene, who had been born nearby so her parents could homestead, there were no friends when she was very young. At first her only playmate was her cat. The cat had a special fondness for Irene, and when Irene was taking her afternoon naps, the cat would wash her head for an hour or more, then lie down beside her head and go to sleep. She left Irene's hair looking as if it had been combed in one direction. When Irene first started to walk, she took her cat by one paw and attempted to get it to walk upright on its hind paws with her. The cat was understandably not fond of this.

Irene has no personal memories of life on their first homestead since they abandoned it in early 1914 when she was two and a half years old. This was a time when even though they seemed removed from nearly all people and even local events, far away conflicts over issues that were totally meaningless to them would determine their fate. In Europe there were two coalitions, the Triple Alliance and the Triple Entente that pitted the dominant power of the

---

189. Loren Eiseley, *All the Strange Hours* (New York: Scribner, 1975), 196.

nineteenth century, Britain, and its allies against the upstart challenger Germany, which also had allies. Developing these alliances and having strength in numbers had perhaps seemed reasonable during the imperialism of the late nineteenth century, when European countries competed to carve up Africa and claim much of Asia where claims could be competitive. When disputes over those claims broke out and people rejected the rule of the countries that claimed them, the advantages turned to dangers.

There likely exists no better example of the danger of competing alliances than what happened in 1914. On June 28, Archduke Franz Ferdinand, heir to the throne of Austria-Hungry, was assassinated by Gavrilo Princip, a Serbian nationalist. After a month of diplomatic blunders, Austria-Hungry attacked Serbia. Within a week, Russia, Belgium, France, Great Britain, and Serbia were at war with Austria-Hungary and Germany. The Great War, World War I, had begun. It eventually involved thirty countries and took the lives of 8,500,000 soldiers.[190] Canada, as a Commonwealth member, sent volunteer soldiers to Britain's aid from the outbreak of the war but did not begin conscription until near the final year. The United States also began conscription after the war had been going on for three years, so Oliver escaped serving, though his brothers volunteered.

As the war approached, living on the homestead that they had taken over from Oliver's brother, things had not gone well. The weather had been bad, with little rain for two growing seasons, then there was the threat of war looming large. Nettie recalled that in August of 1914 Oliver said, "We got to get out of here. War broke out. We'll starve to death. I'm going out to work."[191] They sold their cattle

---

190. Adrian Gilbert, "World War I: Killed, Wounded Missing," Encyclopedia Britannica, https://www.britannica.com/event/World-War-I/Killed-wounded-and-missing.

191. Nettie Fortune, "Transcript of Conversation with Irene Fortune Dodge," 67.

and chickens, and Oliver rented a boxcar to store their machinery and the horses he would need for work. They headed to Milestone, Saskatchewan, where there had been rain. The only furniture they took with them was their bed. Oliver knew someone from Glenburn, North Dakota, who lived in town but had a farm there, and they had harvesting to be done.

In Glenburn, Nettie found a room to rent for Irene and her, while Oliver got a job harvesting and earned a small amount of money. Nettie and Irene slept on quilts on the floor, used wood boxes from one of the stores as furniture, borrowed a cooking range, and bought a few dishes. Irene had never seen sidewalks prior to this. Nettie commented of Irene, "You'd never seen anything but roads, you know. And I couldn't make you walk on the sidewalk. You insisted that roads were meant to walk on."[192] Nettie finally gave up, and roads remained their walkways until they eventually left Canada.

When the weather turned cold, an old friend of Oliver's named Hatfield offered Nettie and Irene a free room. Despite the kindness of this family, Nettie found living conditions difficult. The Hatfields had no running water or indoor toilets. They were living on the second story of a home, and she had to venture out to the outhouse when she needed a lavatory, an unpleasant experience in the Canadian winter. Irene's bodily functions were taken care of with the use of a chamber pot, which Nettie had to carry down to empty in the outdoor toilet.[193]

192. Ibid., 47.
193. Ibid., 49.

*"Irene's chamber pot" - She included the rhyme:
Remember, when you were a wee, wee, tot/ And
someone took you from your warm, warm cot/ and
put you on a cold/cold pot/ and told you to wee wee,
whether you could or not? (Property of the Author)*

After harvest season ended, Oliver said he was going to Minot to auction off the horses and equipment at the livery barn, then look for work. He said it would be cheaper if Nettie and Irene remained in Glenburn, but he would send for them once he had work.

He did get a job, working as a desk clerk at Minot's Lexington Hotel. He got by mainly on coffee and donuts, since he could take what the hotel was providing for its residents. He sent for Nettie and Irene, who came and had a room in the hotel.

"Oliver returns to Minot" - 1915. (Property of the Author)

Nettie bought a meal ticket for eating once a day with Irene and with it, she filled her pockets with milk containers, apples and other fruit, and whatever was available to take to their room. In that location, an event took place one night that was dramatic and for Nettie included what she felt was an insult. Her version of the story is, "A young fellow came to the hotel to register, had a room right across from us. . . All at once I heard, 'bang, bang, bang!' Somebody had shot off a revolver. Gee, I was scared. I called up the office and said, 'Come up here quick. Somebody's shooting across the hall.' Your dad [Oliver] was in the office at the time and he came running. And when I heard him coming I opened my door and I said, 'Don't go in there. You might get shot.' He went, 'Huh, I'm going in.' He went right in there and there the man was, lying across the bed, the revolver beside him, and he was dying. He was past talking. We had to call the police."[194] Nettie and this incident made the front page in North Dakota's largest newspaper, *The Fargo Forum and Daily Republican* under the title, "Minn. Man Took Life at Minot." They reported that fifteen minutes after a man registered as Jack Ford of Minneapolis, "Three shots were heard by Mrs. Oliver Fortune from her room across the hall. She summoned the hotel proprietor and her husband to the scene. . . The first two either went wild or he was testing his gun . . . The third shot sent a bullet into the man's heart."[195] A note found in his pocket said he was Clifford Squires of Cyrus, Minnesota.

When the police had Nettie and Oliver in for questioning immediately following the event, Nettie was taken back by one question. She recounted, "When I called the office, did I call from my room or did I call from his room?"[196] Since this was Minot the implication was clear, and she found it rude.

To survive winter, they went to Wheaton, Minnesota, where Oliver's father Oliver Nels and his wife Hannah took them in. It was Nettie's first time meeting her mother-in-law, who took one look at Nettie and said, "She's no good on a farm; she can't do any work."[197] Later in the winter, they left and headed to the recently established town that had just surpassed 500 people, Mohall, North Dakota, where Oliver found a two-room vacant building to rent. In a very ill-conceived plan, he decided that the family would live in the back room while the front room was turned into a variety store. The back room where they lived was crammed with

---

194. Nettie Fortune, "Transcript of Conversation with Irene Fortune Dodge," 68.

195. "Took Life at Minot," *The Fargo Forum and Daily Republican*, Jan 26, 1915, 1.

196. Nettie Fortune, "Transcript of Conversation with Irene Fortune Dodge," Oct 1974, 68.

197. Irene Fortune Dodge, unpublished memoir, from conversation with her cousin Mildred Wilson, 42.

their table, beds, stove, and all their belongings. Oliver's brother Chris had opened a variety store in nearby Grenburn that was not successful, but which he held onto with determination regardless.

Oliver's store seemed doomed for failure from the start, as he had very little volume in stock of the type of goods sold, there were already stores in Mohall catering to many of the people's needs, and he had no experience in sales or business prior to this. Nettie's observation on Oliver's attempt to start his store was, "Terrible. Nearly everything I could have done so much better. Why start a variety store? Start out with a confectionary store and you've got something that doesn't cost so much, and gradually increase it to a variety store later. Start with candy and peanuts and tobacco and school supplies. You could run a store and that's all you'd need to start with. See how simple that would be? But no, we had to start out getting dishes, all kinds; novelties and so on. We got someone's cat to come over and kill rats. It killed nine rats on the first day."[198]

While Nettie might have had more business sense than Oliver, at least enough to look at what was more affordable and what suited people's needs that could be easily filled, he was not interested in advice from a woman. This failure would not change that, even as he had a second business opportunity and subsequent failure looming in his future in Mohall.

Irene says her dad put every cent he had into building up an inventory. She notes that her father hated to work for anyone else, so trying to start a business after failing at homesteading was not surprising, just unfortunate. His aim, with his lack of understanding, was to substantially undersell other merchants. Her example was that he sold twelve-quart galvanized pails, which farmers bought on most trips into town. Madsen's, a rival store, charged a dollar. Oliver began

---

198. Nettie Fortune, conversation with Irene Dodge 72.

by undercutting them, selling them for twenty-five cents and a loss. She said he never involved himself in maintaining a neat, orderly store, straightening things up or dusting, since this was not "men's work."[199]

There had been a rare good two years with rain in Alberta, and they had missed them by returning to the United States. Oliver's failure of a store following his failure at homesteading had him looking for another option. After two years as a merchant in Mohall, it seemed like homesteading was now the right choice.

---

199. Irene Fortune Dodge, unpublished memoir, 45-46

CHAPTER 9: SECOND ATTEMPT, IRENE'S EARLY LIFE ON THE HOMESTEAD

For five-year-old Irene, the homestead seemed like a wonderful place. Once her father and her uncle had torn down the old shack they had previously lived in and built a small, two-room house with a pitched roof, the family moved in. They had a bleak farmyard to accompany their house. It consisted of a small, crude barn for their two broncos and their cow, a pigpen, a shanty-roof chicken coop, and a granary. All the structures were weather-beaten gray.

Irene's earliest memories are from this time. She was totally unaware of the utter drabness, barrenness, isolation, and poverty of their existence and recalled the time as "exhilarating and joyful."[200] She could not remember living anywhere else, so she had nothing for comparison, and the crystal clear, blue skies of southern Alberta with their puffy white clouds provided her young imagination with wonders and hours of entertainment. She was happy on sunny days, lying on the side of a knoll for hours as she watched shapes of animals, people, and various things coming into shapes, then gradually disintegrating as new shapes emerged.

---

200. This, and most the stories recounted in Chapter 9 come from Irene Fortune Dodge, unpublished memoir.

Where Irene went to lie on a knoll, it would have been close to the Milk River, which was near their homestead and the area where the landscape differed greatly.[201] Sandstone cliffs sit on a hard, dense rock base adjacent to the river and there were some natural grass inclines nearby. Next to that was flat, open prairie.

The bleakness of the landscape that was apparent to her parents seemed lost on Irene. Without trees or shrubs as far as the eye could see, it was unpainted buildings and fence posts, and perpetually brown grass from the shortage of rain, offering little other than monotony. There were no roads, just ruts in the ground from wagon traffic. Russian thistles thrived in the dry climate, reaching up to several feet in diameter. In the fall, the thistles turned brown and brittle and snapped off to become tumbleweeds, rolling in the ever-present wind. Whirlwinds scooped up summer dust and danced across the prairies. On glistening summer days when the sun was beating down, preschool Irene found herself confused by mirages.

What are called mirages can raise the question of whether reality exists externally or in the mind, since when one sees something, it is the person's brain that determines what it is. On a desolate homestead, this is less of an issue. Irene was five when she looked out in their pasture and saw a town. It had a grain elevator, a small store with a barrel in front and a couple other buildings nearby. She ran into their house yelling, "There's a town in our pasture." Surprisingly to her, her mother lacked enthusiasm or excitement about seeing it. Nettie had by this time seen her share of mirages and explained to her daughter what they were. Irene looked again, but the town had faded away. While she experienced other mirages or had hallucinations from heat, dehydration,

---

201. "Item: Oliver Fortune," Microfilm Reel Number: C-6451, Item Number: 281587, *Library and Archives: Canada*, https://www.bac-lac.gc.ca/eng/discover/land/land-grants-western-canada-1870-1930/Pages/item.aspx?IdNumber=281587&.

or fever, there was never another to equal the reality of this first one that she would share.

It would take many years before she could admit that the early solitude had caused her difficulties that she had kept to herself. She finally wrote about the experience, prefacing it with "In over sixty-five years I have never mentioned this to anyone or written a word about it until now." Her long secret memory:

It was in the time before I started school and while I spent a great deal of time by myself on that isolated homestead. I would walk to some favorite spot, like a stone pile quite removed from the house. As I walked I had a sense of a very real personage walking with me—a somewhat nebulous giant of a man, perhaps fifteen or twenty feet tall, with whom I carried on conversations. This was God, and he was very, very real to me.

We never attended church, and could not possibly have done so, even if that had been important to my family. So, it seems strange that I had the real, real experience repeatedly.[202]

The land was rolling and laden with stones and boulders remaining from the retreat of glaciers from the last ice age. It had barely been occupied since the encroachment by White settlers left it abandoned by the Plains Indians. Every gully held stacks of bleached buffalo bones. In a pasture, a ring of stones remained from Indian campgrounds. Irene's father found relics, among them a tomahawk head, a plate, and a sharpening tool that had survived from earlier than 1100 CE, in the pre-Cree Indian era. Arrowheads were strewn around the ground, and Irene constantly played with them, then tossed them away. She never bothered to consider saving them since they were so common.

---

202. Irene Dodge, "The Secret Side of Life," in her unpublished memoir, 57.

The drabness of the house with two rooms was also lost on Irene. The wallpaper was actually insulation designed to help keep in the warmth in winter and keep out the heat in summer. Nails protruded from the walls to serve as hangers. In the bedroom, there was a double bed, a small, three-legged table and a small mirror, Nettie's black trunk, and her Singer sewing machine. The second room was the kitchen, dining room, washroom, and sitting room. It had a rocking chair, coal bucket, kerosene lamp, and a few dishes stored on boards nailed to the wall. It also had a homemade table with a white oilcloth cover, a couple chairs, and the cooking range. The range was lit by cow chip fuel three times per day in the summer, now that they had cattle, and by coal in the winter. One of Irene's jobs was to head out into the pasture with a gunnysack and collect the cow chips.

The range always had three sadirons, heavy chunks of iron that were heated, then clamped onto handles to iron clothes, sitting on it available for use. In winter, the sadirons were wrapped in woolen rags at night and placed at the bottom of the bed, where each pair of feet could reach. In the fall, the house had to be protected against the extreme winter. It was wrapped in tar paper, then "banked" by surrounding it with piled up manure. This provided shelter that allowed for survival in winters that were often bitterly cold. But Alberta lies in a region that is somewhat of a meteorological oddity, in that the winters are interrupted by the "Chinook winds." Chinook is a Native American word meaning "snow eater,"[203] and these are winds that heat the air suddenly as they come down the east side of the Rockies and pass through Alberta thirty to thirty-five times per year. In the winter, they can suddenly raise the temperature dramatically. The most extreme documented Alberta case raised the January temperature 106° Fahrenheit

203. Tiffany Lizée, "Canada's Most Dramatic Temperature Change Recorded 57 Years Ago on Jan. 10 in Alberta," *Global News*, Jan 10, 2019.

in one hour.[204] Later, in the Black Hills of South Dakota, a Chinook caused an increase of 49° F. in two minutes.[205] For the Fortunes, wide open windows and doors in the middle of winter were the pleasant outcomes of these brief interludes in the otherwise harsh, hard winter.

During the challenging, severe day-to-day existence on the open prairie the Fortunes, like all the other Alberta homesteaders, had to make do as best they could. Winter clothing consisted of long, woolen underwear, covered by layer upon layer of scarves, mittens, sweaters, and anything else that was warm that could be wrapped around bodies, until people literally became stiff. The howling winds made keeping all the various layers in place a constant struggle. The heater in the house did not last the night, even though the coals were banked, so the woolen underwear never came off. Water froze in the pail and the basin. When the coal-burning heater was still hot, the family stood around it, turning at regular intervals as they approached scorching one side of their bodies while nearly freezing the other. Blizzards and snow blindness in such isolated conditions presented an ever-present threat of real tragedy, both to people and to the animals that sustained them.

Summers were not much more pleasant. Temperatures often exceeded 100° Fahrenheit, and labor was long and hard. Sleeveless shirts and dresses were not acceptable wear, and straw hats and bandanas were the only clothing concessions to the scorching heat. The air in the house was still, unless the windows were opened. There were partially adjustable screens, but a real breeze necessitated open windows. The tradeoff for the cooling draft was invasion by the multitude of prairie insects.

---

204. Ibid.

205. Rachel Ross, "What Are Chinook Winds?" *Live Science*, https://www.livescience.com/58884-chinook-winds.html, Apr 27, 2017.

To Irene, this was all normal. Her mother and father were working continuously, trying to make a go of a situation that was always threatened by some form of natural disaster and ultimately doomed by the lack of water. Nettie's day started earliest, as she had to have a good breakfast ready for Oliver, whose day involved continuous labor. He needed fuel in him to get the work done. First, the land had to be cleared. This was back-breaking labor, since the rocks and boulders had to be hauled away. Oliver did this with the aid of his pair of broncos, Mutt and Jeff. These horses had grown up on the free range and never really accepted being workhorses. They were wild and unruly, so Oliver's arms were nearly torn from their sockets on a daily basis as he tried to get them to pull the plow and break the sod to turn over an adequate amount of soil that could be planted. The only respite from the continuous work for the horses came on Sundays. It was illegal to work on Sundays in Alberta.

Irene often accompanied her father when he headed out to the fields or pasture. It was her job to bring him morning and afternoon coffee, as well as lunch. Oliver was a good storyteller and conversationalist, and he liked to recount his adventures traveling throughout the west in his younger days. He had an excellent memory and could recite any poem he had learned in his school days, and he was an avid reader despite the dearth of available reading material. Irene found him to be the most interesting person among the limited number of people she knew at that time.

Despite the hardships of life on this homestead, it was initially a happy, hopeful time for the Fortune family. Perhaps it was the best of all times in their rocky history. Oliver and Nettie were struggling together to make a success of something that was their own. There were little surprises for Irene from time to time. Among these were baby rabbits that her father would bring home in his shirt pocket if he happened to plow up a rabbit nest. Although the larger rabbits were used for food, the babies became pets for Irene that she could keep until fall, if they survived that long. At that time, they would have to be let free. The use of rabbits as food came to an end when Irene was six and word went around that rabbits were carrying tuberculosis.

There were also small field animals to entertain Irene. Like many children, she found the gophers and field mice cute and fun to watch. When her parents put out poison to kill them, she would cry. When she was older, she began to realize how destructive the animals were to the family's crops, and she began to snare them and kill them. The government paid a bounty for their tails, so this was a way to earn small change for visits to town. But at age six, her concerns were not for the welfare of the crops, they were for the welfare of the animals.

Rabbits, gophers, and field mice did not make very sociable pets. In the solitude of frontier life, Irene had one close friend, a long-haired, black dog she named Billie Bean. He was a stray that had shown up on the Fortune homestead and was adopted. Although her father was not initially taken with the dog, his attitude changed as a result of an incident that took place one evening. The family was in bed when the dog began barking outside the front door. Oliver got up from his bed and went out to scold Billie Bean. The same thing happened again, further angering Oliver. However, the dog kept at it, and since Billie Bean had never behaved this way before, Oliver went outside to see what the trouble was. In the middle of the night, Billie Bean led Oliver to one of his horses that had broken through the barbed wire enclosure and had fallen, unable to get up. The horse was thrashing in the barbed wire and would have died, had it not been for Billie Bean's intelligence and perseverance. From then on, Oliver was a loyal fan of Billie Bean.

Young Irene was convinced that Billie Bean smiled when she talked to him, and the two of them spent hour after hour together, keeping each other entertained. She also had a second pet, a tomcat. One evening when she was playing with her cat, it bit through one of her fingers. Her father said that once a cat bites, it will bite again, and it would have to go. The next morning, Irene heard a shotgun blast come from behind the barn. She never saw the cat again.

Irene's one great fear regarding her companion Billie Bean was the danger posed by coyotes. Coyotes were very common and would gather in groups in the pasture or field at night and howl at the moon. In the daytime they traveled in twos, and if they came near the farm, Billie Bean would chase after them. The coyotes would split apart, and while Billie Bean was chasing one, the other would get behind him and be chasing Billie Bean. Somehow, the dog always managed to survive unharmed.

"Irene with Billie Bean" - (Property of the Author)

Irene's parents tried to warn her that coyotes were dangerous hunters that could easily prey on small children, but she never feared them. The animals that truly frightened Irene were bulls. Bulls are huge, aggressive animals, and although the Fortunes did not have one, their neighbors did. It would paw the ground and bellow so loudly that it could be heard at the Fortune homestead. Occasionally, it would break through a fence in search of cows, and Irene's family had one cow. Her fear of bulls at such an impressionable age grew so strong that she had frequent nightmares about them, and these nightmares continued to recur into her adult life.

While Billie Bean managed to survive the coyotes, he could not survive the wrath of the neighbors. One family, the Degensteins, was especially protective of their homestead and resented intruders. The Degensteins' female dog was likely what attracted Irene's dog. Billie Bean often returned to the Fortune farm with a bag of rocks tied to his tail. That really irritated Irene but then one day, Billie Bean headed off again and entered Degensteins' property, where he was shot and killed. It was a crushing blow to young Irene. Although her parents got another dog and named it "Billie Bean" again, it was a big disappointment, in that she found it to be a "stupid dog." It could never take the place of the original Billie Bean.

Irene had one memory from this time that reveals how adult conversations sink into children's minds. She wrote, "I recall going to a wedding when I was five or six years old, in a little white wooden one-room Catholic church, where Jack and Mary's hired girl was being married. During the ceremony, I was more interested in trying to figure out where the church was hiding all its guns than I was in the wedding. After all, it was one bare room with no basement, no attic, no door to anything except the one to enter the church. But I'd heard over and over again how the Catholics stored guns in their churches!"[206] The prejudices about religions were prominent not only among homesteaders but with the general public. The nativist view popularized by the Know-Nothing Party at the time Irene's ancestors arrived from Norway that called for a ban of all Catholics from public office and a twenty-one-year naturalization process for immigration among its policies had captured over 100 seats in Congress and won eight governors' victories,[207] was alive and well. In 1912, the year after Irene was born, the House Committee on Immigration debated whether Italians should be considered full-blooded Caucasians and whether immigrants from southern and eastern Europe should be considered less intelligent.[208] Oliver bought stacks of newspapers when he could and read about what was happening. His prejudices were reflected in these developments, which is likely where Irene's idea of Catholics storing guns originated.

Keeping the family fed was a constant struggle, as they had little money to spend on their infrequent visits to town, and no available refrigeration. Vegetables dominated the fare in warm months, while meat was available in winter. What little meat there was in the summer consisted mainly of salt pork, bacon, and an occasional chicken. The drippings from cooked meat, which the family called "smult," was used as a spread on bread. Bread was a constant necessity and a problem to bake, given the unpredictable nature of the heat output of the stove. Pancakes frequently substituted for bread, and ginger snaps and doughnuts provided a sweet break from the monotony of most of the food.

206. Irene Fortune Dodge, unpublished memoir, 49.
207. Lorraine Boissoneault, "How the 19th Century Know Nothing Party Reshaped American Politics," *Smithsonian*, https://www.smithsonianmag.com/history/immigrants-conspiracies-and-secret-society-launched-american-nativism-180961915/, Jan 26, 2017.
208. Ibid.

Gardening was serious and critical, as it provided the family's carrots, lettuce, onions, radishes, cabbage, corn, tomatoes, beets, beans, and peas for summer eating, and potatoes, squash, onions, and citron for fall.

Nettie was an ingenious provider. In early spring, she saved shell halves from the eggs the family chickens produced. She filled them with dirt and planted and sprouted seeds before the weather allowed for their growth outdoors. As the danger of frost passed, she transplanted the young plants into her garden, so they would mature early. It was a constant battle to keep the garden weeded, hoed, and watered, as they lacked so much as a watering can. The water was hauled by bucket from the pump of the cistern.

Water was a problem as there were often long dry periods, so it was stretched as far as possible and often reused. Water for cooking could be used for washing clothes and infrequently bodies, then the floor, or taken out to water plants. The family had a cistern, an underground tank for holding water. The cistern collected water when it rained, but it was sometimes supplemented by ice. They buried snow and ice deep beneath hay and dirt in the winter in large quantities and covered areas that survived into early summer. Much of their water had to be hauled from a slough that was over a mile away. Oliver dug a hole a few feet deep by the slough and bailed out water as the hole filled. He then hauled this water back to the homestead in barrels for the family and the livestock. He had once considered a well but had not had the resources to have one drilled. He attempted digging one but with all else he had to do, the project was soon abandoned.

While a shortage of water leading to drought was a nearly constant danger for the garden and the homestead, there were times when the problem was reversed. The open prairies of the Great Plains allow for the frequent buildup of massive cumulonimbus clouds, which produce spectacular lightning and occasional severe storms. Small whirlwinds frequently danced across the Fortune homestead as the winds gained force during these times, and deadly tornadoes menaced homesteaders, whose flimsy shacks and homes offered little protection. But the greatest fear was the threat of hail. A single storm could destroy a season's efforts to produce a cash crop and the above ground vegetables a family relied on for food.

The battle to make the garden productive was the same in many respects as the battle to make the farm productive. It had to be waged against the insects and worms that could quickly ravage it. Potato bugs were a menace, and these small, yellow-and-black beetles had to be individually picked off the plants, then dropped into a can of kerosene. Cutworms, operating just below the surface of the soil, and cabbage worms that fed on the leaves and heads of cabbages and other vegetables had to be dealt with in the same manner. Most divesting of all were grasshoppers. In years when they came in small numbers, it was possible to cope with the limited destruction they caused, but when the swarms settled in, there was no defense against their voracious appetites. When the massive hordes descended on the Fortune homestead, they surrounded the family with a whirring roar and blocked their view and darkened the sky with millions of airborne attackers.

In the Fortune homestead, a small cellar managed to maintain a few vegetables into the early winter, but more reliance was placed on canned foods. In general, canned vegetables did not survive well. The notable exception was the tomatoes, which Nettie preserved along with large quantities of sugar and slices of lemons. She also made relish of the green tomatoes that had not ripened by the first frost of the fall. Canning and preserving vegetables was the least expensive way to provide variety in the winter diet, but it cut into the Fortunes' small income because it required the purchase of vinegar, salt, and sugar.

Meat was available mainly in the winter, following the butchering of animals that took place once the frost had permanently set in. Steers and pigs provided beef and pork, which was wrapped in paper and buried in the seed grain in the granary for storage. Some chicken was also available, although the "setting hens" were saved to provide the family with eggs.

Preparing a chicken dinner was a gruesome process that yielded delicious results. It began with Nettie catching a chicken, then wringing its neck. After that she would chop the creature's head off, and the headless animal would bounce around on the ground. The next step was to dip the carcass into a pail of boiling water to loosen the feathers for plucking. This completed, Nettie would cut the chicken open to "dress it"—clean out the insides. She attempted to get Irene to assist in this ordeal, but it was more than the young girl could handle. However, once the preparation was done and the chicken was pan-fried, it was a pleasure for the entire family.

Irene lived on milk and milk products more than anything else. At first, the family had only a single cow, Bossie, and Nettie frequently sent Irene to get water for her to drink. Bossie swallowed so much water that it often caused the child to lose her temper, and Irene would kick the animal square in the nose. "You quit drinking water!" she would shout, but the cow would just shake her head, then keep on drinking. Nettie would say, "Don't be kicking Bossie cow. You know she gives us lots of nice milk."[209] Even though she really loved milk, this was not enough of an argument to persuade Irene.

Gradually, the Fortunes increased their herd to four. Whole milk, bread dipped in milk and sprinkled with sugar, and milk with beat up eggs and sugar and nutmeg were all

---

209. Nettie Fortune, conversation with Irene, 67.

basics in their diet. The really special treat was a glass of warm milk straight from the cow's udder.

Since the family lacked a cream separator, some of the milk was poured into flat pans to allow the cream to rise to the top. The cream was then skimmed off and used to enhance the taste of something at nearly every meal. As the remainder soured, its sour cream was skimmed off and churned into butter. This was done first with a dasher churn, the type that consisted of a crock with a lid and a pole that was lifted up and down to agitate the cream, and eventually with a keg churn mounted on a metal rack. Irene earned five cents for each batch of butter she churned, which she saved to buy ice cream cones on her infrequent visits to Bow Island. Nothing went to waste, and the sour milk left over following the butter churning was left out until it curdled into chunks called "clabbers." These were put on a warm burner on the back of the stove to separate into solid parts [cottage cheese], and viscous "clabber." This latter, yoghurt-like substance was used as feed for the animals.

Providing food for the family was one problem; another was turning the homestead into the source of financial security that Oliver and Nettie were seeking. This proved to be unsuccessful, though not because of any lack of effort on Oliver's part. His life consisted of nearly constant backbreaking work, made more difficult by physical ailments. Chores began his day—milking the cow, feeding the stock—followed by breakfast. Then it was out to the fields, dressed in his bib overalls, Panama hat, blue work shirt, and black Blucher boots. In summer, he had a kerchief tied around his neck to keep the sun from burning him and to absorb the heavy sweat. In winter, he was wrapped in his heavy sheep-lined, cotton-covered coat, with four-buckle overshoes protecting his feet.

There was always new land to be broken, along with water to be hauled, barbed wire fence to be repaired, fence post holes to be dug, land to be plowed, seeded, and harrowed, and crops to be harvested. Oliver suffered from "piles," as hemorrhoids were called, making his time sitting on the iron seats of farm machinery pulled by his rowdy horses more miserable. He had three operations for hemorrhoids in Medicine Hat when they were on the homestead. Later, when Irene was in sixth grade, he went to Rochester, Minnesota and had four square inches of his stomach removed, then another hemorrhoid operation several years later.[210]

This was an era when farm machinery came without cabs, so Oliver was constantly exposed to the dusty wind. Every day, he returned from the fields with dirt blown into his nostrils, ears, eyes, mouth, and every crease of his clothing. In spite of all this, the homestead project was doomed from the start by the lack of a reliable source of water.

A great highlight of this homesteading period for Irene was when her parents found it necessary to leave and head to town. In 1932, when she was a freshman at the University of North Dakota, she wrote the following theme called "Going to Town," about her homestead experience of heading to Bow Island.

At four o'clock in the morning the alarm goes off, and we are out of bed ere the first ring ceases. We are going to make one of our monthly trips to town. Town is fifteen miles away. A mere trail, two furrows winding over the country connecting gumbo patches and coulees, connects it to our homestead on the prairies of western Alberta.

It is cold at four o'clock in the morning. Dad rushes out to attend to the chores— milking the cows, seeing that the stock has enough food and water for the day. Mother prepares breakfast with intermittent errands of bringing out the Sunday best clothes, making final checks on the supplies which must be bought, and dressing me, a little five- year-

210. Irene Fortune Dodge, unpublished memoir, 50.

old who stands around in a complete daze after being hurried out of bed at such an hour.

Finally, when the stock has been cared for, when we have bundled ourselves up, and when "Billie Bean," the faithful old black dog, has been fed we are ready to start out for town.

Dad hitches up the two broncos, Mutt and Jeff, to the grain tank which is our only means of conveyance. We start off. The activity and cold crisp air rouse my senses. I am thrilled at the thought of "going to town." It takes four hours to go over the trail and down the ravines to town. The continual jar and bump of the wagon depresses my spirits, but the interesting experience to come continually buoys them up.

At last we arrive. We leave our produce at our chief trading place. Then we all go to Chuck Chune's Cafe for dinner. All cafes in the little town are under Chinese management. The Chinese are wonders to me with their quick short steps, their lack of r's in speech. With dinner over we then do our shopping.

At three o'clock we prepare to go home as there is a four-hour trip ahead and the stock must be cared for by dusk.

It was cold when we started in the morning, but the mercury has been gradually climbing. The sun beats down on the open wagon and we become decidedly warm. It was hot, the day's activity has made me tired, and the continual jolt of the iron wagon irks me. I become cross and teary-eyed. Mother, just as tired and as much jolted and jerked, tries to soothe me.

Then she looks to the purchases to see if everything is all right. There is a basket of fresh tomatoes, or rather there was. Now they are mere skins left. The red juice has trickled down through the box. The jolting had been too much for them.

This sight arouses my self-pity, and a new burst of tears follows. I make this childish vow that I'll never go to town again, if we have to go in that old lumber wagon!

The miles have been creeping by and there a little way ahead is home. At last we arrive, and Billy Bean, tumbling over himself in joy, barks his greeting to us. [211]

Trips to town by this time meant going to Foremost, a new town that was nearer than Bow Island and had emerged since the first time they had homesteaded in the area. It was a real challenge to keep the wagon upright and the horses under control. They did not go often because the constant jolting left them aching and at times, Oliver would make the trip alone. When he did, he would return to hear Bossie bawling to be milked, which would have been the last thing he did before leaving in the morning. Still, there were things that were essential and not available at home. Not forgetting anything on one's shopping list was really important, since another round trip for something forgotten was not going to happen. Basic needs for the kitchen were flour, lard, sugar syrup, baking powder, and soda. Although canned food was viewed with distrust, they sometimes picked some up. For farming they got twine, haywire, bolts, and occasionally overalls. Also, infrequently they had money for cloth and thread.

Another time they took the wagon to town was to bring in the harvest to the elevator, which is why this was the only wagon they had.

---

211. Irene Dodge, "Going to Town," theme submitted for freshman English, University of North Dakota, Nov, 1932.

Homestead Days:

"Nettie with Oliver in overalls and neighbor Glen Dupre holding Irene" - (Property of the Author)

"Fun on the haystack" - (Property of the Author)

"Sharpshooter Nettie" - (Property of the Author)

CHAPTER 10: SCHOOL AND THE NEIGHBORS ON THE HOMESTEAD

Throughout the gradually deteriorating relationship between Oliver and Nettie, one thing they agreed on was the importance of primary education for their daughter. When Irene was six and a half, she was enrolled in school.

Irene's first school was the Charing School, a one-room schoolhouse less than a mile from the Fortune homestead. She did not spend very much time at this school, attending mainly in summer because she had to walk. The Charing School bears little resemblance to modern ideas of a school. It was often closed since there was no electricity and the winter daylight in Canada was short. Like most others living near her, Irene rarely attended school in winter. The little building was difficult to heat, and it was also difficult to find teachers to work in such a remote and lonely place under undesirable conditions.

During the fall and spring, those who could work in the fields were kept home to work. Of the nineteen students, there were no pupils beyond the fourth grade, although some of them were sixteen years old. Canadian law required school attendance until completion of eighth grade or until age sixteen, but regular attendance was unenforceable. A truant officer would show up from time to time to round up the young people who were supposed to be in school, but once the officer left the area, the same students would again leave school. These visits were infrequent, as there was only one school per six-by-six sections of land (thirty-six square miles).

The drinking water for the students was carried to school each day and dumped into a large enamel pail with an enamel dipper. One morning when the teacher, Miss Griffith, came to fill the pail, she discovered that someone had defecated in it, requiring a special session of the school board. This form of "humor" was not uncommon, as Irene discovered soon after school opened. In a one-room school with students ranging from six to sixteen, it might not be surprising if bullying were to occur on occasion. A small, tearful boy approached Miss Griffith to tell her that someone had "diddle-diddled" on his dinner bucket. At the time, Irene was unclear about what it all meant, but her parents explained it to her when she returned home. A more frequently practiced practical joke involved throwing "hoofters," or horseshoes, onto the roof of the school and leaving them for the teacher to retrieve.

Irene's first school day was eventful. Her parents had told her she should raise her hand when she needed to leave and go to the toilet, which she at first refused but soon learned. It was also the first day of school for Tommy Hoefert, the youngest in his family. Tommy was not about to spend his time in school and, when the teacher first turned her back, he hopped out of his seat, jumped out the window, and ran home. The following day, Miss Griffith was prepared for Tommy, who still had no intention of staying. She kept the window closed and tied him to his chair. Tommy was frequently tied to a wagon with a long rope by his mother at home, allowing everyone else in the family to concentrate on their chores, so this method was nothing new to him. The other big event of the first day of school came at lunchtime, when the children opened their lunch pails. When the Beckholtz children opened theirs, Irene and the other students were assaulted by a repulsive smell that enveloped the room. They had stacks of cold pancakes without butter or syrup but packed with garlic, something totally foreign to Irene.

At that time, Irene had two dresses that had been sewn by her mother. Her school dress was black and white gingham, with a white collar and cuffs. The other was very simple, made from a flour sack that Nettie had dyed blue. As soon as Irene returned home from school each day, she would take off her school dress and change into her flour sack one. Her mother would then wash out the gingham dress and hang it out to dry behind the stove. The next morning, Nettie would iron the dress, and it would be ready for Irene to wear again. Her teacher, Miss Griffith, once asked her if she had two identical dresses, since Irene always showed up in freshly laundered clothing. She was surprised and impressed by the dedication to cleanliness that was indicated by the fact that it was always the same garment.

It was required by law that English be the only language used in school. This law was ignored by the Russian students, who continually spoke to each other in their native tongue. The teacher had no idea what was being said much of the time. The large Russian immigrant families who lived in the area generally put little value on education, as the parents were frequently uneducated.

Irene's first teacher stayed with the Whittle family, who had a daughter named Doris. Doris and Irene were the only non-Russians in Charing School. Irene fell ill one day, but there was no way to get her home until the school day came to an end and another student could accompany her. To compensate, the teacher took out her dust cap, put it on Irene's head, and had her keep her head on her desk for the remainder of the day. Dust caps are what women wore during the day when they did their housework or anything that that might raise dust, since they did not wash their hair often. It did little for Irene but it made her feel special. When she finally arrived home she was delirious, and Oliver decided to take her to a doctor in the nearest town. It was a harrowing voyage in the family wagon, a gas tank larger than a regular wagon and designed for hauling grain, heading to the new town of Foremost, twelve miles away. It was the dead of night and there were no roads, only a pair of ruts that passed up and down a steep ravine, and he was attempting to control two skittish horses throughout.

When they arrived, the doctor diagnosed Irene's condition as pneumonia and presented Oliver with a bill for what Irene recalled was $60.[212] That was more cash than Nettie and Oliver earned per month, and Oliver was outraged. He continued to fume for months. It was just one of many problems that began to pile up on the Fortunes, and while Oliver originally held his temper in public, he began to vent his anger on Nettie. The feisty Nettie responded in kind, and the difficulties of life gradually began to take their toll on the Fortune marriage. Irene did not return to school for the remainder of that year, but her mother made her practice writing at home. They had concerns about her spending very much time around the Russian kids.

During the brief period that Irene attended Charing School, the principal school supplies she needed were writing materials. Many of the children occasionally had paper but most relied on slates. Some never had anything other than slates. Irene wanted to be like the others and have a slate, but her parents wanted her to write on the proper material, paper.

Her mother provided her with some of her writing tablets by making use of the squares of tissue paper that had been wrapped around each peach she had bought for canning as food for the winter. She ironed the sheets of tissue as smooth as possible, then stitched stacks of them together with her Singer sewing machine, making a tablet, or "scribbler."

---

212. Irene Fortune Dodge, unpublished memoir, 28.

When Irene ran out of paper, Nettie dug into her trunk and found expensive greeting cards she had received from friends over the years and had saved. She took out the blank pages and gave them to Irene to use for writing practice until they made their next trip to town, when they could buy another tablet. It upset her teacher to see the cards being destroyed, but Nettie felt that the benefits of learning proper penmanship outweighed the loss of the blank portions of her cards.

In other matters, her teacher showed less empathy. Prior to Christmas when money was very scarce and Irene still waited for Santa's visit, Nettie sent Oliver to town to buy a doll. On Christmas Day, Nettie suggested that Irene name the doll Hephzibah. When school reopened in the spring, Irene brought her doll to school to show it off. Her teacher told her that it was the ugliest doll she had ever seen, and that Hephzibah was the ugliest name she had ever heard.

"Irene with her doll Hephzibah" - (Property of the Author)

Teachers did not stay long and were often boarded with families on homesteads near the school. There was a teacherage, a small, absolutely bare, two-room structure available should an adventurous teacher prefer life alone. From the time school began, Irene's mother went over her schoolwork with her. It would prove to give her advantages, especially when unforeseen crisis hit. Nettie also had concerns about Irene's appearance, tying her new front teeth together with a piece of thread every morning to prevent a gap from developing. Braces were not something common people could afford.[213]

While Russian families dominated the area, there was another small segment of the already small Alberta homestead population. This segment consisted of the "remittance men." These were the sons of wealthy families from Canada's east coast. Their parents did not feel their sons were amounting to anything, and the experience of frontier living might change them or at least eliminate them from family concerns. Although the remittance men had to learn to work hard, they had the advantage of regular money coming in from their parents, so homesteading was not the perilous struggle it was to the typical homesteaders. Glen Depery, whose homestead bordered the Fortunes' land, was one of these men. He had a wife when he arrived, but she died shortly after they settled in Alberta.

During the Great War, Glen headed off to fight "for God, for King, and for Country" with the Canadian Expeditionary Force. He kept in touch with Oliver, who was looking after some of his farm equipment. The war did not seem to bother Glen too much, but the conditions did, as he had a difficult time coming up with enough alcohol to keep him happy, and he remained an enlisted man, subject to the orders of officers. All was not misery, however. The post-war song

---

213. Brian Thurman, "The Interesting History of Braces," https://www. thurmanortho.com/the-interesting-history-of-braces/, Aug 31, 2019.

"How ya gonna keep 'em down on the farm / After they've seen Paree"[214] captured the experience of Glen and those like him.

Glen wrote to Oliver from France in 1918, "I have the nicest little French girl you ever saw but it beat hell how much her clothes cost. After the war I take out and let you see her. It funny the way things go. I give her a couple of dollars tell to go out and get grub. Say she can get more grub for a dollar than I can for $10. But give her $10 and send out after clothes and you couldn't cover a ant. As I said it beat hell."[215] The "little French girl" remained in France as the end of the war brought the end of most wartime romances. Glen returned to Alberta and his homestead and married a woman better suited to the life he was to lead. He provided a bit of nearly absent social life for neighbors by having gatherings where he would provide music by playing the harmonica and dance the different women around the floor while their husbands stood or sat indifferently.

Among the more prevalent Russian families were two who were involved in a bizarre feud. These were the Hegels and the Degensteins, both large families. Irene and her parents tried to walk the narrow line of favoring neither and getting along with both. Although the Hegels and Degensteins were sworn enemies and would not tolerate an inch of trespass on their property by any member of the opposite family, they kept very close watch on each other. One family had a baby they named Johnny, so the other family named their next boy Johnny; one had a daughter named Katie, soon followed by the arrival of a Katie in the other family. One family's daughter was christened Abalone, while the other's daughter was called Abelina.

---

214. Walter Donaldson, music, Joe Young and Sam M. Lewis, lyrics, "How You Gonna Keep 'em Down on the Farm," Waterson, Berlin&Snyder, New York, 1919.

215. Glen Deprey, letter from Canadian Expeditionary Force, unknown location, to Oliver Fortune, Oct 18, 1918.

The children attacked each other with rocks fired from slingshots, and the Degensteins had an aggressive dog that would attack anyone or anything, once given the command, "Siccum!" The oldest boy in the Degenstein family was Balzaar. Once he had entered his early teens, his parents viewed him as an adult. They arrived at this conclusion based on his speaking habits. As the parents announced to the Fortune family one day when they were visiting the Degensteins, "Balzaar is grown up now. He can swear just like a man."

The Degensteins lived in a house that Irene's father and other homesteaders found foolish and wasteful, in that they had invested considerable effort into giving it a fancy appearance by adding decorative woodwork to the window and door frames. Like most people in the area, they had little money. Wood was scarce, and non-utilitarian use of it was seen as extravagant. This may have been an accurate opinion regarding the Degensteins. When they needed a granary but could not afford to buy the wood, they were forced to tear up the floor of their home to build it.

Further evidence of their shortage of cash was made clear to the Fortunes when Nettie was visiting with Mrs. Degenstein. Nettie noticed the large number of pigs the Degensteins had, and she asked what the pigs were being fed. As it turned out, the Degensteins did not feed their pigs. They merely let them loose in the nearby coulee, where they scavenged and ate the snakes that were common there.

Shortage of money was not a problem unique to the Degensteins. The Fortunes decided at one point that the time had come for them to rebuild their shack, and they had no money to rent a place to stay. Homesteaders, even those from different countries and cultures, survived by cooperating in times of need. The Fortunes ended up relying on the kindness of the Degensteins, who housed Nettie and Irene while Oliver and his brother Austin rebuilt the shack. It was only one of the expressions of friendliness that the Degensteins demonstrated toward the Fortunes. On another occasion, Mrs. Degenstein arrived at the door of the Fortune homestead with a basket of Easter eggs, each dyed a different color, which she said were "for the baby," Irene. Whatever generosity they may have expressed, it was vastly overshadowed in Irene's mind by the fact that the Degensteins were the ones who had killed her pet and closest companion, Billie Bean.

Mrs. Degenstein was a very stout woman living in an era when fashion dictated the "hour-glass figure" look. Although fashion concerns were not high on the priority list of women on the homesteads, Mrs. Degenstein was jealous of Nettie's petite, natural twenty-three-inch waist. She kept claiming that once they had a good crop, her husband was going to get her a good corset and her waist would be the same as Nettie's small measurement. Her claim asked more than any corset could ever have delivered, and the crop was never good enough to provide that disappointment to the substantial woman.

Her counterpart in this feud was the equally abundant Mrs. Hegel. Irene dined with the Hegels from time to time, and the meals began with Mrs. Hegel standing at the head of the table, holding a fresh loaf of bread to her ample bosom and hacking off slices of it by swinging a butcher knife toward herself. As she sliced off pieces of bread she would fling them, Frisbee style, from one person to the next in order around the table. This penchant for the dangerous handling of knives was not limited to the matron of the family. One of the sons, Johnny, was blind in one eye, but not for the same reason as many of the other young Russian boys. He lost his eye in a fight with his brother, who had a knife and accidentally stuck it in Johnny's eye.

The background to the feud between the Hegels and the Degensteins was not known to the Fortune family, nor to the other area homesteaders. The younger members of the families involved may not have known why they grew up as sworn enemies. For whatever reasons, the families truly despised each other and did what they could to make their adversaries miserable. It seems that of the two, the Degensteins had the greater number of positive qualities. The Hegels were stingy, aggressive people from a family whose father Tony spent his days sitting on porch doing nothing while his boys did all the work, as was his goal in life.

Throughout this time, Oliver had been unable to escape the humiliation and feelings of inferiority that came from his brothers, especially Jack. Their homesteads were not distant from his and were all part of the Bow Island community. Jack's success while Oliver struggled to eat remained painfully obvious. Jack had built a financial empire. His farm included over seventy buildings of various size and function. He had not only acquired the best of the available homestead land, he had diversified to provide the most basic of necessities to other homesteaders—water. He purchased a rig for digging artesian wells on the semi-arid land and offered his service to those whom he knew could afford to pay. While most wells were dug twenty to thirty feet deep into an underground pool of water, artesian wells went down over 1000 feet to tap into the water table. Shallow wells dried up, but artesian wells flowed reliably and continually, making them very valuable.

Like their mother had done years earlier, Jack's wife Mary went to church at every possible opportunity and prayed constantly, in spite of Jack's objections. Unlike Jack and Oliver's mother, her husband was wealthy. She had a hired girl for help, wore elegant furs, and took occasional vacations from prairie life to the cosmopolitan surroundings of Vancouver and Banff in British Colombia. Jack made no pretense about the money he spent on Mary. It was not to make her life happy, but to demonstrate to his relatives and neighbors that he was wealthier than them and could afford to spend money on luxuries they would have seen as frivolous, while they struggled to survive. In keeping with this frame of mind, Jack had the only piano in the area, though neither he nor Mary could play it. Additionally, he was the only person in the area to buy a car.

Perhaps the show of affluence that Jack enjoyed the most took place on Sundays. He frequently invited the many Fortune relatives to his home to eat, during which all sat around a large dining table covered by a white tablecloth. Though his brothers may have resented the obvious display of Jack's success versus their failures, and Oliver certainly did, the offer of a free, high quality meal could not be refused. They also enjoyed the camaraderie the situation provided. Their brother Howard, a stingy bachelor, would intentionally eat so much at these meals that he would become physically ill. Jack sat at the head of the table, holding court by mixing insults concerning other community members with accolades about his own accomplishments. He also set himself apart from the others in other ways at these events. Mary kept a pitcher of milk on the table for the guests to add to their coffee. But when Jack wanted his coffee, he would bellow, "Meery, bring me the cream!" and she would obediently and silently slip away, returning with a small pitcher reserved for Jack alone.

It was not only at the family gatherings that Jack offered his insults about other community members. Once, at a local baseball game, he was loudly complaining to all who would listen about Mr. Hobson, owner of the general store in Bow Island. "That God damn Hobson. He's a son-of-a-bitch!" He realized something was strange when his outburst was greeted with silence. He turned around to find Mr. Hobson sitting directly behind him. Jack's immediate and unapologetic follow up was, "Ain't that right, Hobson!"[216]

One outgrowth of Jack's prosperity was his ability to hire a work force. He eventually hired a girl named Mollie

216. Ibid., 71.

to help with the housework. Mollie was an attractive, coquettish girl, and Jack found her very appealing. In keeping with his doctrine of wealth attitude, he expected that money could buy anything he wanted. He offered Mollie what relatives reported was $1000 if she would have sex with him—an extraordinary sum at that time. However, Mollie refused him, and before long she resigned to look for work in an area that was less isolated and dreary. The next hired girl was considered plain looking, and she was a devout Catholic. Jack's wife Mary may well have had a hand in the hiring of the new girl, Mary Hart, who remained their employee for years.

Word of the episode with Jack and Mollie reinforced the attitude the other Fortune brothers had about Jack. While he saw himself as the head of a clan of Fortunes, they continued to resent him but usually restricted speaking of it to behind his back. Their resentment was tempered by a combination of envy and admiration, since Jack actually achieved what Oliver and several of his brothers dreamed about.

"Wealthy homesteader Jack Fortune and his wife Mary" - (Property of the Author)

Jack's impact was still present in other ways, though again "behind his back." The influence of the Russian environment on the school and community supplied Oliver with the excuse for his failure that he needed. He held out until the fall of 1918 but by then there was no choice, though Nettie and Irene were unaware. Oliver claimed that his daughter Irene was picking up too many bad, un-American habits by spending her formative period surrounded by people like the Degensteins and the Hegels. She had learned several Russian words and phrases from her neighbors, but some Norwegian as well. He announced that his family was leaving their homestead and renting a farm in another region, the Amblie farm. His explanation for leaving their home was, "I signed it over to my brother, because it was such a bad place to live."[217]

In fact, Oliver had not decided to abandon his homestead. He had borrowed money from his brother Jack, after Jack had originally encouraged him to return the homestead. In true Jack fashion, there was no mercy when the payment was due, even though it had been a bad year for crops and the two men were brothers. Jack called in the loan and, when Oliver could not pay, Jack foreclosed on him and added the homestead to his empire.

Oliver's failure to hold onto his homestead was a turning point in the deterioration of his marriage to Nettie. Once again, they were going to be working for someone else. Nettie began to believe Oliver would never amount to anything, and her life's fantasies and aspirations would never be fulfilled. She wondered more regularly why she had married him when she'd had an older, wealthier, and in her view much more successful man interested in her in her time in Minot, North Dakota, just prior to her meeting Oliver. But really? While Nettie had aspirations for herself and was beginning to see disappointment as a pattern, she

---

217. Nettie Fortune, conversation with Irene, 67.

was a strong, independent woman and while she could have had wealth and security, it is difficult to see her having been happy as a trophy wife for a man who was a friend of her father's.

"Nettie second-guessed marrying Oliver having rejected this wealthy friend of her father" - *(Property of the Author)*

CHAPTER 11: THE AMBLIE FARM

In 1918, the family loaded up its small supply of household goods, stock, and machinery, and slowly made its way across the ruts in the prairie that served as roads. Perhaps it was an omen that when they finally arrived where Oliver had been offered employment and lodging, they expected to settle into something comfortable. What they found was that the family occupying their future farm had been quarantined because of some communicable disease and had not been able to leave. Irene, Nettie, and Oliver spent their first few days in their new location of the Amblie farm surviving in a cook car instead of a home.

The Amblie farm's main crops were wheat and oats. Their rent was reminiscent of the archaic feudal system— in exchange for occupying the Amblies' land, the Fortunes were required to give the Amblies one-fourth of the yield of the harvest. Although this was an improved and superior farm that seemed to promise security, there was no escaping the second-class status that came with being renters rather than owners. They were the only renters in the area. As it turned out, even the apparent security was an illusion. Again, Oliver's story was that of being in the wrong place at the wrong time.

In many ways, the farm the Fortunes rented from the Amblie family seemed to offer relief from the hopeless experience on the homestead. Alberta's growth had been extremely rapid since homesteaders first arrived, as census figures put the total number of villages, towns and cities at two in 1890, and that had risen to 160, including six cities by 1916.[218] Though still in Alberta, only fifteen miles north of the homestead, this was in an established farming area. The sod had been broken. There was a good well. The stones in the fields had been hauled away. The yards for the house and barns were separated by fences. The two-story, yellow house they were given as part of the deal was trimmed with white, and had plastered walls, good woodwork, and smooth wood floors. They had acquired a "democrat" so they could travel without their grain wagon. A democrat was the poor man's vehicle of the times until the Model T replaced it. It was a single-seat buggy with room for two or three people and a box in back to haul small loads such as groceries from a trip to town. It had no top so riders were exposed to the elements.

Unlike the Russian community they had recently left, the Amblie farm was in an area populated mainly by "Americans." To the Fortune parents, "America" was synonymous with the United States, though by this time they were Canadian citizens. The "Americans" who surrounded them were mainly Scandinavians; some were first generation, but most had not come directly from Europe. Many had grown up in Minnesota, where their immigrant parents had settled. Most had at least some education, and their customs and manners were similar to what Oliver and Nettie knew from their lives in the United States. They seemed more "civilized" than the Russians the Fortunes had left behind, although their behavior did not always support that view.

Oliver and Nettie were true to their view of the "melting pot." The only language one should speak was English,

218. Eric J. Hanson and Paul Boothe, Heather Edwards eds., *Eric J. Hanson's Financial History of Alberta, 1905-1950* (Calgary, Alberta, Canada, University of Calgary Press, 2003), 28.

and if it was spoken with an accent, it indicated the person speaking was ignorant. Although Oliver had actually learned to speak Norwegian before he learned English, he did not feel that being bilingual was any accomplishment; it was more of a weakness. The Fourth of July and Thanksgiving were holidays he believed were to be celebrated, Dominion Day was not.

Unfortunately, the whims of weather dictate the fate of farmers, and the Fortunes' new farming experience began with extreme drought. In the severe crop failure that followed, there was no harvest to produce a cash crop. There was not even enough grown to provide feed for the animals for the winter to come. Rather than using his harvesting equipment in the fall, Oliver was reduced to using a mower to cut down the hearty weeds that needed so little moisture to thrive in the summer. These weeds, the Russian thistles, had to serve as food for the animals, despite the lack of fondness they displayed for them.

The unharvested thistles broke off and rolled across the prairies as tumbleweeds. The constant wind left them piled up against the fences that surrounded the pastures and fields. Along with the weeds came the dry dirt that blew off the barren land. As the dirt covered the gathered tumbleweeds, it reached the fence tops, eventually providing exit routes for the pent-up cattle and horses, who could walk right over the fences.

The whims of the weather affected the Fortunes in other ways as well. Harvest season was the key season of the year. The farmers on the Amblie farm area had a limited amount of machinery and could not afford to hire "harvest hands." The only other choice was cooperation. The neighboring farmers in the region acted as a single crew, going from farm to farm doing the threshing and harvesting. While drought was the common problem, fall occasionally brought rain to the normally arid area, and cooperative farming amounted to a form of Russian roulette. The work had to be finished before the frost set in, and there was a battle to avoid being one of the last farms serviced. Another problem was that the family whose land was being harvested had to provide the food for the crew. For a farmer whose turn it was, being the victim of rain easily turned to disaster. Crews could only wait a few days before they had to move on, and the poor farm family had to provide food for all, while being doomed to poverty due to the lack of a crop to sell.

One fall when the crew was at the Amblie farm, Oliver began to become more aware of how his desire to be his own man and master of his own destiny was degenerating into a fantasy that could never be fulfilled. An incident that helped crystallize this awareness was an outgrowth of his own nature. Whatever else he may have been, Oliver was a man who found purposeless cruelty to animals repulsive. When the harvest cooperative of farmers was on the land he rented, two of the young sons of one of the neighbors were demonstrating what perhaps they felt was their machismo, or whatever it is that people hope to demonstrate by harming defenseless animals. As Oliver watched with frustration, he saw the boys' efforts to keep their team of horses moving. Rather than flipping the reins, they kept prodding the animals with pokes from the sharp points of pitch forks. Oliver was helpless—someone else's kids, someone else's animals, someone else's farm.

Similarly, Nettie confirmed the same realization for the same reason. The Fortunes had a heifer that had developed "lump jaw," an infection technically known as actinomycosis that comes from bacteria in the soil and can enter a cow's system through an oral wound from a wire or stiff hay and develop into a slow-growing mass that can alter facial appearance and loosen teeth.[219] The animal was

---

219. Geof W. Smith, "Actinomycosis in Cattle, Swine, and Other Animals," *Merck Veterinary Manual*, https://www.merckvetmanual.com/generalized-conditions/actinomycosis/actinomycosis-in-cattle,-swine,-and-other-animals, Oct, 2020.

of little value to the Fortunes and Oliver sold it for a small sum to one of his neighbors. He was away when two of his neighbor's sons came on horseback to pick up the animal. Again, repulsive cruelty was demonstrated. The boys tied a rope around the cow's neck, as one would expect, to lead the animal to their farm. However, rather than walking the heifer at a pace appropriate for it, they took off in a gallop which was beyond the cow's ability to match. When the heifer fell, the boys continued to drag it along the ground toward their farm. Nettie and Irene screamed and pleaded with them to slow down and allow the animal to walk, but the boys merely laughed at them as they continued on their way. Someone else's kids, someone else's cow, someone else's farm.

The Amblie farm was not theirs, they were poor, and they were dependent on people over whom they exercised no control and little influence.

The disappointment and growing feelings of another opportunity gone awry began to wear more and more on the Fortune parents. Oliver usually managed to get along with his neighbors, although he did so by bottling up his anger inside. He reserved his short, explosive temper for Nettie. In the verbal fights that ensued, Irene remained out of the fray. Her father, for all his coarse language, never said a cross word to her. The same cannot be said about her mother, who occasionally vented her anger and eventually, her hopes for a better future, on her daughter.

The anger came first. In an incident that left such a lasting hurt with Irene that she could never forget it, her mother lashed out viciously at her. Irene was seven and with her mother out in the yard. They had a cow tethered to a pole so it could not run off. The cow managed to catch Nettie off guard by walking around her while Nettie was preoccupied. As it continued to walk, the tether wrapped around Nettie, pinning her and leaving her helpless. Nettie's predicament grew worse, and she called for Irene to help. There was little the young girl could do, but Nettie was outraged. She yelled, "Damn you! I hate you! I wish you were dead."[220] Though Nettie eventually freed herself, she had crushed her daughter's spirit, and sorrow began to engulf the entire family.

School, which provided a pleasant and rewarding escape for Irene especially as she grew older, became a diversion for her once the family was settled in at the Amblie farm. Her new school, called Borden School, was an improvement over Charing School. The students were Scandinavian, not first generation, and most had some education. It was still a one-room country schoolhouse, but more spacious and better equipped. Though it lacked a pencil sharpener, that function was taken over by one of the students, Warren Swenumson, who was adept with his pocketknife. The room was heated by a jacketed coal-burning stove, and it had a "library" consisting of two-foot shelves, each four feet long. Best of all, it had a piano. In its eight grades it had forty students, including three Irenes.

Lunch at school remained the same boring fare it had been at Charing School. Sandwiches and water one day, followed by sandwiches and water the next, and the next, and the next. Even the sandwiches were monotonous. Irene's day began with soft-boiled or fried eggs at home in the morning, followed by hard-boiled egg sandwiches every noon. She finally reached a point where she could not eat another egg and actually went for several years after that moment without eating a single egg in any form. Things picked up for her after her refusal to tolerate eggs, and she began to bring sandwiches coated with thick, sweet cream.

Irene's first teacher at Borden School, Velma Peterson, was a pianist and a delight to the students. Most of the students were used to being surrounded by coarse, plain people, and Miss Peterson was anything but that. An

---

220. Irene Fortune Dodge, unpublished memoir, 52.

attractive young woman who dressed in a plumed hat, fox fur, and expensive dark suits that set off white blouses, she was happy and full of laughter and brought light into the children's lives. They loved her. Irene decided that she, too, wanted to be a teacher.

Oliver was initially excited when he first heard about the school's library. Irene asked her teacher if she could pick something out for him and was given *Robinson Crusoe* and *Treasure Island*. When she returned with these, his enthusiasm vanished as he realized there would be no books that he had not already read. Oliver was a voracious reader, given his circumstances, and at one point he borrowed Nettie's family Bible and read it from cover to cover, which led to discussions about Old Testament stories where they spelled words out when Irene was around.

The students celebrated Christmas by presenting a skit for the parents in which Irene and eight others held up the letters that spelled "Christmas" and recited something "meaningful" that began with their letters. Irene's was "I," and her cryptic comment was, "I stands for I, and if I tried, who else could I be?" The big Christmas highlight, though, was the large Christmas tree trimmed with candles. No one had such a tree at home.

Another holiday celebrated at Borden School was Valentine's Day. Irene had never heard of such a thing before her teacher brought it up. Valentine's Day brought out the best in Nettie, who had considerable innate talent for artistic expression. While the other students showed up with lopsided hearts cut from the lined paper of their tablets, Irene's valentines were accurately shaped and cut hearts of firm, colored cardboard taken from catalog covers and embellished with bright red ribbon. When she arrived at school and other people saw one, someone said, "This must be for the teacher." It was not, as she had them for all her friends. They were Nettie's creations, as was the cardboard checkerboard she taught Irene to make.

It was not only with special projects that Nettie helped Irene. Both Nettie and Oliver helped her acquire an education. Although Irene did not necessarily appreciate it at the time, the push she received from her parents served her well, as the quality of the teaching she experienced in Alberta was often minimal.

Not surprisingly, the area failed to attract top quality teachers. It is surprising that it attracted teachers at all, given the lonely life it offered in a remote region with few single people, and the demands of the job, which required the individual to be not only the teacher, but also the janitor and fireman. While Miss Peterson was a charming exception, all but one of Irene's other teachers were sullen or desperate.

Miss Peterson left after Irene's first year, but fortunately, she later returned. Her successor was Miss Penstock, an angry, intolerant woman who, among other things, hit one of the shy girls in the class with the wooden frame of a writing slate for not speaking loudly enough when she recited in class. She apparently incurred the wrath of the school board by requiring the entire school to stay after dismissal time on a Friday. There were four Seventh-day Adventist students who were never on any occasion discipline problems who said they absolutely had to be home before sundown, as it marked the beginning of their Sabbath. This only infuriated the foul-mannered teacher further, and she forbade their departure. They simply walked out, hitched up their buggy, and rode off. The incident was never brought up again, and Miss Penstock was soon replaced by a young, pleasant woman named Miss Spenser.

Miss Spenser's stay at Borden School was very brief and, in the following fall, the students began the year with yet another teacher. It was an unusual choice that perhaps indicates how people had to make do with whatever or whomever they could in this remote, frontier location. The new teacher was Irene Hanson, who had finished eighth grade with the current Borden School students the previous spring. She had spent six weeks at a "normal school" during the summer, which was seen as sufficient qualification. Irene Hanson was a very shy girl, and she had no control over her previous classmates, who often mocked her physical appearance as well as her inability to exercise any authority in the classroom.

"Entire school enrollment near Amblie farm" - (Property of the Author)

Irene Hanson's career as the Borden School teacher came to an abrupt halt as the influence of worldwide events found its way to the tiny Canadian community. World War I, or "The Great War," as it was called, came to an end in 1918. Ten million men had lost their lives. Or was it eleven million? When disasters reach a certain point, the numbers involved begin to become nearly meaningless. It hardly seems to matter what figure is used. At any rate, this was war on a scale the world had never previously seen.

In what had long seemed to appear as a mere footnote to history, a new strain of influenza broke out at the end of the war, catching the weary world unprepared. Whatever number is used for the casualties of the Great War, it is dwarfed by the magnitude of the random assault on the world's population that came with the spread of the new flu. It knew no special enemy, had no interest in boundaries assigned by people, and no special class or group was free from the possibility of its grasp. This was the Spanish Flu, later identified as the H1N1 virus. The name represents a basic misunderstanding. While agreement is not universal, evidence indicates the Spanish Flu actually originated in the United States. The first case apparently occurred in January 1918 at Camp Funston, later Fort Riley, in Kansas. Patient Zero was Private Albert Gitchell.[221] From there, it spread throughout the US Army, then overseas with the American entrance in the war. That would carry it around the world.

Spain was the only major neutral country in Europe and it reported news, which was censored from the combatants. When the flu reached Spain, it was known as the "French Flu."[222] The outside world only received its news of the widespread flu from Spain and inaccurately dubbed it the Spanish Flu. In October of 1918, the Fortunes received a letter their brother Frank, who was in Camp McArthur, Texas, waiting to be shipped out to Europe, but had been put in quarantine because of the flu. He wrote about being

---

221. Jeffrey R. Ryan, ed., *Pandemic Influenza: emergency Planning and Community Preparedness,* (Boca Raton, FLA: CRC Press, 2008), 25-26; John M. Barry, *The Great Influenza: The Epic Story of the Deadliest Plague in History* (London: *Penguin Books*, 2005), 92.

222. Antoni Trilla, Guillem and Carolyn Daer, "The 1918 'Spanish Flu' in Spain," *Clinical Infectious Diseases*, Vol. 47, Iss. 5, Sep 2008, 669.

anxious to go, but the war's end was a month away at the time.[223]

It was a scourge unlike any that preceded it and though estimates vary, with some being twice as large, *The Lancet* put the number killed in 1918 and 1919 at fifty million.[224] The Spanish Flu infected 500 million people globally, which was 33% of the population of the world at the time, and 675, 000 of the deaths were in the United States.[225]

The United States was hit later than Europe but by October of 1918, The *New York Times* carried a story that said, "American communities are now grappling with an epidemic they do not understand well. But we understand it well enough to know that it spreads rapidly where people are crowded together," and added, "Theaters are not allowed to give performances, and it is recommended that the churches hold no services." Area football games had been canceled and area schools were being closed. There was "everywhere, a lamentable lack of doctors, and the supply of skilled nurses is so low that many patients, dangerously ill with influenza, must be left to the care of members of the family, who seldom know anything about the disease."[226]

No place was safe from this disease that spread as soldiers returned and people moved around, and there was no inoculation to protect against it. Even isolation on remote farms and homesteads in Canada, where social distancing was a way of life, did not offer safety. When the flu struck Alberta in 1919, Borden School was closed for the year.

---

223. Frank Fortune, Camp McArthur, Waco, TX, letter to Oli Fortune, Oct 16, 1918.

224. Mark Honigsbaum, "Pandemic," *The Lancet*, https://www. thelancet.com/journals/lancet/article/PIIS0140673609610539/fulltext, Jun 6, 2009.

225. "Spanish Flu," Cleveland Clinic, https://my.clevelandclinic.org/ health/diseases/21777-spanish-flu, Sept 21, 2021.

226. "The Spanish Influenza," The *New York Times*, Oct 7, 1918, 12.

Everyone in the area was required to wear a gauze mask made from cheesecloth when he or she was in a town.

In spite of this precaution, Nettie, Oliver, and Irene all caught the flu. Oliver still had to do his chores through his agony. There was no other way the work would get done. Nettie spent much of her time lying in bed complaining. Irene managed to stoically cope with her suffering. The young girl felt complimented when her frustrated and miserable father said to Nettie, "Why can't you be more patient, like Irene?" This episode did little to narrow the widening gap in the Fortune marriage.

School reopened after the flu epidemic, and another new teacher faced the class. This was Mr. Morgan. Unlike several of his predecessors, Mr. Morgan had no trouble with discipline; unlike previous experiences for most students at Borden School, there was little about interaction with their teacher that they enjoyed. Mr. Morgan was a gruff, unsmiling figure who began his posting at the school by lining up all the students, then sticking his pencil in their mouths as a tongue depressor to examine their throats. Although Irene should have been in the second grade at this time, Nettie sent Mr. Morgan a note saying her daughter had done all the second grade work at home during the flu epidemic, and Irene was allowed to become a third grader. As was true throughout her school days, she had little academic difficulty competing with the more advanced students. She did get mocked by the others for believing in Santa Claus. Her parents thought they could keep a bright spot going as long as possible when instead of candy, nuts, and fruits she found the surprising present of a wooden pencil box. When Irene asked them, following hearing from the children at school, her parents avoided answering until after Christmas.

Another sweeping change aside from the ravages of the epidemic dominated the United States in 1919. The issue of women's suffrage had come to a head after picking up steam following the US entry into the Great War. On the state level, women had begun to gain the vote as early as 1869 in the territory of Wyoming. However, on the national level, the movement had little congressional support even by the presidential election of 1912. Oliver and Nettie always thought of themselves as "Americans," meaning US citizens, and any issue of women's rights was bound to divide them as it did the country. Oliver's view, reminiscent of that of his father and common to Norwegians traditionally[227] was that women were inferior and incompetent to make important decisions. In his words, "I won't make a living for my family if women become allowed to vote. Women are too dumb to vote. That's only for men."[228] Nettie obviously disagreed, and Irene remained caught in her parents' increasing hostility toward each other. Even at school, her usual escape from tension, difficulties were emerging. Although she developed a reputation as a good student, she also came to be known as a bit of a crybaby. For some reason she did not understand, it took very little to make her cry. Once this was discovered by the other children, they displayed the disappointing cruelty of youth by hounding her at every opportunity. After every cry, she would vow to herself that she would never cry again regardless of what happened. But it was only a matter of time until the tears returned, as her classmates knew her too well, and she knew them too well.

School was a considerable distance from the Amblie farm and, in the winter, it was a long, cold walk. Sometimes Irene could get a ride part of the way on a neighbor's sleigh.

---

227. See Karin Bruzelius Heffermehl, "The Status of Women in Norway," *The American Journal of Comparative Law*, Autumn, 1972, for a discussion showing that while Norway has made some strides in advancing legal, educational and social opportunities to women earlier than most other countries, they still lag far behind their male counterparts.
228. Nettie Fortune, "Transcript of Conversation with Irene Fortune Dodge," Oct 1974, 61.

In warmer weather, she would break up the homeward journey by stopping at the farm of the Hoel girls, friends from school who were about her age. This was in violation of a direct order from her mother, who insisted that she head straight home after school. In spite of her mother's instructions, Irene continued to stop to play every day. Each day when she arrived home, her mother would send her outside to get a green branch from the small grove of trees in the yard, with which she would whip Irene. When Irene would see the Hoel girls the following morning they would say they could hear her crying all the way to their farm, but they would not turn her away, and when school came to an end, the whole process was repeated.

What finally put an end to Irene's stops at the Hoels was a present from her father that dramatically changed her life for the better. He came home with an Indian pony for her to ride to school. It was black with a blaze down the front of its head, and white legs up the knees. "White Socks" was the name she gave it, and she considered it the perfect name. They could not afford both a horse and a saddle, so Irene had to learn to ride bareback. When they could finally afford to buy a saddle, Irene was so used to White Socks's back that she refused and said she did not want one. A saddle would have made mounting the horse considerably easier, but Irene had found her own solution to that problem. Whenever she fell off White Socks, she led him to a fence so that she could get high enough to hop on to the horse's back.

White Socks was a small, headstrong horse. He was later listed as 900 pounds, in comparison with the 1600-pound listing for the work horses, Mutt and Jeff. It required a scissor bit for Irene to keep the pony under control. This form of bit was hinged in the middle and pulled up into a "V" when the rider tugged at the reins. The top of the metal "V" pushed against the roof of the horse's mouth, inflicting pain. Oliver warned Irene to use the bit with care, to avoid hurting her horse.

Like the other children, Irene kept her horse in the small barn at the school during the day, where each child had to supply his or her own hay. Every day after school, she hurried home to feed her horse and spend hours brushing him, braiding his tail, and keeping his mane trimmed. White Socks could not be coaxed to leave school during snowstorms or the infrequent downpour of rain. All the children's horses were that way. They eventually figured out that the only way they could get home was to convince one horse to leave the comfort of the school barn and tie their reins together so that all were out in the open, facing the discomfort of the climate. From there, White Socks and the other horses hurried their riders home through the snow or rain, rushing to get to the comfort of their barns on their home farms.

In warm weather, horse racing became the popular noontime activity at school. White Socks loved to run and was a great competitor. The fun came to an end for Irene the day he threw her completely over a barbed wire fence along the side of the road and into a pasture. Although Irene tried to keep news of this from her parents, others who had witnessed it passed the word along. Irene was prohibited from racing her horse anymore.

Oliver the fortune seeker, whose desire in life was to be his own man, was aware after the flu passed that he was no closer, just another worker struggling to get by. He worked hard trying to make someone else rich, and things would never be more than that as long as he was a sharecropper at the Amblie farm. His loathsome brother Jack had stopped by and given him a ride in his new automobile, taking along his daughter to be sure he was really humiliated. Oliver's pot of gold was out there somewhere, he was still convinced. This was not it, so there was nothing to do but have an auction and get as much as he could for everything they owned, then find something new. His failures were mounting and these things required working as a team, but getting support from

Nettie for a new venture could be more difficult than before. Still, he was the man in the house. He wore the pants. Nettie and Irene would have to follow. Also, it was time to be living in the real America.

Irene was told and finally accepted the idea that they would be leaving Canada. Still, she loved her horse just as she had loved her dog Billie Bean. What she could not believe was that her horse was listed among the items up for the auction sale the family was going to hold. Leaflets were printed and posted around neighboring farms that showed her horse was being taken from her like her dog had been when he was shot. Making things worse, on the actual day the auction took place, the auctioneer forced Irene to ride her horse out into the circle of gathered farmers, and she sobbed throughout as they proceeded to bid to take away her closest friend. The $35 bid that won the pony was paid with an I.O.U. that was never made good.

Whites Socks was not all that went under the auctioneer's gavel that day. Mutt and Jeff were sold, along with a cow that was euphemistically listed as "to freshen in March." There were eight horses, all between 1200 and 1300 pounds, nine head of cattle, three dozen chickens, farm equipment and household goods, and a "good democrat," their poor man's buggy.[229] The pigs did not make it to the auction as they were butchered by Oliver and sold to their neighbor beforehand.

229. Fortune Auction poster, 1920.

CHAPTER 12: RETURN TO THE UNITED STATES

In the fall of 1921, the Fortune family retreated from Canada in defeat. They boarded the Canadian Pacific Railroad in Bow Island and headed for North Dakota. North Dakota had changed slightly since they left. In the 1910 census, the year before the family first homesteaded in Canada, Norwegians made up the largest portion of the population with 125,000 residents. There were also other Scandinavians, including 29,000 Swedes and 13,000 Danes[230] in the state's 577,000 people. When they returned, Germans had taken over the top spot, numbering 22% of the state and most outnumbering Norwegians in the state's central area.[231]

On October 21, they stopped at Portal, where Oliver filled out a form of his intent to naturalize as a citizen of the United States. He listed his occupation as a storekeeper who resided in Mohall, North Dakota but was emigrating from Bow Island, Alberta.[232] The storekeeper in Mohall had not been true since 1916 but was apparently adequate. Irene and Nettie got off the train in Minot and remained there with Nettie's Aunt Millie, while Oliver set out once again to find the route to the elusive fortune he was seeking. This time, the pot of gold at the end of the rainbow was once again a retail

---

230. Robinson, *History of North Dakota*, 282.

231. Ibid., 282-283.

232. Oliver Fortune, "Declaration of Intent," United States of America, 14-26786, No. 27214318, May 21, 1921.

variety store in Mohall, North Dakota, which had grown to over 650 people.[233] With almost no money remaining from the auction sale, he managed to rent a two-room house and a small building for a store, "Fortune's Variety Store." Nettie and Irene joined him once he was settled.

There was very little money for furniture, as Oliver spent nearly all they had in an attempt to build up an inventory. Additionally, there was no running water or sewer, in a town where most houses had both. The lack of creature comforts meant little to Oliver, but the same could not be said for Nettie. She directed her ingenuity to seeing what could be made from available materials. Nettie's admirable creativity to improve their home and store was impressive. She used the sturdy wooden crates wholesalers used to ship goods at the time. She found she could get a large wooden crate which had been used to ship dishes and put wholesale Diamond ("farmer") match boxes for the store into a large wooden crate on wooden runners for containers in drawers. They sold small, black kettle knobs and she took some, which she attached to the drawers, then she painted the entire project white. A very sturdy, practical piece of furniture was born. Very clever, but her neurosis as a hoarder perhaps began here. Over sixty years later, Irene would discover this chest from that time in her mother's Berthold home.

Nettie also used saw, nails, and paint to create other storage spaces for the store. In her ambition to improve things, she studied the Sears Roebuck Catalog and the pre-cut lumber offered along with other supplies for making one's own house. Though it would be less expensive than the cost of having a new house built, it was still far more than they could afford, and her hopes and plans came to nothing. At least, they seemed to be collaborating on attempting to improve their situation.

---

233. "Total Population for North Dakota Cities: 1920 - 2000," https://www.ndsu.edu/sdc/publications/census/NDcities1920to2000.pdf.

As he had previously, Oliver lacked competence as a businessman. His strategy was once again to undersell his local competition, an approach he carried much too far with disastrous effects. He often ended up selling his limited inventory at a very tiny margin of profit, or even at a loss. To compound his problems, on three occasions he headed to the Mohall Bank in the morning to find signs that said, "The bank's closed." In each of those cases, what operating cash he had was lost, and he never received a penny back once the bank reopened. By the third such experience, his anger and discouragement were running high.

The story of the bank closures was one of greed by bankers who hoped to take advantage of the rural community and embezzle money while counting on their customers' confidence. In this case, Oliver's frustration was shared by others and though Oliver and his business were victims, the bankers this time did not get off unnoticed and without consequences. The story of the bankers during Oliver's years when he was attempting to get his store going as a business was reported in the major paper of the area, Minot's *Ward County Independent.* On its front page of November 25, 1920, was the headline, "GLENBURN, MOHALL AND COLUMBUS BANKS CLOSE THIS WEEK."

The story said the Mohall bank had closed on Wednesday with a capital of $25,000 while a year earlier, it had deposits of $630,000. The article closed with, "There is no cause for alarm because a few of the banks have been closed. A number of others are apt to follow. Nobody is going to lose a cent and many of these banks that have closed will within a short time be doing business again."[234] On December 21 of the next year, also on the first page but with a small headline in a string of stories, "First National Bank of

---

234. "GLENBURN, MOHALL AND COLUMBUS BANKS CLOSE THIS WEEK," *Ward County Independent* [Minot, ND], Nov 25, 1920, 1.

Mohall Closes," stated bank officers said that, "abnormal demand for deposits was the cause if its closing."[235]

April 13 of 1922 revealed that there was more to the story than local residents knew. An article with the headline, "Mohall Bankers Charged with Misuse of Mails," revealed that the president, vice-president, and cashier of the bank had been charged and arrested for distributing postal fraud for misleading mail and motion pictures nationwide showing Mohall in the vicinity of gas and oil wells to request deposits in the defunct bank. There were also state charges that the bank had issued worthless certificates of deposit of meaningless paper but guaranteed to pay a rate of over 6% annually.[236] By October of 1923, things had moved dramatically as the *Independent* carried the banner headline, "Peters, Wiebe, Bergman Plead Guilty in Mohall Bank Case."[237] The officers of the bank had hired a Minneapolis lawyer to defend them, but the district attorney had evidence they had sent out false information on the condition of the bank. Especially galling was included the State charge that they had accepted Liberty bonds at par in exchange for worthless certificates of deposit. The paper concluded, "Resulting from their practices, a great deal of money was lost by many who had dealings with the concern."[238]

Oliver was not alone in losing money while dealing with the bank. There was one more story that year that did not make the front page and many might have missed it. For those who noticed, perhaps it offered some satisfaction. The headline was, "Upton Takes Three Mohall Bankers to Leavenworth Prison." Their times there would be four

---

235. "First National Bank of Mohall Closes," *Ward County Independent,* Dec 1, 1921, 1.

236. "Mohall Bankers Charged With Misuse of Mails," *Ward County Independent,* Apr 13, 1922, 4.

237. "Peters, Wiebe, Bergman Plead Guilty In Mohall Bank Case," *Ward County Independent,* Oct 19, 1922, 1.

238. Ibid.

years, two years, and one year and a day.[239] A deputy marshal dropped the bankers off at a federal penitentiary that had over 4000 other inmates at the time, including those who had committed the most heinous crimes.[240]

Mohall was involved in another financial crisis at this time that left a lasting impression on Irene. While natural gas had been found in the area before 1910, in 1919, a state geological survey determined the likelihood of underground oil in the area. The Great American Gas Company decided drilling for oil in Mohall could bring great profit and initiated a campaign to attract investors for exploration and drilling. They hired a firm named Publicity Film Company to make promotional films featuring scenes from downtown Mohall and gas-operated products. They distributed flyers with photographs of farm machinery powered by gas, gas cooking ranges, gas-powered wells, an oil well derrick with the caption "one of Mohall's gushers." Stock started at $1 per share and rose to $5 as drilling began. Special big investors were taken to the country to see spectacular, bright burning gas at night against the dark sky without ambient light. The company did not drill deep and the drillers left for Montana, so it was all a bust.[241]

For Mohall it was a failure, but it was the first of North Dakota's oil booms in the surrounding area. A story Irene recalled is, "One hot July day back in the mid-1920s, a bulk oil tank located near the center of town blew up in Minot, North Dakota. Minot is about forty-five miles from Mohall. By miraculous good fortune it occurred at the noon hour, when only one lone office worker was in the adjoining offices of the company. Everyone else had gone for lunch.

239. "Upton Takes Three Mohall Bankers to Leavenworth Prison," *Ward County Independent,* Nov 9, 1922, 5.

240. Ibid.

241. John P. Bluemle, *The 50th Anniversary of the Discovery of Oil in North Dakota*, North Dakota Geographical Survey, Manuscript Series No. 89, 2001, 12-17.

The *Minot Daily News* carried a big headline story, of course. It told how the woman's remains were picked up in a bucket. It was gruesome and has left an imprint in my memory for some sixty years."[242]

For Oliver, it was again wrong place, wrong time. That was of little solace. Throughout his life, Oliver had been a hard worker, and he had expected that hard work to pay off. It was the American Dream, the Protestant Work Ethic—work hard, prosper, be master of your own destiny. You do not need to have your future determined by someone else by being forced to work for someone else. That's what it was really all about—personal independence, self-reliance. Hard work was not keeping its promise. In his frustration, this is when he began to turn to alcohol for relief and escape.

In his new commercial effort, another attitude Oliver had developed early in life, that of the proper role of women, contributed to his failure and the snowballing deterioration of his already shaky marriage. For him there was men's work, which included running the business and making the decisions; and women's work, which included cleaning, dusting, scrubbing, washing clothes, and cooking.

He made no attempt to keep his store neat and orderly, even though Nettie pointed out that the business was more likely to be successful if he did. She had the instincts to operate a more successful business than he had, but any suggestion she made was automatically ignored with comments such as, "You are so dumb, you don't know anything." Before long, she intentionally ceased keeping the store dusted and straightened out.

The move to a new location peopled with strangers freed Irene from the expectations of those who had known her in Alberta. This gave her a chance to change one aspect of her life that had been a source of anxiety at Borden School—her reputation of a crybaby. Upon leaving Canada,

---

242. Irene Fortune, Memoire, Appendix D.

she made up her mind that the time had come to cope with life's challenges without letting her tears make them worse.

The acid test came when she started fourth grade in Mohall. She was nearly eleven at the time. It was noon of her first day, and time for her to head home for lunch. A school bully, Oscar Handy, slipped up behind her and pushed her down a flight of outdoor stairs. She tumbled to the bottom headfirst, tearing large holes in her stockings and bruising and scraping her knees as she fell. But when she lay shaking on the ground, she did not cry or say a word. It was her moment of truth establishing herself among new people in a new location, and she was never thought of as a crybaby again. The bully did not bother her and she felt confident. Her newfound strength was to prove valuable as her life at home continued to grow more and more unpleasant.

The new school in Mohall was a big change from her earlier county schools. It seemed huge to the young girl, as it was a large, three-story brick structure built to house students bused in from the surrounding area. It was also an accredited school, so its standards of teacher qualifications, equipment, and community support were considerable improvements.

"Mohall high school" - 1911. (Property of the Author)

"Irene at 11 when she began school in
Mohall"- (Property of the Author)

As before, Irene had little difficulty standing out academically. From the very beginning, as an eleven-year-old girl, she had to pull her own weight working in the store. She waited on customers, unpacked and shelved goods, and did whatever odd jobs there were that needed doing. The store was open six days a week, in the evening as well as in the daytime, so there was little time for her to do much else. Saturdays were especially long days, as the store stayed open as long as farmers remained in town, which could be as late as 2:00 a.m. Though she was never paid for her work, she was allowed to take as much candy as she wanted.

Even though she could have all she wanted once she returned home, Irene became so obsessed with having candy that by sixth grade, she brought a bag of it to school every day to eat during recess time. Once other students became aware of this, her candy sack began to vanish from her coat pocket before she went outside. Irene reported this to Nettie, who contrived a scheme for putting an end to the problem. She removed the bottoms from some chocolate drops and licorice cigarettes, filled them with red chili pepper powder, then replaced the bottoms. She repeated the process for several days and, after that, although Irene continued to bring her candy to school, it was never again stolen.

Irene's early years in Mohall were much like those of farming community children everywhere in the Midwest of 1920. Sledding was popular in winter, roller skating, with clap-ons, in summer. Visits to other cousins in Minot afforded opportunities to watch for the ice wagon, then run after it to gather bits of ice that chipped off the chunks. Halloween brought the usual pranks—heavy farm equipment on the school steps, even a plow on the roof, a cow with a week's worth of hay in the lower entrance to the hotel's bowling alley. Irene was never allowed the opportunity to become involved in these nuisances, as Nettie would not allow her out of the house on Halloween.

It was in seventh grade that sorrow and confusion entered Irene's life. One aspect of it was minor, although it did not seem so to her at the time—her hairy arms. It seemed unimportant to her family, but it was so embarrassing to the young girl that she would not wear short-sleeved dresses, regardless of the temperature. She insisted that her mother make her only long-sleeved apparel. Another aspect was much more devastating. It was the year her father's regular drinking began.

Mohall had a pool hall, and one thing Oliver had been since years earlier was an excellent pool player. American author and essayist Larry Aasen wrote in *Images of America: North Dakota,* "From 1900 to 1940, pool halls were very popular places in North Dakota towns for young men and boys. Some considered these pool halls sinful places, where idle youth wasted time and smoked cigarettes."[243] Oliver would stop in and play for some money, spending little or nothing, while managing to regularly walk out with enough to pay for the coffee he and some of the other businessmen liked to gather for to take a break. If, in Irene's words, "some 'expert' came to town and wanted to show the local yokels up, someone would immediately come to get Dad."[244]

In 1926, Oliver managed to buy a lot across the street and build a tile and brick store. He built it on the slimmest of resources but managed to complete the project. He acquired a variety of merchandise, including dishes, pots and pans, household equipment, hardware from nuts and bolts to shovels, farm clothing, school supplies, a wide line of candy, also cigars, cigarettes, toys, sundry goods, notions for personal use, and more. He also managed to pay off the mortgage after several years and owned it clear.

This was a time when the general store was also a place to congregate for social interaction, and many people still spoke Norwegian. While Oliver and Nettie had been quick to assimilate, Oliver had learned Norwegian when he was young. It was useful for a businessman in a small community such as his, just as German continued to be the common language spoken in town in other parts of the state in small communities where German settlers were predominant. A study done of Norwegian small towns in the upper-Midwest in 1941 observed that while the residents might by then all speak English, "The Norwegian language also thrives in the taverns, the post office, and the general store, where old, retired farmers and shopkeepers assemble to gossip."[245] These times seemed to hold some promise.

---

243. Larry Aasen, *Images of America: North Dakota* (Charleston, SC: Arcadia Publishing, 2000), 11.

244. Irene Fortune Dodge, unpublished memoir, 50.

245. Marjorie M. Kimmerle, "Norwegian-American Surnames in Transition," *American Speech*, Vol.17, No.3, Oct 1943, 161.

*"Nettie in front of new store" - 1926.
(Property of the Author)*

*"Irene playing tennis on dirt near
school" - (Property of the Author)*

Oliver was an honest man other than about drinking. With the new store, there was one place he felt operating illegally was justified. If one could do the government out of some money, he thought that was not being dishonest, just practical. His opportunity was on the cigarette tax. Each pack required a ten-cent government tax stamp. The rule was that when a merchant opened a new carton he applied a stamp to each pack. Oliver's method was to open two cartons at a time and stamp the packs from one but not the other. He then appraised each customer who came in asking for cigarettes and if he thought the person would keep his mouth shut and not report him, Oliver would sell them an unstamped pack. It was not big money, but it was something.

While the store started off with mild success, Oliver's drinking grew worse rapidly, and the condition of the store became embarrassing to Irene as she was entering her teens. Her friends and their parents were often customers. She methodically cleaned the shelves every day after school in a losing battle to keep up appearances. Even more embarrassing were the frequent and vocal public shouting matches between Nettie and Oliver. The comments, as recorded by Nettie, degenerated from, "It's none of your damn business how much I drink," to "I'll send you to an asylum," and "I'll knock out all your teeth,"[246] which were heard by many in the small town.

These bitter quarrels were generally followed by feelings of remorse from Oliver, when he would offer to do anything for reconciliation. However, they led Nettie more and more to a hardened and generalized attitude about men that had been waiting to congeal since she was a young girl. She was not just coming to hate her husband, she was coming to hate men. Of course, Oliver remained the primary focus, and Irene became a victim of this. Nettie began to blame Irene for keeping her bound to Oliver. If Irene had

---

246. Nettie Fortune, conversation with Irene, 66.

never been born, she could have left him long ago, but her responsibilities as a mother prevented her from doing so. Once Irene finished high school, though, that was going to be it.

This hatred of males was imposed more and more on the teenaged Irene. She was severely scolded if she so much as said "hello" to a boy in her class in the presence of her mother. What brought on real expressions of anger was any hint by Irene, no matter how obscure, that she might someday get married. To Nettie, marriage had been a terrible trap, a condemnation to a life of misery brought on by one brief indiscretion of youth. Nettie's attitude began to take a dangerous twist, from Irene's point of view, as high school passed by.

Irene made a conscious decision when she was a sophomore in high school that affected her life from that point on. Perhaps that drop of Viking blood in her heritage had at last found its way to the surface for her. At that time, her life was filled with situations that made it difficult, and she was often uncomfortable and embarrassed. But "I decided then and there that there was nothing I could do about those problems. So, my only solution was to be responsible for myself. Therefore, I would make no excuses nor would I try to hide or evade the problems. Instead, I would be pleasant and helpful; work hard at whatever I did."[247] In her words, "It was one of the wisest decisions I've ever made. It gave me an inner strength, got me out of a useless apologetic frame of mind, and quickly won respect, appreciation, and friends. Best of all, it felt right."[248]

Irene proved to be a very bright student, the best in her consolidated school district. Mohall awarded a loving-cup trophy for the top high school student each year and, contrary to tradition, it went to the same person two years in a row:

---

247. Irene Fortune Dodge, unpublished memoir., 57.
248. Ibid.

Irene as a junior and as a senior. Oliver's regular response to customers who came into the store to congratulate him on his daughter's success was, "She does well, for a girl."[249] He had valued her getting an education and told her she would get a car once she actually achieved it. Whether that was just talk would never be known, because outside circumstances had changed things for everyone by then, as the Great Depression had begun. To Nettie, having such a capable daughter came to look less and less like a curse that had bound her to Oliver. It began to look like a possibility for an escape from her situation.

"Irene with All-High School Scholarship trophy presented to top student by Superintendent Earl Abrahamson" - 1929. She received it again in 1930. (Property of the Author)

More and more it became, "When you finish college and get a job, *we* can get our own place to live far away from

---

249. Ibid., 50.

here." It was Nettie's plan that once Irene was an employed college graduate, she would move in with her daughter as the housekeeper.

Irene graduated from high school in Mohall as the valedictorian of the class of 1930.

"Irene's high school senior photo" - 1930. (Property of the Author)

The already poor Fortune family suffered like everyone else as the Stock Market Crash of 1929 dragged the country into the Great Depression.

"Nettie in early 1930s when Irene was about to leave Mohall" - (Property of the Author)

CHAPTER 13: LIFE IN THE GREAT DEPRESSION

Irene was intent on going to college, and both her parents encouraged her although they could not afford to finance the endeavor. The young woman followed her own advice to be responsible for herself and spent the two years following her high school graduation working in clerical jobs in Mohall, first at the Renville County Treasurer's Office, then as bookkeeper for Gifford Chevrolet Co., to save her own money for her education. Herbert Hoover, who had been in office when the stock market crashed and had seen the nation descend into depression, was in his final year of his term in 1932. New ideas were being sought to deal with the unprecedented event and subsequent consequences. The state's oldest paper, the *Bismarck Tribune*, made its position clear in timeless arguments, stating:

"Nineteen thirty-two may be a crucial year in the history of the United States. . . we have endured one of the most severe and prolonged general depressions of all time . . .The greatest danger of a depression is that we may lose our heads . . .The new congress, before it has completed its session, will be swamped with suggestions for relieving the unemployed with gigantic bond issues; for helping the farmer with government subsidies and attempts at price fixing; for helping small business at the expense of large one; for helping the poor and those of moderate means by overtaxing the wealthy.

"Prosperity will return as the result of stimulated employment, buying, trade and building. . . Business can do this better than government."[250]

The *Tribune*'s fears would become realities following the November election of Franklin D. Roosevelt and his program, the New Deal.

In September of 1932, Irene left Mohall for Grand Forks, North Dakota, a city of over 17,000 people and site of the University of North Dakota. Her reflection on her movements back and forth between Mohall and the Canadian homestead, then the Canadian sharecropping was, "Short stays, all of them, yet they left me with the impression of long periods of time in my early years."[251]

She was nineteen at the time and soon turned twenty. In Grand Forks she met another freshman, a six-foot, three-inch, lanky fifteen-year-old who soon turned sixteen named Vincent Dodge. Starting college when he was fifteen did not indicate that he was a child prodigy. It meant that in his one-room school he had completed all they had to teach, so they had no alternative but to pass him on to university. Irene had heard of him before he arrived through the grapevine of the time that emerged through church camps. While she did not attend, Vincent was the son of a Methodist minister and his ringing tenor voice had been discussed by those around the state who heard him sing at camps, including friends of Irene's. He would soon be the tenor soloist in the university's chorus while winning the conference in tennis and competing on the track team. Despite the four-year gap in their ages they soon began dating and, in spite of the

250. "Looking Forward," The *Bismarck Tribune* [ND], Jan, 8 1932, 4.
251. Irene Dodge, "The Slow Tomes of Childhood" in personal memoir.

hardships brought on by the Great Depression, university life was great fun for Irene.

The times brought out the comradery that sometimes accompanies a shared experience of adversity. People made their own fun by doing things together, rather than spending money to watch things done or prepared by others. Irene's secretarial skills managed to keep her financially independent, as she typed theses for graduate students and took other odd jobs.

"Irene's homemade fun in Depression"
- (Property of the Author)

In some ways, Irene's absence removed a buffer that had helped prevent the complete deterioration of the Fortune family. She had been Nettie's hope for an escape to a new life, but her involvement with Vincent had become a threat to that. Additionally, Irene had always been a calming influence on her father. Although he had frequent temperamental verbal outbursts directed against Nettie, he never lost his temper with his daughter.

The Great Depression hit North Dakota especially hard. Combined with the economic collapse there was extreme weather, including the years from 1934-36 that saw an especially severe drought. During this time, grass and crops did not grow. Drifts of fine prairie soil piled up and were carried off on the flat prairie. The clouds that appeared in the skies were made up of many millions of grasshoppers that finished off whatever growth remained. The result was that thousands of cattle had to be sold while some died of starvation. Many farmers lost their land to banks through foreclosures, and throughout the 1930s, 121,000 people left the sparsely populated state.[252]

In other ways, the desperation of the times seemed to bring some softness to the relationship between Nettie and Oliver. In the best of times, the Fortunes had struggled to make ends meet in their incompetently run store. As falling prices, vanishing credit, failing banks, and weather that ranged from record highs in the summers to record lows in the winters combined to destroy the agricultural economy, people in the Mohall area had very little to spend. The store, which in Oliver's dreams was to be his ticket to wealth and comfort, could not provide enough of a return to keep Nettie and him fed, although he somehow found enough money to continue to drink. By this time, he had moved beyond being able to tell himself he was a social drinker. Oliver was an alcoholic.

By 1934, Oliver was frequently away from Mohall. Like many others of that era, he was forced to head out to seek whatever work he could find. His absence brought out a sentimental side of Oliver, and a mildly tolerant side of Nettie. First, he went back to the family farm in Wheaton, Minnesota. He looked for work as a farm hand there but had

252. "Section 15: Farm Depression, 1930s," in "Part 1: North Dakota Agriculture," State Historical Society of North Dakota, https://www. ndstudies.gov/gr4/north-dakota-agriculture/part-1-north-dakota-agriculture/section-15-farm-depression-1930s.

no success. Most of his brothers had returned to Wheaton as well. In early 1934, he wrote to Nettie, "Dad and boys not getting along and won't." He claimed it was because of arguments about medicine to give their mother, who was seriously ill. He also asked Nettie to send him some money for cigarettes.[253] He stayed on, since there they had shelter and food and could commiserate and attempt to help each other find work. They could also spend time with their ailing mother. Then, on October 3 of that year, he wrote, "Mother passed away peacefully at 2:15 today. As she wished, all the boys were around her bedside. The doctor said it was like a clock running down."[254] That seemed an apt description, whether or not it captured the cause of death. Born in Norway, she came to America as a young girl, then spent a life of overwork where Oliver had never seen her walk. She did all the housework for her husband and their seven sons as they claimed land and built farms in Minnesota. Life had worn her out and finally taken its toll.

"Fortune brothers at their mother's funeral" - (Property of the Author)

253. Oliver Fortune, Wheaton, MN, letter to Nettie Fortune, Mohall.
254. Oliver Fortune, Wheaton, MN, letter to Nettie Fortune, Mohall, Oct 3, 1934.

Oliver Nels, now left without his wife who had been his servant for sixty years, hired a housekeeper not long after as his health was also declining. Oliver described her to Nettie: "She is an old maid seventy years of age. She has a crooked back. Her name is Annie Nelson and was a great friend of mother and was with her when most of us were born."[255]

Oliver apparently had a somewhat confused understanding of Social Security and was still not in Mohall regularly. His letter indicates he learned from Nettie and Irene that he might be eligible for some benefits, so he looked into it. He wrote, "I note what you say about the Social Security party. It seems as if I will have to live across the line to get the $25."[256] He was claiming he would need to not live in their home but in a cabin sixteen miles away. This was in 1935, and his alcoholism was serious. Perhaps he thought an escape from his home would make hiding things easier.

"Vincent Dodge, Irene Fortune, senior year in college" - 1935. (Property of the Author)

---

255. Oliver Fortune, Wheaton, MN, letter to Nettie Fortune, Mohall, Aug 27, 1935.
256. Oliver Fortune, Wheaton, MN, letter to Irene and Nettie Fortune, Mohall, Aug 28, 1935.

During this time, Oliver sank further and further into the grips of alcoholism. During Christmas, Irene returned home from the University of North Dakota for a two-week holiday. She never saw her father sober throughout the entire time. She said, "It's as though I hadn't had a visit with him at all."[257] It was a turning point that left Irene self-reliant. In spite of her love for her parents, it was time to go her own way.

Irene remained in Grand Forks during summers when possible, even though she was impoverished and found paying for meals a challenge, at times resorting to soup kitchens. She took on work even as a volunteer. Among the jobs she took, where her participation was mentioned in the Bismarck paper, was assisting incoming freshman girls in getting oriented, registering, and learning about campus activities.[258] Her boyfriend Vincent took work in the New Deal's Civilian Conservation Corps, or CCC for some needed income. There, he did a study in the Badlands of North Dakota that was likely never read. The highlight of the experience was an encounter with a rattlesnake.

Irene's final college year was made a bit easier by an unexpected surprise. In January, she received a letter from Oliver Nels, her grandfather that her father had been unwilling to introduce her mother to years earlier. His letter began, "My dear granddaughter, I herewith enclose my check for $200.00, which I think will carry you through the term."[259] He closed with, "Best wishes and lots of love from your Grandpa." He would not be as generous with his son as he was apparently aware of his condition and impressed by Irene's academic achievements. She had several jobs scheduled for her final semester but canceled them.

---

257. Irene Fortune Dodge, unpublished memoir, 56.

258. "Bismarck Co-eds to Assist 'U' Freshmen," *Bismarck* [ND] *Tribune,* Aug 31, 1935, 5.

259. Oliver Nels Fortune, Wheaton, MN, letter to Nettie Fortune, Grand Forks, ND, Jan 14, 1936.

As Irene had her final college year in 1936, Oliver attempted to participate in New Deal jobs for some sort of income. He headed west to Montana as fall was fading into winter. With no job, he was willing to take anything he could find. He had left Wheaton and decided against returning to Mohall in the hopes he could find work and get back on his feet again. It was the depths of the Depression and the wrong time for this choice. In the summer, there had been 10,000 jobs in the New Deal, but when Oliver arrived only 2800 were on the payroll and hiring was infrequent, as winter was coming and projects were closing down. On November of that miserable winter, he wrote Nettie a seven-page letter on lined paper outlining the miseries he was facing that he was sharing with many other desperate people. He wrote, "It looks so hopeless here," and "I see so many people living in poverty such as we have never seen." His conditions were dismal, noting, "I've never been in a country when the wind blows like here. The bad winds of North Dakota would seem like a gentle breeze here, and it don't go down at night." The temperature fell to -62° Fahrenheit the previous winter so with the wind, things were going to be dangerous. He said he had "not spent one cent in restaurants for lunches or meals except to have a few cups of coffee." He told his wife, "I want to promise you one thing. Not one cent of my money will be spent for liquor, beer, or cigars."[260]

He was surviving these conditions while living in the cab of his truck, as he had no money to stay in any better shelter. What little he had, which was the occasional dollar or two he received from Nettie, plus anything he earned from very infrequent work, went mainly for food. But his not spending money on liquor proved to be a hollow promise. He began selling his possessions, including his prized Colt revolver,

---

260. Oliver Fortune, unknown location in Montana, letter to Nettie Fortune, Mohall, Nov 19, 1936.

to provide himself with the money he needed to sustain his habit.

In his final semester at the University of North Dakota, Vincent was defending conference champion on the tennis team and still throwing javelin on the track team. In a real North Dakota oddity, since an African-American had never graduated from a college or university in the state to that time,[261] a Black hurdler had joined the track team the previous year as well as the football team. Though he had never played tennis previously, Vincent convinced him to come to try it after track practice, and before long he could beat everyone on the team, including Vincent. Fritz Pollard, Jr., went on to win a medal in the 1936 Berlin Olympics the following summer as one of the group headed by Jesse Owens that shattered Hitler's dream of demonstrating his racial superiority of Germans.

Irene graduated with a degree in commerce and Vincent graduated as a science major and trained to teach. In the fall, nineteen-year-old Vincent moved to Bathgate, a town of about 300 inhabitants and farms surrounding it in northeastern North Dakota, where he began as the high school principal. He was the only teacher on the faculty with a college degree, while all the others had attended some school up to and possibly including high school, and many had received teacher training at normal school. He also coached and directed the choir. Several of his students were older than he was, since they only attended school when it did not interfere with farm work.

In the summer of 1936, Oliver was still attempting to improve business in the variety store they owned. He contacted the owner of The Palace Theater and Confectionery in Wildrose, North Dakota, who had advertised what he described as a Butterkist popcorn machine in "A1 shape"

---

261. Stephanie Abbott Roper, dis, "African-Americans in North Dakota 1800-1940, University of North Dakota, 1988, 88-89.

for which he claimed to have paid $417 plus freight. Oliver offered to give him a quarter carat diamond in exchange, which the seller found satisfactory, if it was good quality.[262] This remained a mystery for quite some time as Irene never spoke or wrote of the store having a popcorn machine and where Oliver would have obtained such a diamond, unless it was Nettie's or inherited from the wealthy grandmother who raised his wife early on, is unclear. Oliver did request money from his father, who sent him $50 on November 1, 1936, in a letter written in elegant script.[263] Many years later, it became clear that such an extravagant transaction took place during the most desperate time in the Depression, though the source of the information was a surprise.

Irene and Vincent were married on September 5, 1937, and settled in Bathgate. They always kept one can of beans at the back of the cupboard to be sure there was something to eat, as having food was not guaranteed.

Oliver was forced to swallow his pride and once again return to Wheaton, where his relatives provided food and board, but he never received anything from his father like Irene had. In Wheaton, he set about an unsuccessful job search while the store remained in Nettie's hands. His letters to her from this time are affectionate, showing concern over her welfare as well as Irene's, and providing no indication of the animosity that existed between them when they were together. At times, he seemed thoughtful and introspective about how things had turned out. In 1939, he wrote Nettie, "I wrote a few words to Irene some time ago and had a nice letter from her. Such things make a fellow realize what is worthwhile."[264]

---

262. C.L Larson, Wildrose, ND, letters to Oliver Fortune, Mohall, Aug 21, 1936 and Aug 27, 1936.

263. Oliver Nelson Fortune, Wheaton, MN, letter to Oliver Fortune, Mohall, Nov 1, 1936.

264. Oliver Fortune, Wheaton, letter to Nettie Fortune, Mohall, June 15, 1939.

CHAPTER 14: SECOND WORLD WAR, FAMILY CHANGES

The Depression was brought to an end by World War II. Irene and Vincent moved to North Dakota's largest city, Fargo, in 1939. There they started their own family with the birth of a son, Larry. Later in the year, war broke out in Europe. North Dakota had been mainly isolationist during the rise of Hitler and fascists in Italy and Japan, influenced by Senator Gerald P. Nye and his commission hearings, blaming banking and munitions profiteering for getting the United States involved in World War I.

With the United States not initially in the war, Oliver moved back and forth between Mohall and Wheaton, where his father's health was in decline. While his personal story was of weakness and regret, Oliver found it difficult to see the strong man who had created a successful farm out of wilderness and raised such a brood of men reduced to a disoriented, incoherent shell. What his father's condition was remains a mystery, but he was delirious, seeing small people and animals in the room with him that became his companions, and rarely lucid with his sons, who were in the area and frequent visitors. Some hints come from a letter Nettie wrote to Oliver in January of 1943 that he might as well stay in Wheaton with his father. It is apparent she is responding to Oliver's description of his father's condition when she mentions an "electric treatment" she had read about being helpful for arteries and suggested he ask a pharmacist "about there being any danger of the continued use of Phenobarbital."[265]

Phenobarbital was used mainly to control seizures in people who had epilepsy. There is no other evidence that Oliver Nels had developed epilepsy, and people with the condition were being confined at the nearby asylum in Fergus Falls at the time, so it may have been a family secret to the degree possible. It is also possible that he was the victim of some condition associated with aging that now has a name but had not been labeled at the time. The loss of his wife might have exacerbated whatever the illness was that was transforming him into an invalid.

With the bombing of Pearl Harbor on December 7, 1941, the United States entered the war. Oliver was called to register for the draft. He weighed 138 pounds and where the registration asked, "Place of Employment or Business," he left an empty space.[266] It appears he had given up and admitted that Fortune's Variety Store had been a failure. The war put North Dakotans in a bit of a peculiar position. Germans constituted the largest share of the population and when Germany moved to attack Norway, the country was taken over by a German collaborator, Vidkun Quisling, who sided with the Nazis. Soon after Quisling took power, the *Bismarck Tribune*, paper for North Dakota's capital and in a German majority area, had a front page headline, "Quisling Assails Norse Clergy." The story said that the Norwegian clergymen who resigned over new state regulations of young people following alignment with the Nazis "must without

---

265. Nettie Fortune, Mohall, letter to Oliver Fortune, Wheaton, Jan 9, 1943.

266. World War II Draft Registration, "Registration Card: Men born on or after April 27, 1877 and on or before February 16, 1897," Serial Number U 347, Oliver Fortune, Mohall, Renville, ND.

ceremony be treated as traitors."[267] Later, when Quisling was about to be tried as a traitor himself, coverage of him in rural North Dakota was anecdotal. The *Hope Pioneer* reported that a woman in Bottineau had been a classmate of Quisling's father's and stated that he was "a very fine man and was active in Norwegian life."[268]

One thing that should not go unmentioned at this point is that there were Norwegians who fought bravely on the Allied side during the war, in spite of Quisling's government. Notable is the 99th Battalion, made up of Norwegians living in the United States and American citizens of Norwegian ancestry.[269]

Oliver returned to Mohall soon to make it his permanent place of residence again after the United States entered the war. He claimed to have desires of saving his marriage to Nettie. Previously, he repeatedly said that he hoped to die before he turned fifty, and at times he seemed to invite situations that would allow that wish to be fulfilled. Now he was waiting to see if his father would survive, while Nettie remained someone with whom he could share confidences. She had been happier living on her own. He knew he had failed at everything he tried and talked about death, hoping he would have a heart attack and go quickly, but expecting he would get cancer and suffer a long, lingering end.

The main reason Nettie had not wanted him around was his drinking. Although he began telling her that he was done, was going to quit drinking, he returned home drunk

---

267. "Quisling Assails Norse Clergymen," *Bismarck Tribune*, Apr 8, 1942, 1.

268. "N.D. Woman Knows Quisling's Father," *Hope Pioneer* [ND], May 31, 1945, 2.

269. "The Vikings of World War II, "Norwegian American, https://www.norwegianamerican.com/the-vikings-of-world-war-ii/, Oct 8, 2014.

each evening. Eventually and ominously, he began every day by bidding his wife a final farewell.[270]

One early May evening, Oliver was in Mohall, drinking, as usual. It was an unusually cold May, with temperatures below freezing. Oliver eventually headed off in the direction of home but never reached his destination. Perhaps that was never really his intent. He was found the following morning beside a path, dead from exposure or frozen to death. The examining doctor ruled that his death by exposure could have been preceded by a heart attack, though there was no reason to think so, and that appears to have been a final act of kindness in a close-knit rural community.

In Nettie's words, "He seemed to have planned to be drunk enough so he could fall down and not get up and die in his sleep. Which he did."[271] She added, "He even told me he wanted me to be happy."[272] Most surprisingly, her letter stated, "Let me tell you what your dad said a couple of years before he died. He said don't feel sorry about people dying of a heart attack. They are lucky. He thought he had to die of cancer. He was so sure he would die of cancer that he wanted to die before that time came, and I feel sure that he planned his own death."[273]

There are mysteries here. Nettie wrote her comments about Oliver's view on "don't feel sorry about people dying of a heart attack" to Irene on November 5, 1979. Her daughter's husband had died three days earlier from a heart attack. While they no doubt had a phone call soon after, there is no remaining mail mentioning a conversation or expression of consolation for her only child or for the man

270. Nettie Fortune, Berthold, ND, letter to Irene Fortune Dodge, Mar 31, 1975.

271. Nettie Fortune, Berthold, ND, letter to Irene Fortune Dodge, Nov 5, 1979.

272. Ibid.

273. Ibid.

whose salary had been supporting her, just a comment about not feeling sorry for such people.

Could it be that her aversion for men had actually reached a point where she felt her daughter would be better off without her husband? Vincent was not Oliver and while Nettie's treatment and abandonment certainly explained some of her views, they seemed specific, as she always felt the "right" man could have made her life more what she had once hoped for. It also seems unreasonable that she could still harbor her hopes from Irene going to college of her plan for being Irene's maid and the two of them living together without men. The final line, "He even told me he wanted me to be happy," raises a different issue. This couple had brief moments when they were working together for common goals, both on the homestead and the second attempt at a general store, and they also cooperated on educating their daughter. If somehow these moments of cooperation and common interest had become what guided their relationship, both individuals might have ended living happier, more fulfilling lives. How easy it is to change things after the fact.

As it was, the date of Oliver Fortune's death was May 7, 1943. His father outlived him, dying seven months later on December 9. For Nettie, a new chapter began without the millstone around her neck that had been holding her back since she was nineteen. If only life were so simple.

CHAPTER 15: END OF THE HOMESTEADING GENERATION

Nettie lived on her own in Mohall following Oliver's death. She turned into more and more of a recluse as years passed by. During this time, she remained in contact with Irene, who had two more children, Pat or Patty in 1943, and Bob or Robert in 1945. Irene informed Nettie of her grandchildren's progress as babies while she and Vincent began sending her monthly checks to help with what expenses she might have. Irene made several drives of over 310 miles northwest across the vast plains of North Dakota to visit her mother in the summers of these years, taking the opportunity on one occasion to attend an all-year reunion and reconnect with her one real friend from high school, Vi.

By the early 1950s for reasons unknown, years after Oliver died, Nettie became very interested in her family's history. For twenty years, this would be a continuing activity that occupied her, writing to all the relatives she could locate and requesting information. She received many responses and saved them, though often without the envelopes, the specifics of who had sent them, or the person's relationship to her. She also saved personal correspondence from her husband from before they were married and he was "riding the rails" at the beginning of the twentieth century, when he was seeking work in Montana and elsewhere during the

Depression, and letters to Irene, documents from the US and Canadian governments, as well as a sales announcement for an auction, copied records maintained in a family Bible, drawing books, and other personal items from their homesteading days. Some items had specifics of location and date, and others were just the letters. She gathered photographs going back to the second generation following her family's settlement in America.

She also was curious about Oliver's heritage but knew far fewer people to contact about their Norwegian background or settlement in Minnesota. She never set about organizing all the material she gathered in any way or putting it together to be meaningful to anyone else. These letters, while personal memories, left some of her history unclear. Ole Olson, for example, who married Inga in Iowa following the Civil War, was described by his grandchildren who met him when they were very young as coming from just outside of Oslo, and by others as from the Førde farm on the west coast. Letters give the time of his enlistment in the Union forces as 1858 and 1863 and his marriage date with equal disparity. Nettie also was interviewed about her early life and Irene's younger days by her daughter, who recorded her responses, then transcribed the answers.

During this time, Nettie was capable of communicating rationally. However, she became more and more neurotic and perhaps psychotic in certain ways, in that she was at times detached from reality. While there are no obvious reasons to assign her behavior to this category, it is one realistic possibility that the years of solitude and isolation on the plains with a young daughter and husband, neither of whom provided companionship, might have affected her in ways that presented themselves later. Though this story recounts her life interacting with others, Nettie had spent much of her life alone.

The challenges of life on the plains were many, including the hard work to make a living, but the fact of living in isolation affected people. People used the term "prairie madness" for the mental illness that accompanied the loneliness of existing in isolated cabins while weather came in extremes of cold, heat, and continuous wind that kept them confined from interaction with others. "Cabin fever" was an expression for a less developed form of the condition. Many were institutionalized on the Great Plains as "lunatics" during these years as a result of this, but not Nettie. In her communities of Mohall and Bathgate it came to be commonly assumed that she was mentally ill.

This was not a new phenomenon. E.V. Smalley's 1893 *Atlantic* article written after ten years in Nebraska and the Dakotas described the conditions that led to this well. It began, "In no civilized country have cultivators of the soil adapted to their home life so badly to the conditions of nature as have the people of our great Northwest."[274] He contrasted this with European peasants living in villages active with social life. He continued, "On every hand the treeless plain stretches away to the horizon . . . The new settler is too poor to build of brick or stone. He hauls a few loads of lumber from the nearest railway station and puts up a frail little house of two, three, four rooms that looks as though the prairie winds would blow it away."[275] This was followed by how those living there were confined together for much of the time and how there were no social gatherings, neighbors rarely dropping by during long periods of winter weather, what neighbors there were constituted a sprinkling of nationalities, while life was "bleak and dispiriting." He stated, "An alarming amount of insanity occurs in the new prairie states among farmers and their wives. In proportion

---

274. E.V. Smalley, "The Isolation of Life on Prairie Farms, *Atlantic,* September, 1893, 378.
275. Ibid., 379.

to their numbers, Scandinavian settlers furnish the largest contingent to the asylums."[276]

During Nettie's time shuttered up in her home in Mohall, she first became a hoarder and shut-in. By the time her granddaughter Patty had reached upper elementary school age, Nettie was likely neurotic to a point where she was somewhat agoraphobic, among other things. Patty went to a Methodist church camp, Wesley Acres, which was attended by young people from around the state. She met girls from Mohall at the camp and social person that she was, she told them she had a grandmother who lived in the town. When she told them who it was, they said, "She's the crazy lady."[277] Patty's brother Bob had a similar experience years later when he began teaching in West Fargo, North Dakota. One of his social studies colleagues resigned in hopes of earning a more substantial income and took a job as an insurance salesman. His territory included Ward, Renville, and other western counties. They got together socially and Bob mentioned to his former coworker that his grandmother Nettie lived in Berthold. The immediate response was, "Oh, you mean the crazy lady." Apparently, that name was well established.

Nettie had left her longtime home of Mohall by the time Bob spoke with his former colleague, moving thirty miles south to Berthold. A pharmacist offered to buy the store she owned and in eliminating her past life, she sold it and could afford down payment on a small house. Oscar, her long lost brother who had briefly reentered her life after a ten-year separation when they had been split up as children, then embarrassed her badly by his boorish behavior that drove out customers at the dining hall where she worked in Garrison, once again established contact. This time it

---

276. Ibid., 380.

277. Patricia Dodge Stocker, telephone conversation with Robert Dodge, Sept 5, 2020.

was different. It had been over forty years and Oscar began sending her money. Like Oliver's brothers, he might have served in World War I, although he would have been young to have done so. He was living in the Old Soldiers' Home in Marshalltown, Iowa on a military pension and not allowed to accumulate over a certain amount of cash. In the late 1950s, when Nettie bought her house, she was receiving monthly checks from Oscar that covered her payments.

Irene and Vincent visited Oscar when they were on a trip in 1965. Irene said she felt very uneasy about it, since she had heard only negative comments about him from her mother. He, however, while deaf and frail, took great pleasure in introducing her to everyone. Meanwhile, she noted, "A nurse there was less pleasant to me, a niece who had neglected her uncle all those years!"[278]

Nettie was among the town's 398 residents by 1970.[279] Her mail that she was still receiving from relatives was postmarked Berthold following this. Nettie continued to do things she had done since homesteading, including carefully not wasting material and planting a small garden next to her house that would grow edible vegetables for her.

She had a preoccupation about citizenship and having a birth certificate for proof of being born in the United States for both herself and Irene. That is evident in her correspondence with Irene through the 1950s, 1960s, and early 1970s. Nettie's was resolved by her diligent efforts to find proof she had been born in Madison, South Dakota. She obtained her baptismal certificate, an affidavit of parentage, and found an insurance policy that had her place and date of birth. This was sufficient for her to receive a certificate of citizenship from the US government, undoing the incidental

---

278. Irene Fortune Dodge, unpublished memoir, 73.

279. "Supplementary Report: 1970 Census of Population: 1970 Population of North Dakota by Township and City," U.S. Department of Commerce: Bureau of the Census, https://www2.census.gov/prod2/ decennial/documents/31679801n104-107ch3.pdf, Dec 1976.

change caused by her husband.[280] She also carried on with her fixation on Irene's birth certificate, sending her letters about contacting Portal, North Dakota for when the family crossed to enter Canada and entering the United States. Perhaps they retained records from 1911 that listed Nettie and Oliver as citizens of the United States, which would make their daughter a citizen and list a date of Irene's birth to support her claim for a birth certificate. She also suggested homestead records from Oliver at Ryder, their wedding in Minot, hospital insurance, and more.

That changed completely in the mid-1970s, when Irene actually needed a birth certificate to apply for a passport. Her son Larry was living and working in Rome, and Vincent and Irene planned to visit him and include it in a trip through Europe. Nettie then wrote to Irene, "Why don't you just give up on your plans? It isn't as if Larry and his wife were there permanently. I would feel terrible if you got stuck over there and couldn't get back until a lot of red tape had been wrangled over. If Vincent wants to go, he could go, then come back and tell you about it."[281]

About this time, Nettie received a letter from one of her brother Oscar's daughters, informing her that he was dead and the Veterans Home said he had left $351.44, which would be split equally between his two daughters.[282] Irene and Vincent made her modest home payment as well as continuing to send her a monthly check for personal expenses.

On a trip to Berthold to visit her mother, Irene made a disturbing discovery. Nettie threw nothing away and

---

280. "Certificate of Citizenship," No. 4191098, Petition No. 179, The United States of America.
Irene Fortune Dodge, unpublished memoir, 73.
281. Nettie Fortune, Berthold, ND, letter to Irene Fortune Dodge, Mar 31, 1975.
282. Bernese Johnson, Aberdeen, South Dakota. letter to Nettie Fortune. Feb 23, 1973.

kept everything in her house, which held the furniture she had shipped from Mohall. She received a daily newspaper and had never disposed of a copy. They were just piled up randomly on her floor. All mail that arrived, including the letters from relatives with information she had requested, was dumped in the house, not opened. Vincent and Irene had sent her gifts such as a toaster and other small household items. The packages had never been opened but were mixed in with all the new and old clutter overwhelming the small amount of square footage in the house. When Irene came, she could not stay with her mother but had to get a room at the town's hotel.

The situation rapidly grew worse as Nettie developed what psychologists term a hoarding disorder. This had long been included as a category of obsessive-compulsive disorder, or OCD, but in 2013 the American Psychiatric Association's *Diagnostic and Statistical Manual of Mental Disorders* assigned it a unique diagnosis.[283] This word is used frequently to describe a person who accumulates or collects things but as a disorder, it has a specific meaning. The Mayo Clinic states, "Hoarding disorder is a persistent difficulty discarding or parting with possessions because of a perceived need to save them." They add, "Hoarding often creates such cramped living conditions that homes may be filled to capacity, with only narrow pathways winding through stacks of clutter."[284]

The final sentence is what came to describe Nettie's home. Irene worried about her mother for living in a fire hazard, the dangers of her falling and being hurt, the unsanitariness as rodents found homes in the piles or

283. American Psychiatric Association, *Diagnostic and Statistical Manual of Mental Disorders*, *5th Edition* (Washington, D.C.: American Psychiatric Publishing, 2013.

284. "Hoarding Disorder," Mayo Clinic, https://www.mayoclinic.org/diseases-conditions/hoarding-disorder/symptoms-causes/syc-20356056.

hoarded materials, and her mental health. By continuing to accumulate trash and unread newspapers, Nettie had reduced her home to a warehouse of useless trash, piled high, with a single passageway that led to her bed, another to her toilet, and one to a small section in her kitchen.

Nettie ventured out once daily to a small cafe nearby for a single meal. A good-hearted waitress whose name has been lost from memory treated her well and took care of her, aware of her eccentricities and frailties. One other issue also exposed things about her personality that may have resulted from the challenges of her early upbringing or from the isolation of living on homesteads alone without regular companionship. Her exception to only venturing out to the cafe was that she began attending funerals of people she did not know, merely to hear the soloists sing, having long enjoyed music.

While Nettie continued to carry on in this manner for some time, she had some ailment that required her hospitalization. Irene drove from Fargo to be with her and realized this was an opportunity. She found a couple high school boys who had a truck and hired them to go to Nettie's house. They emptied almost everything out of the house and hauled it to the trash. The process took most of a week with Irene working alongside the boys. It would have gone faster, but Nettie had no arrangement at all in her clutter. One example was that mixed in with the many old newspapers, Irene found the deed to her house. It meant she needed to actually inspect the trash as the boys emptied the house. She worked hard physically as well and returned to Fargo twenty pounds lighter. She mentioned to her daughter that she wished her husband could see her since it had been years since her weight had been as low. His early death prevented this.

When Nettie returned home, not surprisingly, she was outraged. The evidence indicates that Irene, rather than admitting what she had done, told her mother that some teenage boys had broken into her house, taken things, and broken her furniture. Nettie wrote to Irene later, "You know how badly those high school boys tore everything up in my house, emptied out all dresser drawers, threw everything all over the floor, pictures, silverware, letters, broke up nearly everything." She added that they, "Broke up that big popcorn machine so it wasn't any good either."[285]

Apparently, years earlier Oliver had gone ahead with exchanging the diamond for the popcorn machine. The dresser drawers that had been emptied before the dresser was taken to the dump was the one Nettie had constructed from a wooden shipping container when they returned to the United States because of the threat of World War I.

While Nettie wanted to continue living on her own and did so briefly, her daughter finally convinced her that her life would be much easier in a nursing home, where she would have someone to look after her. While her hoarding behavior was no longer tolerated, her mental illness began to show itself in other ways. She was a woman who felt persecuted and was not pleasant. When Irene came to visit, she told others "about when Irene tried to push her down a flight of stairs to hurt her."[286] Of course, they never had a flight of stairs and she had spent her life for as long as Irene could remember attempting to control her daughter. Whether Nettie actually believed this or was inventing it to insult her daughter in front of other residents of the nursing home is unclear, but neither option sheds a positive light on Nettie's status as she neared the age of ninety.

285. Nettie Fortune, Berthold, ND, letter to Irene Fortune Dodge, Nov 15,1975.
286. Patricia Dodge Stocker, telephone conversation, Sept 5, 2022.

CHAPTER 16: REFLECTION

This story is not meant to be representative of Norwegian immigrants to America and especially those who settled in North Dakota. At the time Oliver first homesteaded in Ryder and when Nettie moved to a homestead near Garrison, 78% of North Dakotans, excluding Native Americans, were immigrants or of foreign parentage, the largest figure for any state in the nation.[287] Of the Scandinavian people who settled the Great Plains states, the Norwegians were the most populous group and over half settled in North Dakota, where they became the largest ethnic group.[288]

These people turned the prairie in the land that became North Dakota into an agricultural breadbasket that now leads the nation in production of spring wheat, durum wheat, dry edible peas, and dry edible beans.[289] Alberta, where Oliver, Nettie, and Irene spent most of their homesteading years, is also a major wheat producer with its annual ten million tons of wheat being exported to seventy countries.[290] This production no longer comes from small farmers. Back in 2011, the figure was already up to 98% of America's food

---

287. Luebke, "Ethnic Group Settlement on the Great Plains," 405-406.

288. Ibid., 417.

289. North Dakota Facts," *North Dakota*, https://www.ndtourism.com/articles/north-dakota-facts.

290. "Alberta Wheat," *Canada: Alberta*, https://open.alberta.ca/dataset/5e2d6a5c-5446-4630-9232-da3a0cfa5f6f/resource/7c86b5df-76ad-4792-b5de-f694eb6798a5/download/af-alberta-wheat-2020-english.pdf.

supply being produced by agribusinesses,[291] so the family farms and the small towns that developed to support them have largely faded away.

The words "pioneer" and "frontier" that are associated with the homesteaders continue to be celebrated, as in the names of small-town newspapers, many taverns, an airline, and a ride at Disneyworld. Some did succeed for a time and their success is admirable. The story for others, however, was not of such achievement. What should not be lost is the memory of those for whom it was more than they could handle and what happened when they were overcome by it all. This is a true account of the evolution of a Norwegian family from its time in Norway through its relocation in America and westward movement, that disintegrated in many ways as it was unable to tolerate the demands of resettlement on the prairie. One thing that might have seemed incidentally surprising was the number of mentions of children who did not survive childbirth or died at a very early age. There were many. That was the normal situation for the time. In 1900, deaths of children under the age of five constituted 30% of all deaths in the nation. That figure, fortunately, had been reduced to 1.4% before the century ended.[292]

Irene, who put together reflections on homesteading life and included interviews of her mother about her life that she transcribed, offered a commentary on it in 1984:

"Had I started to write this account several years ago, it would likely have sounded quite different. I realize it would

291. Melanie J. Wender, "Goodbye Family Farms and Hello Argibusiness: The Story of How Agricultural Policy is Destroying Family Farms and the Environment," *Villanova Environmental Law Journal*, Vol. 22, Iss. 1, Art. 6, 2011, 140-141.

292. Marilyn J. Fields and Richard E. Behrman, eds., *When Children Die: Improving Palliative and End-of-Life Care for Children and Their Families* (Washington, D C: National Academies Press, 2003), https://www.ncbi.nlm.nih.gov/books/NBK220806/.

have been harsher on my parents than this, because I was still feeling the hurts from my life at home. I had not yet been able to stand back and be objective. My mind was filled with all the negatives of my home situation and somehow I didn't recognize that there were many positive aspects which might not necessarily have existed.

"I hadn't factored in all the experiences my parents had had during their childhood and youth, and those experiences did indeed have an impact on them. I'm not suggesting that I think people should be excused for whatever behavior they exhibit, simply because of their past. On the other hand, it is important, for better understanding, for us to see why such reactionary behavior takes place. It is all too easy to sluff off other people's hardships, which they've endured over a long, continual time, and decide that such people should behave ideally later.

"I'm reminded of a couple of quotes, which I can't quite recall accurately. One is about walking in someone else's moccasins. The other is from an old radio show, where a character by the name of Baron Munchausen (I think) was always piercing someone's complacency with the question, Vas you dare, Charlie?"[293]

Nettie died in September of 1989, less than two years short of her 100th birthday. The span of her life began twenty-six years following the end of the Civil War, when Manifest Destiny was in full force. Born and growing up during horse and buggy days, she survived to the time of Apple and McIntosh. She celebrated the arrival of the twentieth century and was fourteen when the Wright brothers made their famous first flight at Kitty Hawk, North Carolina. She lived through both World Wars and the Depression and twenty-one different presidents. Whether she did more good than damage depends on when in that long span the question is asked. She did leave behind Irene,

---

293. Irene Fortune Dodge, unpublished memoir, 86.

which is her positive contribution, even if at times she made that a serious challenge.

Irene's life began to change in the late 1960s. Having escaped the continuing attempted dominance by her mother, she largely abandoned her past and lived in the present with her family. She had, like many Norwegian women, led a life where she was helpmate to her husband, though to less of a degree than many of her generation. She and Vincent continued the family with three children: Larry, Patty, and Bob. Vincent began his Fargo career, teaching science at Agassiz Junior High School, the junior high for the south side of the city, in 1939. It was a position he enjoyed greatly, sitting on top of his teacher's desk where he could see what all the class members were doing and explaining different areas of science. He had completed a master's degree in science by this time and became president of the North Dakota Classroom Teachers' Association and a member of the National Education Association (NEA) Executive Committee. Once all their children were school age, Irene also took a job at Agassiz as a secretary. This was convenient, since the school occupied a full block and also had an elementary school attached, which was where Patty and Bob were enrolled while Larry attended junior high there as well from grades seven through nine. It was only two blocks from their home and nearly all the block that was not school was a large playground, where the boys learned to play baseball and which became a large skating rink when the weather turned cold, so all skated daily.

Though Irene was not trained or certified and such things had become required in many places, the principal asked her to teach junior high school mathematics to those who found it challenging. Vincent went on to become an elementary school principal, though he would have preferred to remain a teacher. The salary was higher and he thought the tradeoff worth it. He eventually served as National President of the Department of Elementary Principals. Throughout his life in Fargo, he remained a well-known figure in area music circles as a tenor soloist and especially conductor, conducting youth and adult choirs at First Methodist Church as well as women's and men's barbershop choruses. He is remembered as a good and multi-talented man who attempted to bring out the best in people by being positive and encouraging. A heart attack brought his life to an end on November 2, 1979. He had just turned sixty-four and they had begun plans for retirement, possibly moving to Arizona where he could play golf regularly, but that was suddenly abandoned. Even though her younger son Bob and his wife had moved to London the year Vincent died, Irene made the trip on her own to visit them the following year.

Back in the late 1960s to 1970, Irene had begun to move out of her husband's shadow. She and Vincent had joined First Methodist Church in Fargo in 1939, and she continued her active participation there until her death. She became an active member of a number of organizations, including the American Association of University Women, (AAUW), where she served as president of the Fargo branch from 1969-1971. She also attended two AAUW National Conventions. When Common Cause was first organized by John Gardner, Secretary of Health, Education, and Welfare under President Lyndon Johnson in 1970 as the "citizens lobby," it had its own slate of candidates to accompany Gardner as director.

Irene believed citizens needed more voice in politics and that commercial lobbies had too much influence. She boldly put herself forward, touting her credentials as "a housewife from North Dakota," and representative of regular people more than the impressively credentialed people on the list. She was elected to the National Governing Board of Common Cause and became a frequent visitor to Washington, DC to attend Board meetings. She served as a member of the chair selection committee to replace Gardner and also chaired the Membership and Communications Committee of the

Board. Irene was also appointed by former Governor Sinner as a charter member of the North Dakota Commission on Judicial Qualifications. A strong advocate of conservation, she was active in the environmental movement and local organizations. She was having an impact.

After her husband died, Irene moved to Denver and rented an apartment near her daughter Pat's home. While she attended church and her daughter included her in many activities, she never felt like she belonged. Still independent minded, she chose to live where she felt most useful and alive and returned to in an apartment in Fargo, North Dakota, where so much of her life had been. There, she carried on with activities that mattered to her, including the Fargo Fine Arts Club Literature Section, which naturally suited her lifelong appetite for books and reading. She also involved herself with membership and leadership roles in the Cass County Retired Teachers Association.

Her children visited, one from the east coast, one from the west coast, one from overseas, occasionally with spouses and grandchildren. The constant the three children shared is that they all played Scrabble with Irene. As she grew older and reached ninety, one might have expected that her college educated children would "let her win" as an act of kindness. Irene and Vincent had played Scrabble socially for years before he died. When Bob returned to visit from Singapore on Christmas vacation of 2002 and played repeated games with his ninety-two-year-old mother, she often pointed out how he might have used his letters more wisely and made plays with words that only Scrabble players know exist. She was keeping the score respectable so as not to embarrass him and certainly needed no help.

Irene, the daughter of an alcoholic who always dreamed of great success but continually failed at all he tried and the "crazy lady" who hoarded everything, then became delusional in her paranoia, was a strong, determined woman. She had every excuse to be otherwise. Her daughter Pat, like the women before her, is a strong, determined woman. Pat was the appropriate one to see that her mother was treated well and cared for in her final years, which she did despite living a considerable distance away, taking time from her busy schedule.

Irene had become a woman devoted to lifelong learning for herself and others, supportive of other people and their educational endeavors, and continually involved in making her community of Fargo, North Dakota a better place to live while remaining involved as long as possible with international issues.

Irene died peacefully on February 24, 2003, in Fargo. Her funeral was held at the First Methodist Church and featured music arranged by her husband. All arrangements were handled by her daughter, the next woman to carry on in her manner of stepping up and seeing that all continued, regardless of the external factors. On a small table at the entry to the sanctuary was a holder for Scrabble letters placed by her eldest son. Spelled out on the holder, he had written in Scrabble tiles, "GOOD LIFE." It was a succinct summary that she would very likely have thought summed everything up ideally, despite the many rough spots she had on the way. Like the Norwegian ancestors before her, she had persevered and found satisfaction in life on the desolate, cold prairie and remained strong to the end.

EPILOGUE

The story does not end with Irene's death. This has been a history of Norwegian immigration to the northern Great Plains through the lens of a single family—the author's family. While there was considerable firsthand material to rely on, I have also expanded considerably on the memories of my ancestors and added historical context to their stories. In the earliest years where information is very limited, gaps were filled with probabilities based on the known locations and movements of individuals. Much of this included history would have likely been unknown and meant little to the individuals at the time, or what they knew would have been viewed from a different perspective. The interrelation of westward movement with Indian displacement and genocide is mentioned without any blame assigned to my ancestors or their fellow settlers, who emigrated without current awareness. They were a part of larger stories that influenced them and that they unknowingly influenced.

An important point is that this is very much a women's story. Of course, it recounts the lives of men, which were often better preserved in records, and men were admirable in the challenges of resettlement, the hard labor of breaking the soil and creating farms from prairie land. There were also stories of couples who worked in tandem for survival in challenging times and situations. However, it was strong women who kept the story moving and allowed the lineage from Norway to survive to the present. When the few men came up short or disaster struck, these women carried on even if it destroyed them, preserving families that would have died out after husbands abandoned them or circumstances left women alone to raise children.

With Irene's passing, what remained in the direct lineage of Viking på Torsnes from the 1100s were her three children, Robert [Bob], Pat [Patty], and Lawrence [Larry]. I am Robert, and my wife Jane and I have an adopted child who certainly is in the mold of the strong women who prevail in the face of adversity. Her Scandinavian mother raised her to be that way. Larry also has no direct descendants, but stepchildren of a strong woman. Again, it is the datter, Pat, who, like Inga Vikingsdatter Torsnes a thousand years earlier, will keep the direct lineage alive. Pat has three children, and all of them have children, so grandchildren abound, all carrying the Fortune blood from Norway into the uncharted future. Hopefully, there is a drop of that Viking heritage that remains intact for them to help navigate the inevitable challenges with the aid of unbound courage.

SOURCES

Aasen, Larry. *Images of America: North Dakota.* Charleston, SC: Arcadia Publishing, 2000.

Ablavsky, Gregory. "Making Indians 'White': The Judicial Abolition of Native American Slavery in Revolutionary Virginia and Its Racial Legacy." *University of Pennsylvania Law Review,* Vol. 159, No. 5, Apr 2011.

Act of May 20, 1862 (Homestead Act), Ch. LVIIIV, Sec. 2 General Records of the United States Government, Record Group 11; National Archives Building, Washington, DC. https://www.archives.gov/milestone-documents/homestead-act#transcript.

"The Age of Jackson," *U.S. History,* https://www.ushistory.org/us/24f.asp.

Agrippa, Henry Cornelius. *Three Books of Occult Philosophy.* London: Gregory Moule, 1651.

"Alberta Wheat," *Canada: Alberta,* https://open.alberta.ca/dataset/5e2d6a5c-5446-4630-9232-da3a0cfa5f6f/resource/7c86b5df-76ad-4792-b5de-f694eb6798a5/download/af-alberta-wheat-2020-english.pdf.

Alexander VI, Pope. Papal Bull *Inter Caetera,* 1493.

Allen, Douglas W. "Homesteading and Property Rights; Or, 'How the West Was Really Won.'" *Journal of Law & Economics,* Vol. 34, No.1, Apr 1991.

American Psychiatric Association. *Diagnostic and Statistical Manual of Mental Disorders, 5th Edition.* Washington, D.C.: American Psychiatric Publishing, 2013.

Andersen, Arlow William. "Venturing into Politics: The Norwegian-American Press of the 1850s." *Wisconsin Magazine of History,*

September 1948, Vol. 32, No. 1, September 1,1948.

-------- "American Politics in 1980: Norwegian Observations," *Scandinavian Studies*, Vol. 40, No. 3, August 1968.

Anderson, Harry H. "Deadwood Effort at Stability." *Montana: The Magazine of Western History,* Winter, *1970.*

Andersson, Rani-Henrik. The Lakota Ghost Dance of 1890. Lincoln, Neb: University of Nebraska Press, 2008.

Andrist, Ralph K. T*he Long Death: The Last Days of the Plains Indians.* New York: Collier Books, 1969.

Anserude, Violet. Letter to Nettie Fortune, "Family Tree of Halvor Finne." RR#2, Case Lake, Minnesota, May 5, 1978.

"Arriving Passenger and Crew List," *Virgo*, June 24, 1853, Castle Garden and Ellis Island, New York, *National Archives and Records Administration.*

Barry, John M. *The Great Influenza: The Epic Story of the Deadliest Plague in History.* London: *Penguin Books*, 2005.

Bø, Gudleiv. "The History of a Norwegian National Identity." University of Oslo, https://www.tsu.ge/data/file_db/scandinavian-studies/ Nation-building-the-Norwegian-way.pdf.

Bennet's Handbook for Travelers in Norway with Through Routes to Sweden and Denmark. London: Simpkin, Marshall, Hamilton, Kent, and Co. 1913.

Beuermann, Ian. "The Norwegian Attack on Iona in 2009-10: The Las Viking Raid?," *Medievalists.net*, https://www.medievalists. net/2016/02/the-norwegian-attack-on-iona-in-1209-10-the-last-viking-raid/, April 11, 2012.

"Bismarck Co-eds to Assist 'U' Freshmen." *Bismarck* [ND] *Tribune.* August 31, 1935.

Blegen, Theodore C. "The Early Norwegian Press in America*,"* *Minnesota History Bulletin*, Vol. 3, No. 8, November 1920.

Bluemle, John P. *The 50th Anniversary of the Discovery of Oil in North Dakota.* North Dakota Geographical Survey, Manuscript Series No. 89, 2001.

Boissoneault, Lorraine. "How the 19th Century Know Nothing Party Reshaped American Politics." *Smithsonian*, https://www. smithsonianmag.com/history/immigrants-conspiracies-and-secret-society-launched-american-nativism-180961915/, January 26,

2017.

Bruns, Roger. *Knights of the Road: A Hobo History.* London: Methuen Publishing, 1980.

The Bull *Romanus Pontifex* (Nicholas V). January 8, 1455. http://caid.ca/Bull_Romanus_Pontifex_1455.pdf.

Burke, Peter. "Popular Culture in Norway and Sweden." *History Workshop Journal*, Vol. 3, Iss. 1, March 1, 1977.

"Certificate of Citizenship," No. 4191098, Petition No. 179, The United States of America.

Christian, Lewis Clark. "Mormon Foreknowledge of the West." *BYU Studies Quarterly*, Vol. 21, Iss. 4, 1981.

Clerk of Courts, Lake County, South Dakota, Affidavit of Parentage, Nettie Williams as daughter of Caroline Olson and Austin Williams, verified by Jim Creek, uncle, December 1, 1953.

Clerk of Courts, Lake County, South Dakota, Certified Copy of Birth Transcript for Nettie L. Williams, November 2, 1956.

Cobb, Russell. *The Great Oklahoma Swindle.* Lincoln, NE, Bison Books, 2020.

Cohen, Brenda and Cohen, Paul. "The Leprosy Museum at St. George's Hospital in Bergen: Tracing the Roots of a Dreaded Disease in Norway." *Journal of College Science Teaching*, Vol. 28, No. 1, September/October, 1998.

"The Constitution of the United States: A Transcription," Article I§ 8, *National Archives*, https://www.archives.gov/founding-docs/constitution-transcript.

Custer, Elizabeth B. *Boots and Saddles.* New York: Harper & Brothers, 1885.

"Custer's Expedition: Its Objects, Equipment, and Personnel," *New York Times*, July 5, 1874.

Danielsen, Dag Arne. *Ancestors of Irene F. Fortune.* Florvåg, Norway, self-published, 2020.

DeMallie, Raymond J. "The Lakota Ghost Dance: An Ethnohistorical Account," *Pacific Historical Review*, November, 1982.

Department of Health, Education, and Welfare. Social Security Administration Kansas City, Missouri. May 4, 1967.

d'Ericco, Peter. "Jeffrey Amherst and Smallpox Blankets: Lord Jeffrey Amherst's Letters Discussing Germ Warfare Against American

Indians." https://people.umass.edu/derrico/amherst/lord_jeff.html.

de Tocqueville, Alexis. *Democracy in America, Vol. I*, [originally London: *De la démocratie en Amérique:* Saunders and Otley, 1835]. Trans to English by Henry Reeve, Cambridge: Sever & Francis, 1862.

Diamond, Jared. *Guns, Germs, and Steel: The Fates of Human Societies.* New York: W. W. Norton & Company, 1999.

Diffendarfer, Joel. "Hobo Code: The Signs and Symbols Used by Travelers of Old." *Owlcation*, July 13, 2022, https://owlcation.com/humanities/All-things-HOBO-signs-and-symbols.

"Disorderly Houses: An Ordinance Related to Disorderly Houses, and Houses of Ill-Fame and Common Prostitutes." *Ward County Independent* (ND). September 20,1906.

"Do Cows Drink Their Own Milk," *AgricAite.com,* https://agricsite.com/do-cows-drink-their-own-milk/.

Dodge, Irene Fortune. Interviewed by Robert Dodge. Fargo, North Dakota, 1995.

--------- Dodge, Irene Fortune, "Unpublished Memoir," 1984.

--------- "Going to Town," theme submitted for freshman English, University of North Dakota, November, 1932.

--------- unpublished memoir, from conversation with her cousin Mildred Wilson.

Donovan, Jim. *Custer and the Little Bighorn: The Man, the Myth the Mystery.* Minneapolis: Voyageur Press, 2001.

Dörr, Dieter. "The Background of the Theory of Discovery." *American Indian Law Review*, Vol. 38, No. 2.

Duprey, Glen. Letter to Oliver Fortune, Winnipeg, Manitoba. October 18, no year stated.

Editors of Britannica. "California Gold Rush." *Britannica*, https://www.britannica.com/topic/California-Gold-Rush.

Eigen, Lewis and Siegel, Jonathan. *The Macmillan Dictionary of Political Quotations.* New York: Macmillan Publishing Company, 1993.

Eiseley, Loren. *All the Strange Hours.* New York: Scribner, 1975.

Eitrheim, Oyvid, Klovland , Jan T. and Qvigstad, Jan F. eds. *Historical Monetary Statistics for Norway 1819-2003.* Oslo: Norges Bank,

2004.

Faragher, John Mack. "History from the Inside-Out: Writing the History of Women in Rural America." *American Quarterly*, Vol. 33, No. 5, Winter 1981.

Fauve-Chamoux, Antoinette, Ed. *Domestic Service and the Formation of European Identity*. Bern: Peter Lang AG, 2004.

Fields, Marilyn J. and Behrman, Richard E. eds. *When Children Die: Improving Palliative and End-of-Life Care for Children and Their Families* (Washington, D C: National Academies Press, 2003). https://www.ncbi.nlm.nih.gov/books/NBK220806/.

Fiske, Frank. *The Taming of the Sioux,* Bismarck, ND: Bismarck Tribune, 1917.

"First Account of the Custer Massacre," Bismarck *Tribune Extra*, July 6, 1876.

"First National Bank of Mohall Closes," *Ward County Independent,* December 1, 1921.

Folger, Tim. "Why Did Greenland's Vikings Vanish," *Smithsonian Magazine*. March 2017.

Fortune Auction Poster, 1920.

Fortune, Frank. Letter to Allie Fortune. Camp MacArthur, Waco, Texas. October 16, 1918.

Fortune, Nettie, Certificate of Citizenship, U.S. Department of Labor, May 21, 1937.

-------- Fortune, Nettie, Transcripts of Conversations with Irene Fortune Dodge conducted Oct 1974, Oct 2, 1979, June, 1980, April 1983.

--------- "Personal Memories." Transcription of interview of with Irene Dodge. Mohall, ND, Oct 22, 1979.

--------- Undated memoirs in three sections. Berthold, North Dakota.

--------- Letter to Oliver Fortune. Mohall, North Dakota, January 9, 1943.

--------- Letter to Oliver Fortune. Mohall, North Dakota, January 12, 1943.

-------- Letter to Oliver Fortune. No location given, January 7, no year stated.

-------- Letter to Irene Fortune Dodge. Berthold, North Dakota, October

29, 1970.

-------- Letter to Irene Dodge. Letter including family history. Berthold, North Dakota, December 9, 1970.

-------- Letter to Irene Fortune Dodge. Berthold, North Dakota, March 31, 1975.

-------- Letter to Irene Fortune Dodge, Fargo, ND, April 1, 1975.

-------- Letter to Irene Fortune Dodge. Berthold, North Dakota, November, 1979.

-------- Letter to Irene Dodge, letter including family history, Berthold, North Dakota, November 19, 1970.

-------- Letter to Irene Dodge. Letter including family history. Berthold, North Dakota, November 21, 1970

------- Letter to her sister Millie, letter including family history, February, 23, 1955.

------- Letter to Bernese Johnson of Aberdeen, South Dakota. February 24, 1973.

------- Letter to Cousin Norma. Letter including family history. Berthold, North Dakota, February 12, 1980.

------- Letter to Unknown Person and Address.

------- Letter to Unknown Person and Address.

Fortune, Oliver. Emigration from Canada to United States, Naturalization Service. U.S. Department of Labor, June 25, 1923.

------- "Declaration of Intent." United States of America, 14-26786, No. 27214318, May 21, 1921.

------- Certificate of Citizenship. U.S. Department of Labor. May 22, 1936.

------- Letter to Nettie Fortune. Wheaton Minnesota. September 26, 1934.

------- Letter to Irene Fortune. Wheaton Minnesota. October 3, 1934.

------- Letter to Nettie Fortune. Wheaton Minnesota. October 3, 1934.

------- Letter to Nettie Fortune. Wheaton Minnesota. August 27, 1935.

------- Letter to Nettie Fortune. Wheaton Minnesota. August 28, 1935.

------- Letter to Nettie Fortune and Irene Fortune. Wheaton Minnesota. September 2, 1935.

------- Letter to Nettie Fortune. New Deal, Montana, November 12,

1936

-------- Letter to Nettie Fortune. New Deal, Montana, November 19, 1936.

-------- Letter to Nettie Fortune. Wheaton Minnesota. June 14, 1939.

-------- Letter to Nettie Fortune. Wheaton Minnesota. June 15, 1939.

-------- Letter to Nettie Fortune. Wheaton Minnesota. June 21, 1939.

-------- Letter to Nettie Fortune. Wheaton Minnesota. January 2, 1943.

-------- Letter to Nettie Fortune. No location given. Undated.

Fortune, Oliver Nels. Wheaton, MN, letter to Nettie Fortune, Grand Forks, ND. January 14, 1936.

"Fortune Rites Friday," Article from unknown, undated newspaper concerning John Richard "Jack" Fortune, age 86.

"Fugitive Slave Act 1850." *The Avalon Project: Documents in Law, History and Diplomacy.* https://avalon.law.yale.edu/19th_century/fugitive.asp.

"Funeral Rites Held Sunday for Oliver Fortune," *Renville County Farmer* [Mohall, ND], May 13, 1943.

"Funeral Rites for Oliver N. Fortune Held Sunday." Article from unknown, undated newspaper.

Fur, Gunlög, "Indians and Immigrants - Entangled Histories," *Journal of American Ethnic History,* Vol. 33, No. 3, Spring 2014.

"Genocide of Indigenous People." *Holocaust Museum Houston.* https://hmh.org/library/research/genocide-of-indigenous-peoples-guide/.

"The Geographical Origins of the German Speaking Immigrants." *AlbertaHistory.* https://sites.ualberta.ca/~german/AlbertaHistory/Georigin.htm.

Gevikm, Brian. "Think Deadwood was wild in the 1870s? Try Yankton." *South Dakota Public Broadcasting,* https://www.sdpb.org/blogs/images-of-the-past/think-deadwood-was-wild-in-the-1870s-try-yankton/ May 5, 2022.

Gilbert, Adrian. "World War I: Killed, Wounded Missing." Encyclopedia Britannica, https://www.britannica.com/event/World-War-I/Killed-wounded-and-missing.

Gjerde, Jon and McCants, Anne. "Fertility, Marriage and Culture: Demographic Processes Among Norwegian Immigrants to the Middle West." *Journal of Economic History*, Vo. 55, No. 4,

December 1995.

Graven, Andreas R. "The Horrific Disease That Won't Die." *sciencenor. no*, https://sciencenorway.no/bacteria-diseases-forskningno/the-horrific-disease-that-wont-die/1464510, April 13, 2012.

Grimley, Daniel M. *Grieg: Music, Landscape and Norwegian Identity.* Rochester, NY: Boydell & Brewer, Boydell Press, 2006.

Grinnell, George Bird. "Account of the Northern Cheyennes concerning the Messiah Superstition." *The Journal of American Folklore*, Jan. – March, 1891.

Hanson Eric J., Boothe, Paul and Edwards Heather eds. *Eric J. Hanson's Financial History of Alberta, 1905-1950.* Calgary, Alberta, Canada, University of Calgary Press, 2003.

Harari, Yuval. "Moses, the Sword, and The Sword of Moses: Between Rabbinical and Magical Traditions." *Jewish Studies Quarterly*, Vol. 12, No. 4.

Harrisse, Henry. *The Diplomatic History of America: Its First Chapter.* London: B.F. Stevens, Publisher, 1897.

Haugesund, Reidgar Østensjø. "The Spring Herring Fishing and the Industrial Revolution in Western Norway in the Nineteenth Century." *Scandinavian Economic History Review*, Vol.11, No. 2, December 20, 2011.

Heike, Paul. *The Myths that Made America: An Introduction to American Studies.* New York: Columbia Publishing, 2014.

Helm, Merry. "Colonel Lounsberry Scoops Bighorn." *Prairie Public NewsRoom*, https://news.prairiepublic.org/show/dakota-datebook-archive/2022-04-25/colonel-lounsberry-scoops-bighorn, April 25, 2022.

Hedren, Paul L. *Fort Laramie and the Great Sioux War.* Norman, OK: University of Oklahoma Press, 1998.

Heffermehl, Karin Bruzelius. "The Status of Women in Norway." *The American Journal of Comparative Law*, Autumn, 1972.

Hipple, Annika S. "Exploring Norway's Fjords: The Sognefjord." *Real Scandinavia*, http://realscandinavia.com/exploring-the-norwegian-fjords-the-sognefjord/.

"History." *Bow Island.* https://www.bowisland.com/history.

History.com Editors, "Oregon," *History*, https://www.history.com/

topics/us-states/oregon, Nov 4, 2019.

\--------- "Battle of the Little Bighorn," *History*, https://www.history.com/this-day-in-history/battle-of-little-bighorn, July 1, 2022.

Hix, Lisa. "Don't Call Them Bums: The Unsung History of America's Hard-Working Hoboes." *Collectors Weekly*, Apr 16, 2015, https://www.collectorsweekly.com/articles/dont-call-them-bums-the-unsung-history-of-americas-hard-working-hoboes/.

Hjelde, Anrnstein and Jansson, Benthe Kolberg. "Language Reforms in Norway and Their Acceptance and Use in the Norwegian American Community." https://library.oapen.org/bitstream/handle/20.500.12657/54132/external_content.pdf?sequence=1#page=297, 2016.

"Hoarding Disorder," *Mayo Clinic*, https://www.mayoclinic.org/diseases-conditions/hoarding-disorder/symptoms-causes/syc-20356056.

Holmsen, Andreas, "The Old Norwegian Peasant Community: Investigations Undertaken by the Institute for Comparative Research in Human Culture," *Scandinavian Economic History Review*, Vol. 4, No. 1, 1956. Published online December 20, 2011.

Homstad, Daniel W. "Abraham Lincoln: Deciding the Fate of 300 Indians Convicted of War Crimes in Minnesota's Great Sioux Uprising." *Historynet*, https://www.historynet.com/abraham-lincoln-deciding-the-fate-of-300-indians-convicted-of-war-crimes-in-minnesotas-great-sioux-uprising.htm, December 2001.

Hoverstad, Torger Anderson. "*The Norwegian Farmers in the United States.* Fargo, ND: H. Jervell Publishing Company, 1915.

Hudson, Myles and Ray, Michael. "Wounded Knee Massacre." *Encyclopædia Britannica*, https://www.britannica.com/event/Wounded-Knee-Massacre, December 22, 2021.

"Indian Deserves the Same Rights," *Winona Daily News* (Winona, MN), November 22, 1972.

"Item: Oliver Fortune." Microfilm Reel Number: C-6451, Item Number: 281587, *Library and Archives: Canada.* https://www.bac-lac.gc.ca/eng/discover/land/land-grants-western-canada-1870-1930/Pages/item.aspx? Id Number=281587&.

Johnson, Bernese. Letter to Nettie Fortune. Aberdeen, South Dakota. February 23, 1973.

Kasasa. "Boomers, Gen X, Gen Y, Gen Z, and Gen A Explained." The

Kasasa Exchange, https://www.kasasa.com/exchange/articles/generations/gen-x-gen-y-gen-z, July 6, 2021.

Keel, Terence D. "Religion, Polygenism and the Early Science of Human Origins." *History of the Human Sciences*, Vol. 26, No. 2, April 1, 2013.

Kimmerle, Marjorie M. "Norwegian-American Surnames in Transition." *American Speech*, Vol.17, No.3, October 1943.

Klein, Christopher. "The Viking Explorer Who Beat Columbus to America," *History*. https://www.history.com/news/the-viking-explorer-who-beat-columbus-to-america. September 2, 2020.

Kristiansen, Roald E. "Two Northern Grimoires: The Trondenes and the Vesteaålen Black Books." *Acta Borealia*, Vol. 30, No. 2, December 2013.

Kuitems, Margot. *et al.* "Evidence for European Presence in the Americas in AD 1021," *Nature.* Vol. 60, Oct 20, 2021.

Kuntz, Kristine. "High Third Street." Oral history special collection HQ146.M65 K86 2002, Minot State University, March 5, 2002.

Land Title Office, Calgary, Canada. To Oliver Fortune. Notice of arrears of taxes and costs due on parcel of land to be paid to prevent forfeiture of title to land, April 22, 1927.

Lantow, Glen. Letter including family history to Nettie Fortune, Fredericksburg, Iowa, March `30, 1982.

Larson, C.I. Letter to Oliver Fortune. Wildrose, North Dakota, August 21, 1936.

-------- Letter to Oliver Fortune. Wildrose, North Dakota, August 28, 1936.

Lee, Sandra Soo-Jin, Mountain, Joanna and Koenig, Barbara A. "The Meanings of 'Race' in the New Genomics: Implications for Health Disparities Research." *Yale Journal of Health Policy, Law, Ethics*, Vol. 1, Art. 3, 2001.

Linneaus, Carolus. *Systema Naturae*. Leiden: Johann Wilhelm de Groot for Theodor Haak, 1735.

Lizée, Tiffany. "Canada's Most Dramatic Temperature Change Recorded 57 Years Ago on January 10 in Alberta." *Global News*, January 10, 2019.

Longfellow, Henry W. "The Revenge of Rain-in-the- Face," Henry

Wadsworth Longfellow.

<http://www.hwlongfellow.org/poems_poem.php?pid=208>.

"Looking Forward," The *Bismarck Tribune* [ND], January 8, 1932.

"Lorna Doone" National Style Book. Including sketches by Nettie L. Williams age 16, 1907. Schoolwork and personal drawings.

Lovoll, Odd S. *The Promise of America: A History of the Norwegian-American People*. Minneapolis: University of Minnesota Press, 1999.

Luebke, Frederick C. "Ethnic Group Settlement on the Great Plains." *Faculty Publications, Department of History*, DigitalCommons@ University of Nebraska - Lincoln, 1977.

Lueck, Dean. "The Extermination and Conservation of the American Bison." *Journal of Legal Studies*, Volume 31, Number S2, June 2002.

Lydia [no last name given], letter to Nettie Fortune. Hawkeye, Iowa. May 4, 1976.

Lydia, K. Letter to Nettie Fortune including family history, Hawkeye, Iowa, July 1955.

Marshall, John. *United States v. Rogers*, 30 US 1, 1831.

Meyers, John and Anna. Letter to Nettie Fortune. Bow Island, Alberta, Canada. February 10, 1959.

Miller, Robert J. "The International Law of Colonialism: A Comparative Analysis." *Lewis & Clark Law Review*, Vol. 15, No. 4, Winter 2011.

Miller, Ella Wickham. Letter including family history to Nettie Fortune. Cedar Rapids, Iowa, April 24, 1952.

Miller, Mrs. Ed. Letter including family history, Hawkeye, Iowa, April 24, 1952.

-------- Letter including family history to Nettie Fortune. Hawkeye, Iowa, June 4, 1952.

-------- Letter to Nettie Fortune. Hawkeye, Iowa. March 4, 1954.

-------- Letter to Nettie Fortune. Hawkeye, Iowa., 1955, no date stated.

-------- Letter to Nettie Fortune. Hawkeye, Iowa. August 29, 1956.

Millett, Francis Davis. "The Treaty of Traverse des Sioux." *Minnesota State Capitol,* https://www.mnhs.org/capitol/learn/art/8961, 2005.

Miscali, Monica. "What Happened in the North? Servants and Rural Workers in Norway." *Mundo Agrario*, Vol. 18, No. 39, December

2017.

"Mohall Bankers Charged With Misuse of Mails." *Ward County Independent.* April 13, 1922.

Mooney, L. Wilma and Mike, letter Nettie Fortune including family history, compiled by Jedediah and Vea Mae Hills, with handwritten additions of unknown authorship.

MS.801059 «Vinjeboka». - *Nasjonalbbibliotetek.* https://www.nb.no/nbsok/nb/c596c7c4925c127cdef017847b5b17ad?index=1#0.

Municipal District Court of Forty Mile No. 64, certificate of local tax payment, Mabel, Alberta, Canada, September 14, 1920.

Myhre, Jan Eivind. "Emigration from Norway 1830-1920." *nordics info.* https://nordics.info/show/artikel/emigration-from-norway-1830-1920, September 8, 2021.

National Archives. Census of 1870. Inhabitants of the Township of Pleasant, County of Winneshiek, Iowa, June 20, 1870.

National Archives, Civil War Pension Records, Ole Olson, born 1839, Washington D.C.

U.S. department of Labor, Declaration of Intention to become a citizen of the United States, June 25, 1929.

"N.C. Fortune, Glenburn, Dies," *Minot Daily News* [Minot, ND], July 14, 1943.

"N.D. Woman Knows Quisling's Father." *Hope Pioneer* [ND]. May 31, 1945.

Nichols, David A. "The Other Civil War: Lincoln and the Indians." *Minnesota History*, Spring 1974.

Nilsen, Lars. "Norway's Presence in New York City - The Norwegian Immigration Association, Inc." *Scandinavia Review* in *NIA*, https://niahistory.org.

"North Dakota Facts." *North Dakota.* https://www.ndtourism.com/articles/north-dakota-facts.

Nunn, Nathan and Qian, Nancy. "The Columbian Exchange: A History of Disease, Food, and Ideas." *Journal of Economic Perspectives*, Vol. 24, No. 2, Spring 2010.

O'Neill, Aaron. "Life Expectancy in Norway, 1765-2020." *Statista*, https://www.statista.com/statistics/1041314/life-expectancy-norway-all-time/, September 19, 2019.

"Order for Hearing on Partition for Administration, Limiting Time to

File Claims and for Hearing Thereof." Probate Court of Traverse County, Minnesota. December 15, 1943.

"Oscar Williams of ISH [Iowa Soldiers' Home] Dies," Article from unknown, undated newspaper.

Østenjø, Reidar. «The Spring Herring Fishing and the Industrial Revolution in Western Norway in the Nineteenth Century," *Scandinavian Historical History Review*. Vol. 11, No. 2, Published online December 20, 2011.

Ostler, Jeffrey. "Conquest and the State: Why the United States Employed Massive Military Force to Suppress the Lakota Ghost Dance." *Pacific Historical Review*, Vol. 65, No.2, May 1996.

"Passenger List 1853 -brig Virgo." *Norway Heritage*, NARA Roll # 128, arr. no. 600. http://www.norwayheritage.com/p_list.asp?jo=2045.

"Peters, Wiebe, Bergman Plead Guilty In Mohall Bank Case." *Ward County Independent* [ND]. October 19, 1922.

Pintner, Walter M. "The Burden of Defense in Imperial Russia." *The Russian Review*, Vol.49, No.3, July 1984.

"Pioneer Settler Dies Thursday at Age of 91." Article from unknown, undated newspaper about Oliver N. Fortune of Wheaton, Minnesota.

Population and Development Review. Vol.37, No.1. March 20, 2011.

"Quisling Assails Norse Clergymen." *Bismarck Tribune* [ND]. April 8, 1942.

Ranlet, Philip. "The British, the Indians, and Smallpox: What Really Happened at Fort Pitt in 1763." *Pennsylvania History*, Vol. 67, No. 3, Summer 2000.

Reher, David S. "Reflections on the Fate of the Indigenous Populations of America." *Population and Development Review*, Vol.37, No.1, Mar 20, 2011.

"Return of the Seventh." *Press and Daily Dakotaian* [Yankton, Dakota Terr]. October 26, 1876.

Robinson, Doane. *A History of the Dakota or Sioux Indians*. Aberdeen [SD]: State of South Dakota, 1904.

Robinson, Elwyn B. *History of North Dakota*. Lincoln, University of Nebraska Press, 1966.

Roper, Stephanie Abbott. dis, "African-Americans in North Dakota 1800-1940." University of North Dakota, 1988.

Ross, Rachel. "What Are Chinook Winds?" *Live Science*. https://www.

livescience.com/58884-chinook-winds.html, April 27, 2017.

Russo, Priscilla Ann. "The Time to Speak Is Over: The Onset of the Sioux Uprising." *Minnesota History*, Fall 1976.

Rustad, Mary S. *The Black Books of Elverum.* Lakerville, MN: Galde Press, Inc., 2009.

Ruster, Mildred (Millie) Wilson [Nellie's first cousin]. Letter including family history, to Millie Purdy, March 21, 1954.

-------- Letter to Nettie Fortune including family as told to her by her mother.

Ryan, Jeffrey R. ed., *Pandemic Influenza: emergency Planning and Community Preparedness.* Boca Raton, FLA: CRC Press, 2008.

Rynning, Ole. *True Account of America.* Christiana, Norway: 1838.

-------- *True Account of America,* Theodore Christian Biegen English translation. Minneapolis: Norwegian-American Historical Association, 1926.

Sandoz, Mari. *The Battle of the Little Bighorn.* Lincoln, Neb: Bison Books, 1978.

Scholnick, Robert J. "Extermination and Democracy: O'Sullivan, the Democratic Review, and Empire, 1837-1840." *American Periodicals,* Vol. 15, No.2, 2005.

"Section 15: Farm Depression, 1930s." in "Part 1: North Dakota Agriculture," State Historical Society of North Dakota. https://www.ndstudies.gov/gr4/north-dakota-agriculture/part-1-north-dakota-agriculture/section-15-farm-depression-1930s.

Semminsen, Ingrid. "The Long Journey." in *Norway to America: A History of the Migration*, Minneapolis: University of Minnesota Press, 1975.

Shaw, James H. "How Many Bison Originally Populated Western Rangelands?" *Rangelands,*

Volume 17, Number 5, October 1995.

Sherman, Bill "Tracing the Treaties: How They Affected American Indians and Iowa." *Iowa History Journal*, http://iowahistoryjournal.com/tracing-treaties-affected-american-indians-iowa/, January 7, 2022.

Simmingsen, Ingrid. *Norway to America.* Minneapolis: University of Minnesota Press, 1978.

Smalley, E.V. "The Isolation of Life on Prairie Farms. *Atlantic,*

September, 1893.

Smith, Geof W. Actiomycosis in Cattle, Swine, and Other Animals." *Merck Veterinary Manual*, https://www.merckvetmanual.com/ generalized-conditions/actinomycosis/actinomycosis-in-cattle,- swine,-and-other-animals, October, 2020.

Smith, O.K. {Nettie Fortune's cousin), Nevsho, letter including family history, Missouri, May 25, 1952.

Solveig Wikstrøm, "Surnames and Identities," *Names and Identities, Oslo Studies in Language*, Vol. 4, No. 2, 2012.

"The Spanish Influenza." *The New York Times*. October 7, 1918, 12.

Star Journal Research Staff. "Indian Meeting Won't Match Old Days." *The Minneapolis Star*, September 12, 1941.

Stinson, Bertha. Letter to Nettie Fortune Including Family History. Wheeler, New York, July 7, 1952.

Stocker, Patricia Dodge. Telephone conversation with Robert Dodge. September 5, 2020.

Stokker, Kathleen. "Narratives of Magic and Healing: *Oldtidens Sortebog* in Norway and New the New Land." *Scandinavian Studies*, Vol. 73, No. 3, Fall 2001.

Stromsodt, P. Sherman, Letter including family history. Box 105, Wimbledon, North Dakota, March 18, 1978.

"Supplementary Report: 1970 Census of Population: 1970 Population of North Dakota by Township and City." U.S. Department of Commerce: Bureau of the Census. https://www2.census.gov/prod2/ decennial/documents/31679801n104-107ch3.pdf, December 1976.

Taney, Roger. *United States v. Rogers*. 45 US 567, 1846.

Thirteenth Census of the United States, 1900. National Archives and Records Administration, Census Place: Clifton, Traverse, Minnesota, Page 2. Enumeration District: 0285; FHL microfilm:1240794.

Thornton, Russell. "Cherokee Population Losses During the Trail of Tears: a New Perspective and Estimate." *Ethnology*, Vol. 31, No. 4, 1984.

"Took Life at Minot." *The Fargo Forum and Daily Republican*. January 26, 1915.

"Total Population for North Dakota Cities: 1920 - 2000." https://www.

ndsu.edu/sdc/publications/census/NDcities1920to2000.pdf.

"Transcript of Fort Laramie Treaty (1868)." U.S. National Archives.
<http://www.ourdocuments.gov/doc.
php?flash=true&doc=42&page=transcript >.

Trenerry, Walter N. "The Shooting of Little Crow: Heroism of Murder?"
Minnesota History. Vol. 38, No. 3.

Trilla, Antoni, Guillem, Trilla and Daer, Carolyn. "The 1918 'Spanish
Flu' in Spain." *Clinical Infectious Diseases*, Vol. 47, Iss. 5,
September 2008.

Thurman, Brian. "The Interesting History of Braces." https://www.
thurmanortho.com/the-interesting-history-of-braces/, August 31,
2019.

Trost, Jan. "A Renewed Social Institution: Non-Marital Cohabitation."
Acta Sociologica, Vol. 24, No. 4, October 1, 1978.

Turner, Frederick J. "The Significance of the Frontier in American
History." *American Historical Association*, https://www.historians.
org/about-aha-and-membership/aha-history-and-archives/
historical-archives/the-significance-of-the-frontier-in-american-
history-(1893). Chicago, 1893.

"Upton Takes Three Mohall Bankers to Leavenworth Prison." *Ward
County Independent* [ND]. November 9, 1922.

"Vinjeboka: The Very Oldest Svartebok Manuscript, 1480 - 1520."
Grimoire Archives. https://booksofmagick.com/vinjeboka/ /. Oct
24, 2020.

"The Vikings of World War II." Norwegian American,

https://www.norwegianamerican.com/the-vikings-of-world-war-ii/.
October 8, 2014.

Walchester, Kathryn. "Pioneers and Adventuresses." Chapter from
*Gamle Norge and Nineteenth-Century British Women Travelers in
Norway*. New York: Anthem Press, 2014.

Wahlgren, Erik. "The Case of the Kensington Rune Stone," American
Heritage. Vol.10, Iss.3, https://www.americanheritage.com/case-
kensington-rune-stone, April 1959.

Wallace, Brigitta. "The Norse in Newfoundland: "'L'Anse aux
Meadows and Vinland," *Newfoundland and Labrador Studies*.
https://journals.lib.unb.ca/index.php/nflds/article/view/140/236.

Washburn, Walter L. "Leprosy Among Scandinavian Settlers in the

Upper Mississippi Valley, 1864-1932." *Bulletin of the History of Medicine*, Vol. 24, No. 2, March/April, 1950.

Waters, Michael R. "Late Pleistocene Exploration and Settlement of the Americas by Modern Humans." *Science*, Vol. 365, No. 6449, July 12, 2019.

Weatherbee, Edgar. "Rapid Development." *Ward County Independent* (ND), October 4, 1905.

Wender Melanie J., "Goodbye Family Farms and Hello Argibusiness: The Story of How Agricultural Policy is Destroying Family Farms and the Environment." *Villanova Environmental Law Journal*, Vol. 22, Iss. 1, Art. 6, 2011.

Whitman, Walt. "A Death-Sonnet for Custer," *The Walt Whitman Archive*.

<http://www.whitmanarchive.org/published/periodical/poems/per.00142>.

Williams, Henrik. "The Kensington Runestone: Fact and Fiction, "*The Swedish-American Historical Quarterly*, Vol 63, No. 1, January 2012 .

Williams, Jr., Robert A. *The American Indian in Western Legal Thought: The Discourses of Conquest.* New York: Oxford University Press, 1992.

Wilson, Mildred (Millie) Reister. Nellie Fortune's first cousin, letter including family history, to Millie Purdy.

World War II Draft Registration. "Registration Card: Men born on or after April 27, 1877 and on or before February 16, 1897." Serial Number U 347, Oliver Fortune, Mohall, Renville, ND.

For More News About Robert Dodge,
Signup For Our Newsletter:

http://wbp.bz/newsletter

Word-of-mouth is critical to an author's long-term success. If you appreciated this book please leave a review on the Amazon sales page:

http://wbp.bz/fortune

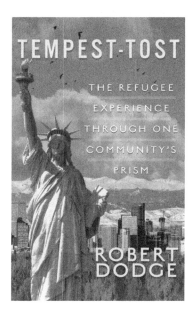
Preface

This is a book on refugees, a subject that elicits considerable reaction and divided, often impassioned opinion. It is based on the personal stories and experiences of refugees, including the conditions they fled and their transition to life in the U.S.

It is an educational book with background material based on evidence that comes from scholarly literature, including peer reviewed journals and academic publications offered in support of ideas presented, as well as sources cited for numbers mentioned and statistics discussed which can be verified. To prevent this material from impeding the telling of the many personal stories and interrupting the narrative, all the notes come at the end of the book. This adds a number of pages for a limited audience. The reader will only be distracted by small numbers which are endnotes so that those so inclined can seek to find where data was located or in some cases discover additional information on a topic being discussed. While the author's interviews and research led him to reach conclusions, the book is based on the evidence cited.

Chapter One: Introduction

"The ordeals refugees survive and the aspirations they hold resonate with us as Americans. This country was built by people who fled oppression and war, leapt at opportunity, and worked day and night to remake themselves in this new land. The refugees who arrive in the United States today continue this tradition, bringing fresh dreams and energy and renewing the qualities that help forge our national identity and make our country strong." This was how Barack Obama described refugees in 2014 as the United States welcomed 70,000 new residents who were fleeing oppression and war. A year later Donald Trump was on the scene and he said, "So we have a president that wants to take hundreds of thousands of people and move them into our country." He ominously warned that refugees, "…could be a better, bigger more horrible version than the legendary Trojan horse ever was."

A heated national debate has emerged over refugees coming to the U.S. in recent years. There are those who present refugees as a threat to security in America, while others view welcoming refugees as the tradition that made the country strong and diverse. This book looks at refugees who have settled in Colorado, focusing on the Denver metropolitan area.

Colorado is a swing state that presents a microcosm of America and the broader refugee experience. The intent is to elevate the discussion by helping the reader realize what people endured before becoming refugees and how they have managed since arriving in America. To consider the role refugees have played and should play in America, it is of value to hear their stories and understand their struggles, what they contribute, and what problems they face that could represent problems to the communities in which they are settled.

A point sometimes ignored in the current discussion is that the original English settlers in New England were refugees. While many have fled war and abuse throughout history, the word "refugee" entered the language during the religious wars in Europe following the Protestant Reformation. That Reformation came to England with Henry VIII who broke with the Catholic Church and declared himself the head of the Church of England.

Some felt the new English church remained too similar to Catholicism and hoped to bring it closer to Calvinism and purify it, earning themselves the name Puritans. Those Puritans who were willing to remain within the Anglican Church and work to change it were the Nonconformists. A second group of Puritans chose to remove itself completely from the Church of England, and these were the Separatist. This group was especially persecuted. Pilgrim leader and *Mayflower* passenger William Bradford reported that during the reign of Queen Elizabeth many Separatists were imprisoned and murdered, and survivors petitioned the Queen, "that they may not be 'murdered' by 'hunger and cold, and stifled in loathsome dungeons.'" When James I came to the throne following the death of Elizabeth, the situation grew worse, and Separatist groups became refugees. A group left England in 1608 and secured a settlement in Holland. In 1620, a Separatist group led by Bradford became refugees from England and boarded the *Mayflower*, reaching North America after over two months at sea, and they created the colony of Plymouth. There exists a myth that they came for religious freedom, but they came to practice their own religion and established an intolerant theocracy.

This second permanent British colony in America was founded by refugees from religious persecution and physical abuse who were seeking a better life and set the model for the colony, which would become a recurring pattern throughout U.S. history.

Since Plymouth there has been a home in America for those fleeing danger and persecution. It wasn't until after World War II when 250,000 refugees came to the U.S. that the country passed its first law specifically allowing for the admission of displaced people. This was followed by the Cold War and laws were passed to allow the admission of those fleeing Communist countries. Those escaping countries behind the Iron Curtain were joined by refugees from China, North Korea and many Cubans. The fall of Saigon in 1975 led to the challenge of resettling hundreds of thousands of refugees from Vietnam. Congress responded by passing the *Refugee Act of 1980*. In passing the Act, Congress standardized the definition and government supported services available for refugees.

The *Refugee Act* specified five categories of persecution a person might suffer from that would qualify them for refugee status: race, religion, nationality, membership in a particular social group, and political opinion. Proof of being a victim of one of these would be a requirement when applying for admission to the U.S. Also included was considerable specific direction to states accepting refugees regarding assistance and monitoring, as well as obligations for refugees to follow. From 1975 when the Vietnamese resettlement began through mid-2015, the U.S. resettled over three million refugees in its borders from over 70 nations.

While that has been substantial, it is not in keeping with the recent increase in displacement of people from their homes. Civil wars and famine have resulted in unprecedented numbers of refugees in recent years and as 2016 began 65.3 million people were displaced from their homes. New refugees are added at a rate of 24 per minute and their numbers approach one percent of the earth's population. A limit of 50,000 refugees per year was set in the original Act, subject to change "as the President determines, before the beginning of the fiscal year…is justified by humanitarian concerns or is otherwise in the national interest."

Humanitarian concern has seen the number of refugees admitted vary considerably over the years. In 1980 when the Act was passed, an all-time high of over 207,000 were taken into the country. This included the Vietnamese "boat people" and others escaping from communist Southeast Asia. The numbers soon were lowered, but when the Soviet Union collapsed in 1989, there were again well over 100,000 refugees entering the U.S. annually for several years, with a large influx of Russians and others from Eastern European counties that had been part of the Soviet Block. This was followed by a brief spike in 1999 following the genocide in Kosovo.

Following 9/11 and the *Patriot Act*, admission of refugees dropped to an all-time low of 27,000 in 2002. President Bush called for 70,000 for 2007, but Congress reduced that number to 50,000. In 2008 refugee status was granted to thousands of Burmese and Bhutanese, and within years Burma annually ranked first or second as the country of origin for refugees, while Bhutan ranged from third to fifth. The civil war in Syria resulting in millions of refugees who flooded Europe. German Chancellor Angela Merkel opened the doors and welcomed them.

Named *Time* magazine's Person of the Year for 2015, Merkel said, "If we now have to start apologizing for showing a friendly face in response to emergency situations, then that's not my country." President Obama increased the refugee number to be admitted and added 10,000 Syrian refugees in his 2015 proposal. The governors of 24 states responded by saying their states would not accept any. Obama admitted 85,000 refugees in his final year of office and, for the first time in history, Muslims admitted outnumbered Christians (46% to 44%). There was a drumbeat of alarm over the admission of Syrians and Muslims from other countries and often the entire program of refugee admissions became related to the issues associated with these concerns.

One of the states that has been willing to accept refugees since the program was formalized is Colorado. When many state governors had said they would not allow any Syrian refugees within their borders, Governor Hickenlooper of Colorado accepted them and called for the state to "provide a place where the world's most vulnerable can rebuild their lives." Since the *Refugee Act* in 1980 through 2015 the state of Colorado processed 50,207 refugees for resettlement and the state receives approximately 2,500 refugees per year from countries worldwide. The largest number has come from Vietnam, where nearly 110,000 have resettled. The "first generation" refugees, whose incoming numbers began to decline in the 1980s, were down to double digits in the 90s. By 2010 there were no new Vietnamese arrivals and many in Colorado are largely adapted to U.S. life. The second largest group has been the 6,000 from the Soviet Union/Russian Republic, most arriving in the 1990s. This dropped off in the new millennium and was down to single digit arrivals following 2010.

While many came to Colorado from Somalia at the beginning of the twenty-first century, the large influx of refugees in recent years has come from Burma and Bhutan with thousands of each arriving in the years since 2007. The vast majority of these newcomers have been settling in the Denver-Aurora metropolitan area.

Denver, called "The Mile-High City," is connected to Aurora with a combined population of a million people. They are located on the front range of the Rocky Mountains and have mainly sunny days and a dry climate. The mountainous terrain near Denver and Aurora make the location not quite so dramatic a change for one group that has been placed there for resettlement from a much more mountainous region, the Bhutanese.

In the current controversy, there are claims that refugees represent a general threat, stemming from several incidents of terrorism. These have not involved refugees. The threat posed by refugees is not borne out by evidence, only suggestions of possibilities, as the right-wing leaning CATO Institute pointed out in a recent study noted: "the chance of an American being murdered in a terrorist attack caused by a refugee is 1 in 3.64 *billion* per year."

http://wbp.bz/tta

Preface

I'm trapped inside a catacomb. The vaults above take a direct hit from Russian projectiles and erupt into flames. Clouds of ink-black smoke snake through the underground corridors.

I choke for breath as Russian soldiers pour inside, pointing assault rifles at civilians and indiscriminately shooting, the seamless line of bullets crackling in quick succession.

BRRRRRRRRRRRRRRRRRRRRTTTTTTTTTTTTTT!

BRRRRRRRRRRRRRRRRTTTTTTTTTTTTTTTT!

A Russian soldier chases after me. I race up the stairway and flee into the street. Outside, the air is cold, yet fire is everywhere. A murder of crows perches above the skeletal framework of tall-standing megaliths. Russian soldiers approach from behind. They pull out plastic water guns and shoot me in the back. *Splash!*

"You got me!" I shout.

I wake up laughing crazed, maniacal laughter. *That was one hell of a nightmare.* Eyes still shut, I go about mentally preparing for my day. I have only two days left of vacation, so I had better hurry up and get to work on renovating the bathroom. After that, I'll take Yola for a walk in City Theater Square.

I open my eyes. Reality intervenes. I'm not in the bedroom of my apartment in Mariupol. I lay inside the attic of a refugee hostel in the Czech Republic. *It wasn't a dream,* I realize dismally. *The nightmare was real.*

***

My name is Adoriana Marik. I'm a thirty-two-year-old tattoo artist and merchandiser who lived in the once beautiful port city of Mariupol, Ukraine. The life I enjoyed in Mariupol seems like a far-off dream to me now. It was by no means a perfect existence, but I was safe and free. I had friends, family, and my beloved dog, a husky named Yola. In those simple things, I saw a full-fledged and peaceful life that no one could take away from me. Overnight, my world was permanently and tragically altered by the Russian invasion. Today, I am a refugee.

This is my story. I do not speak for all Ukrainian refugees, nor do I pretend to be a scholar on the facts surrounding Russia's brutal invasion of Ukraine. I am simply one woman with a story to share with those who are willing to listen.

Chapter One

I was born in June 1990. At the time, my parents and two elder siblings lived in an unassuming three-bedroom apartment in a modernized section of Mariupol. A balcony overlooked a road where pedestrians bustled past, and a loggia hovered above a grassy courtyard.

Most of the buildings in the twenty-third micro-district had nine stories, with fourteen-storied buildings located a few blocks away. In those days, the visual appeal of Mariupol was far less alluring than what it would become in subsequent decades. The brutalist architecture was ugly and plain. Buildings were slabs of concrete with raw textures, designed for utilitarian purposes. There were few parks where trees and flowers could grow, and even fewer foreign restaurants.

The palatial Drama Theater located in Teatral'na Square was an exception to this uncultivated and coarse character. With its brick-red roof, towering white walls, beveled columns, and rudimentary arches, the colossal structure evoked the Mediterranean Sea and Roman times. Every Christmas season, a giant, fresh-cut evergreen tree, laced with ornamental bulbs and glowing lights, was placed outside the theater.

I recall walking past the Drama Theater as a small child. My mother exclaimed, *"Moya vyshen'ka*, look at the beautiful tree!" *Moya vyshen'ka*—meaning "my little cherry"—was her affectionate pet name for me. It was a uniquely Ukrainian endearment; cherries are our national fruit and constitute the main ingredient of many of our recipes, including the traditional Ukrainian varenyky, a crescent-shaped dough similar to ravioli, stuffed with sweet, syrupy cherries, or other items like potato, cabbage, or salo (pork meat). Cherry varenyky are best complemented by sour cream. If varenyky are not your style, you can always try traditional cherry *babka* ("cake").

In 1990, the first competitive elections to the Ukrainian parliament resulted in the establishment of parliamentary opposition and declaration of the sovereignty of the republic still within the USSR. My parents later told me about how different Ukrainian life had been under Soviet control. Everyone had a job, they said, and everyone was busy. Ukrainian citizens lived modestly but their essential needs were met. It sounded to me like there was a herd mindset in which no one stood out or questioned the commands of Soviet leadership.

In comparison, the Ukrainian democratic government that followed the fall of the Soviet Union in 1991 brought with it a daunting host of new demands. It was difficult for many Ukrainians to make the transition from being given instructions from autocratic leaders on how to live their day-to-day lives to suddenly needing to work more with their brains and not their hands. Under the new democratic rule, Ukrainians were instantly allowed the freedom to choose for themselves how they wished to live and seek self-expression. It was as though everyone was collectively pushed off a pier and forced to sink or swim.

Most Ukrainians learned to swim, taking great satisfaction in knowing they could question their leaders and vote for better ones if they were not happy with the direction the country was moving in. As we bathed in the waters of democracy, we realized that everything depends on the individual and their choices. Why purchase Soviet bread buns for three kopecks when you can open a bakery and make your own?

That is not to say that the waters of democracy equated with smooth sailing. There were many political storms— some of them were Category 5 hurricanes. In 2004, when I was thirteen years old, the Democratic Orange Revolution commenced. Ukrainians protested the government's corruption and Russian interference in our electoral process. The Orange Revolution resulted in the installation of a pro-reform and pro-Western government led by President Viktor Yushchenko.

Still, Ukrainians were not one hundred percent united in the spirit of democracy. People squabbled amongst themselves without attempting to look at issues from a global perspective. I remember one girl at school criticizing me for wearing an orange sweater, claiming it represented my support for the Orange Revolution. It was an absurd accusation. I was simply wearing an orange sweater. On that day, I learned an important lesson: Rats live amongst us. Certain minds are not healthy. They seek to exchange our hard-won freedoms and nostalgically revert to a Soviet-controlled past.

My early childhood was defined by loneliness and boredom. My father worked long hours to provide for our family, and my sister and brother were teenagers, already absorbed in their activities. I spent many hours alone in the apartment as my mother made the two-hour journey to care for her elderly parents in an outlying village.

When I returned from school each day, I roamed the streets in search of a stray dog I had named Lassie. A cross between a German shepherd and a mongrel, Lassie was a titanic black dog who quickly attached herself to me. Everyone told me to stay away from her, but I refused. I walked everywhere with Lassie and even purchased a collar for her using my pocket money.

I was not allowed to bring Lassie home, so I took food from our apartment and brought it to her in the street. Once, as Lassie was eating some meat and bread crusts I had placed on the pavement, another dog, belonging to a local woman, attacked. The dog was a fighting breed. He ferociously dove at Lassie's neck, tearing into it with his teeth.

I attempted to separate the dogs, but the woman who owned the other dog grabbed me and would not let me intervene. A man approached. He lifted a large brick from the ground and threw it at the head of the attacking dog. Only then did the dog remove his teeth from Lassie's neck. The owner hooked her dog on a leash and marched off.

Lassie writhed on the ground in pain. I knelt beside her and stroked her blood-streaked pelt. My parents emerged from the apartment building and took me home, leaving Lassie wounded and alone in the street. I searched the following day and found her surrounded by a crowd of boys in the yard where we played. They were laughing and throwing stones at her. She scurried away, her tail locked between her legs, and went to die under the porch of a house. The heartless boys pursued her and continued to throw stones.

In a fit of rage, I grabbed a large tree branch and drove away the savage thugs, knocking out the tooth of one of them in the process. I then crawled beneath the porch and treated Lassie's wounds, which were already infested with maggots.

When my parents found out about the incident, they were shocked. "You cannot walk that dog anymore!" they ordered.

Defiant, I told them I would not return home if they forbade me to walk Lassie. To my surprise, they relented. After that, I did not have many friends in the neighborhood. I was fine with that so long as I had Lassie at my side. Her wounds gradually healed, although one of her torn ears was permanently damaged and sagged at an awkward angle, giving her a funny look.

The boy whose tooth I knocked out threatened to poison Lassie when I was not around. One day, animal control arrived. Lassie was taken to the animal shelter and euthanized for allegedly biting one of the boys. I wept as I discovered her collar in the street. I held on to it as a keepsake, storing it in the little drawer of my night table.

http://wbp.bz/mariupol

MARGARITA NELIPA

KILLING
RASPUTIN

THE MURDER THAT ENDED
THE RUSSIAN EMPIRE

KILLING RASPUTIN by MARGARITA NELIPA

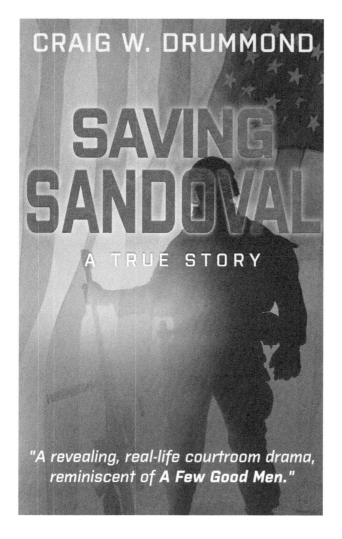

Made in the USA
Middletown, DE
08 November 2023

42195055R00149